ROUTLEDGE LIBRARY EDITIONS:
DEVELOPMENT

DEVELOPMENT POLICY IN SMALL COUNTRIES

DEVELOPMENT POLICY IN SMALL COUNTRIES

Edited by
PERCY SELWYN

Volume 56

Routledge
Taylor & Francis Group

LONDON AND NEW YORK

First published in 1975

This edition first published in 2011
by Routledge
2 Park Square, Milton Park, Abingdon, Oxon, OX14 4RN

Simultaneously published in the USA and Canada
by Routledge
270 Madison Avenue, New York, NY 10016

Routledge is an imprint of the Taylor & Francis Group, an informa business

© 1975 Institute of Development Studies

British Library Cataloguing in Publication Data
A catalogue record for this book is available from the British Library

ISBN 13: 978-0-415-58414-2 (Set)
eISBN 13: 978-0-203-84035-1 (Set)
ISBN 13: 978-0-415-59666-4 (Volume 56)
eISBN 13: 978-0-203-83834-1 (Volume 56)

Publisher's Note
The publisher has gone to great lengths to ensure the quality of this reprint but
points out that some imperfections in the original copies may be apparent.

Disclaimer
The publisher has made every effort to trace copyright holders and welcomes
correspondence from those they have been unable to contact.

DEVELOPMENT POLICY IN SMALL COUNTRIES

EDITED BY PERCY SELWYN

CROOM HELM LONDON
in association with
THE INSTITUTE OF DEVELOPMENT STUDIES, SUSSEX

First published 1975

©1975 Institute of Development Studies
University of Sussex

Croom Helm Ltd.
2-10 St John's Road London SW11

ISBN: 0-85664-282-7

Reprinted 1977

CONTENTS

PREFACE

The papers in this collection were prepared for a Conference on Problems of Small Developing Countries organised by the Institute of Development Studies in August 1972 at the Centre for Multi-Racial Studies at the University of the West Indies in Barbados.

Much of the work on small country problems over the past decade has been carried out in the Caribbean. Apart from the pioneering study of William Demas, there have been major contributions by West Indian social scientists, mainly within the University of the West Indies. But not only have small countries been a subject of academic study; there has also developed a wealth of expertise on the day-to-day problems of planning in small countries. Thus the Caribbean was an ideal site for a conference drawing on both academics and practitioners. The Institute of Development Studies was also able to draw in people whose experience had been in small countries in other parts of the world, and especially in Africa and the South Pacific.

The emphasis of the Conference was practical. The central question it posed was this: what constraints are faced by small countries on possible policies and actions merely by virtue of their size, and what is their scope for independent action? This emphasis is reflected in the papers. These make no claim at a complete coverage of the issues raised by small country size. Their main contribution is in this narrower, more policy-oriented area.

The Conference organisers would like to express their thanks to the Prime Minister of Barbados, the Rt. Hon. Earl Barrow, and to officials of the Barbados Government, for their cooperation and assistance; and to our chairman, Mr. Arthur Brown, of the Bank of Jamaica. Although the Conference was not officially sponsored by the University of the West Indies, there was invaluable participation by social scientists from the University, as well as by officials of governments and public sector organisations in the Caribbean.

Finally we should like to express our thanks to the Centre for Multi-Racial Studies — especially to its secretary, Mrs. Joy Allsopp — and to the Conference secretary, Mrs. Eve Johnson. They all helped in making the Conference a success.

Institute of Development Studies
University of Sussex.

INTRODUCTION: ROOM FOR MANOEUVRE? *

Percy Selwyn

The problem of country size attracted little attention in development literature until the 1960s. As far back as Marshall there had been some analysis of the implications of the size of country for economic structure, but the first general attempt to look at size as a problem in itself was made in the International Economic Association's Conference in 1957 (Robinson, 1960). Although the main emphasis of the conference was on developed countries, papers by Vakil and Brahmananda, Pinto and others looked specifically at problems of development, and the paper by Kuznets in particular laid the foundation for a good deal of later statistical work on the implications of country size.

Since then, there has been a substantial expansion of work in this field. This has taken several forms. First, there has been further statistical work on the implications of country size for economic structure and growth (Chenery and Taylor, 1968; Erb and Schiavo-Campo, 1969; Kuznets, 1971). Much of this has yielded negative results. Thus no association has been found between size (however defined) and income per head or rate of growth. The only important associations have been between size (in population terms) and import and export coefficients and (to a limited extent) degrees of industrialisation. Secondly, there have been continuing discussions on various aspects of smallness, such as the 1963 seminar of the Institute of Commonwealth Studies of the University of London (Benedict, 1967). Possibly of most importance, there has been the continuing debate, especially in the Caribbean and largely (although not entirely) by West Indian economists, about both the economic implications of small size and the problems of particular kinds of small economies − e.g. oil economies, plantation economies and so on. Here the pioneering work was that of Demas (1965), but there are also major contributions by Seers (1964), Kennedy (1966), Best (1966 and 1968), Beckford (1972) and many others.

Growing appreciation of the importance of size of country in development reflects several trends of the period since the Second World War. First the process of decolonisation led to the emergence of large numbers of countries which were small in terms of population, area, productive capacity, or all three. Secondly there has been a substantial shift in views about the role of government in the development process. Many (though by no means all) governments of poor countries in the 1920s and 1930s could regard their role basically as that of maintaining law and order and providing a

*I have had valuable comments from Jake Jacobs, Bernard Schaffer, Dudley Seers and John White.

minimum social and economic infrastructure, while leaving such questions as the general level of the national income or its distribution to market forces. Since the war and especially since the virtual ending of the old colonial system, this has become very much a minority view, confined to such outposts of the free market as Hong Kong. More recently, growing urban unemployment in many countries has led to demands for further government action covering a wide range of policy areas. (I.L.O. 1970, 1971, 1972.) Thus more complex and wide-ranging decisions and policies are expected from governments in the economic and social field. The scope for and constraints on such decisions have therefore become of greater significance. Both possibilities and limitations are fundamentally influenced by the size of the country over which government has authority. One particular aspect of government policy has been of central concern. Growing disenchantment with raw material exports as an engine of growth gave rise in the 1950s to a body of arguments (mainly associated with Prebisch and the Economic Commission for Latin America) in favour of industrialisation based on import-substitution policies. But for such policies to succeed, the size of country is critical. This was recognised by the theorists of ECLA and was the intellectual basis for their promotion of regional integration schemes. (United Nations, 1967.)

A further element in the growing interest in country size has been the revival — especially over the past decade — of theories of dependence as a major element in underdevelopment. There are various possible meanings of dependence. Much recent writing is concerned with a world system of inequality, whereby poor countries are both exploited and inhibited from developing. Many elements in this dominance/dependence system have been identified — the concentration of decision-making in the developed countries, the international forces making for the polarisation of industry in rich countries, the operations of the multinational corporations, the alleged control of world prices by rich countries, the technological monopoly of the developed countries and the terms on which technology is transferred to poor countries, and cultural dependence. (See, for example, Sunkel, 1969.)

But these are problems facing all developing countries. When we describe small countries as dependent by virtue of their size, we have more limited meanings in mind. Various interpretations have been suggested. Thus we have Schaffer's notion of 'score', by which it is possible to range countries into some kind of international pecking order, with the most dependent countries at the bottom. Such a score might take account of such elements as degrees of autonomy in decision-making, internal integration, the existence of military or political client status, isolation, or poverty. We may be describing a situation of asymmetry in the ability to take autonomous decisions, where external decisions and events have a far greater effect inside the

9

country than internal decisions and events have outside the country. Or we may be concerned with the absolute constraints on decision-making.

There can be little question that size is an important element in determining the extent of a country's dependence or independence in these more limited senses. Small countries are more likely to be clients of big countries than big countries are of small countries (although as Schaffer points out, political dependence is also influenced by a wide range of other factors). In economic terms, small countries may be more weakly integrated internally and more dependent on foreign trade and capital markets. The total size of their economies may be small in relation to that of the international corporations with which they have dealings. They may have a dependent relationship with aid donors. They may have little influence on the markets in which they sell their goods and services. Therefore an interpretation of underdevelopment in terms of dependence will call special attention to the situation of small countries.

A last element in the growing attention to country size has been the emergence at UNCTAD of concern with the situation of the so-called least developed countries. Work which has been carried out so far on the identification of such countries has produced a list of 25 'hard-core' least developed countries, nearly all of which are small. (United Nations, 1971.) Part of the reason for this coincidence of least developed status and small size lies in the criteria employed (Selwyn, 1973), but the existence of this list has undoubtedly directed attention to the problems of small countries.

My own personal interest in this field goes back to the days when I was an economist in the British Colonial Office. In the last years of the Colonial Office's existence, when the larger colonies had become independent, a steadily increasing part of our concern was with small — and occasionally minuscule — territories. So we found ourselves involved with the problems of Mauritius, Malta, Zanzibar, the smaller islands of the Caribbean and the South Pacific, Gibraltar, the High Commission Territories, and so on. But the then conventional wisdom about paths of development as well as about planning aims or systems appeared to have little relevance to the problems of such places, and indeed was frequently downright misleading. This view was confirmed when I later spent two years with the Central Planning and Development Office in Lesotho. A good deal of thought had however been given in the Caribbean area to the whole range of issues relating to country size, and it appeared that there would be a substantial advantage in organising a conference on small developing countries in the Caribbean where we could draw on the experience of West Indian social scientists and practitioners, but where we could also bring people whose experience had been

been in other regions, so as to arrive at conclusions with a wider relevance.

Before describing the conference discussions, it is necessary to point to an ambiguity in the subject itself. What do we mean by country size? As Schiavo-Campo points out, the way we define it will depend on the context within which we are working. If we are concerned with constraints resulting from a narrow range of resources, we may identify size with physical area. If we are concerned with manpower limitations of the small clientele for public and other services, we will measure size in terms of population. If we are concerned with the market for industrial products, we will identify size with GNP. Throughout our discussions, it was apparent that size was being used in different ways according to the context. This ambiguity may however be less important than it may appear; many of the countries with which we were concerned were in fact small on any measure. But it was recognised that the nature of the political, social and economic problems will vary according to the scale according to which a country is small.

The conference was intended to be policy-oriented — to examine what room for manoeuvre small countries have in highly dependent situations. It was in this respect that it broke new ground; while continuing the process of analysis, it was concerned with practical issues. In this we were helped by the presence of participants from governments or parastatal bodies, and it was this which gave it a special character.

The conference had one other distinguishing characteristic. Much discussion in the past has been concerned with small countries as a 'problem'; it has been assumed that there were disadvantages in smallness or, looked at in another way, that there were virtues in size. (This is of course the implicit assumption behind arguments in favour of regional integration in Europe.) As little as ten years ago, much of the discussion on small countries would have assumed this without question; indeed, a conference organised by the then Secretary of State for the Colonies in the mid-1960s on the future of the smaller colonial territories did take it for granted that many of the smaller colonies would not be 'viable' as independent countries, and that they would suffer from insuperable problems as separate states.

This was not the assumption of the Barbados conference. The recent emergence of many small countries is not only part of the reaction against colonialism, but can also reflect positive values — and in particular the desire of people to have a national unit with which they can identify, as opposed to the 'anonymity of the mass society'. The small country thus has a value in itself. Indeed some participants argued that the 'quality of life' is in some sense superior in small countries to that in large countries — though the question 'quality of life from whom?' was not clearly answered. These views, which are reflected in Abbott's paper in this symposium, reject the notion of viability as the justification for the separate existence of states. Viability has no meaning except in relation to the purposes of the citizens of a country, and in the last resort any national unit which can maintain its separate existence is *ipso facto* viable.

There is much force in this view. The notion of viability has proved extremely slippery. It was firmly believed ten or fifteen years ago that many small territories would be unviable as separate countries (principally because they were in receipt of budgetary aid). Most of them now exist as nation states and as members of the United Nations. Not only do they exist, but they show every sign of continuing to exist. But even so, there are substantial difficulties in arguing that any group which feels that it should exist as a separate nation should do so. Is there no lower limit in terms of population or area or resources below which the establishment of a nation state would not be justified? Is the fact of separate existence the only possible criterion for viability?

If it is, we are centrally concerned with those factors which enable small countries to exist and to continue to exist. Here the analysis by Schaffer — and in particular the notion of 'extantism' — provides a valuable framework for examining the issue. The international ideology which supports the status quo on international frontiers is a major support for new states once they have been established. Equally it acts as a limitation on the splitting-up of existing states save in extreme circumstances. Moreover the existence of small countries might be tolerated by the main decision-makers in the international community (the large powers and the multinational corporations) and this existence might even be to their advantage, in so far as the strength and bargaining power of small countries is less than that of large countries. In other words, the existence of large numbers of small countries is a support for neo-colonial relations.

But although small countries can exist, and have a value as primary loyalty units, there may be many purposes of its citizens which can be achieved only in the context of larger areas. There is thus what one of our participants described as a dialectical conflict between bigness, associated with possibilities of economic growth and power, and smallness associated with the ability of people to define their own nationalism. Is it possible to get the best of both worlds by combining large functional units with small loyalty units? Or is the separate existence of small loyalty units a barrier to the establishment of larger functional units? This is a point to which we returned in our discussion

12

of regional policies.

Granted that many small countries exist and are likely to continue to exist, and that small size is significant in some sense, are small countries as such a useful field of study? In what sense are small countries a useful classification? They are clearly far from homogeneous. Unfortunately the conference lacked a paper on a typology of small countries (the nearest approach to one being the broad classification in Ward's paper). But it is apparent that there are few general propositions that can be made about small countries as such. Moreover political, social and economic problems can be studied at various levels — at the international or regional level, in terms of the multinational firm and its operations, at a national or local level, or in terms of individuals and social groups. The nation is important as a level at which certain decisions are taken (e.g. about taxation, monetary matters, external trade, foreign relations, security and the legal framework), but for many purposes — and especially in small countries — decisions at other levels may also be of critical importance. Thus it could be argued that classification in terms of countries may be misleading, and countries may be a less useful unit of study than either smaller or larger areas or groups. In fact what we were concerned with was *problems* which might be affected by small country size. Thus there was general concern with how far problems of poverty might be aggravated by smallness, or how far smallness imposes *constraints* on relevant policies.

When we consider the problem in terms of constraints, we are brought back to the question of dependence. As is pointed out earlier, there are senses in which we may consider that small countries are more likely to be dependent than large countries and hence subject to more constraints on possible policies. Much of this is spelled out in the papers by Demas, Schaffer and Ward. But although it might be generally agreed that small countries are more likely to be dependent than large countries, the conference was strongly divided on the implications of such dependence. At one extreme there were those who saw dependence as the overwhelming fact of small country situations and the room for manoeuvre of their decision-makers as correspondingly narrow. At the other extreme it was argued that the concept of dependence is empty and useless in an analysis of small country problems; decision-makers have to live with it but it has no operational significance. The real issue is what cards do small countries have to play and how can they best play them. Far more useful than a study of dependence then, is an examination of the methods of bargaining open to small countries. In such an examination, nothing can be taken as fixed — even country size is not a datum. Size is an outcome of a particular process. A successful small country will attract population and resources; an unsuccessful country will lose both. Even physical size can in the last resort be changed by forms of political association.

Partly this argument may have been one about time scales. In the short
and medium term, with which planners and decision-makers are mainly
concerned, size and its related constraints have to be taken as a datum,
whatever might be true in the longer run. This view was expressed
strongly by some (though not all) of those more closely involved in the
planning process. Clearly they were made aware in their day-to-day work
of the powerful constraints under which they operated. As against this
it was argued that the distinction between the short and the long run
is meaningless and that long-term changes are the result of a succession
of cumulative short-term measures of the right kind. This view has been
expressed by Best (1966):

'. . . economic development is a problem of management — of
timing, sequencing and manipulation in an unending effort to
perceive or create, and, in any case, to exploit a multiplicity of
little openings and opportunities.'

In this sense, a successful policy depends on an awareness of what is the
last card which small countries have to play — and if possible to change
the rules of the international game, as did the oil-producing countries
by the establishment of OPEC, and as Malta did by opening up new
options in the strategic base game. Such a succession of cumulative
short-term measures might not however add up to a sound long-term
strategy. Without such a strategy, this kind of opportunism could lead
to increased long-term dependence; equally it is the fact of dependence
and its associated uncertainties which makes the formulation of a
long-term strategy extremely difficult.

The discussion ranged over a wide range of possible room for
manoeuvre. There are five areas where small countries are believed
to be particularly dependent. These are political status, trade,
monetary policies, aid, and the operations of the multinational
corporations.

In political terms, poor small countries may be client states of rich
large countries, and may have thus lost any power of independent
action. But this is not inevitable. Various options may be open even to
a small country which appears to be in a very weak international
position. National independence is weakest where a country has
forgone all options except one by its acceptance of decisions imposed
on it by a powerful large country. It is strongest where a range of
options remains open. This involves skilful manoeuvring between
alternative large countries, and not closing options with any of them.
If a small country is in a position which a great power considers to be
strategic, this may be difficult; the large power may use all means
from internal subversion to direct aggression to inhibit possible
alternative choices. But there are many recent examples of skilful
political manoeuvring by small countries in what might appear to be
highly unfavourable circumstances.

The heavy dependence of small countries on external trade is well

14

documented, as well as their lack of influence over the markets in which their exports are sold. This dependence may be compounded by extreme export specialisation (although as Brookfield points out, data on export specialisation may give an exaggerated view of the extent of specialisation in the economy as a whole). In extreme cases, the level of economic activity, incomes and employment may be almost totally dependent on the level of exports in general, and of one or two exports in particular. In so far as it is possible to distinguish between 'structural' and 'contingent' dependence, this is part of structural dependence — that is, it is inherent in the fact of small country size. In particular, there are severe constraints on the possibility of industrial development through import substitution in small countries, but the alternative strategy of the promotion of industrial exports on the basis of a very small home market also presents difficulties. The creation of regional markets for manufactures is beset with many problems, and in any event tends to benefit the more advanced countries rather than the poorer ones. But some small countries such as Singapore have successfully built up industrial exports on the basis of narrow home markets. Is there a trick which can be learned by other small countries, or are the possibilities peculiar to specific economic, social or political structures and situations?

Although small countries are also dependent in respect of monetary policy, this is an area in which there may be more room for manoeuvre. First, although many countries tie the value of their currencies to some international currency such as the dollar, the franc or sterling, there is no reason why they should do so. And indeed the recent world monetary crisis has compelled small countries to rethink such policies. Again, although monetary systems are frequently dominated by foreign banks, these can be localised at little cost (amounting to only the surplus of the banks' local assets over their local liabilities). Ally, basing his views on the experience of the Bank of Jamaica, points out a number of possible areas of action. Where a country is too small to afford the cost of specialised institutions designed to mobilise local savings (a point made in de Vries' paper), such institutions can, at least in principle, be provided on a regional basis, and there is room for other forms of monetary cooperation between small countries.

The aid relationhsip between 'donor' countries and agencies and small recipient countries may well be one of dominance and dependence. As de Vries points out, small countries tend to get more aid per head and in relation to their national income than larger countries (although there was some difference of opinion on the implications of this situation — a dispute reflected in Schiavo-Campo's comment on de Vries' paper). But this may at least partly reflect their greater dependence. De Vries refers to the willingness of a recipient country to 'work with' donor agencies and suggests that small countries may be more interested in building up more effective donor-recipient relationships. But this relationship might — and frequently does — take the form of donors imposing their own criteria and programmes on the recipients; the smaller and weaker the recipient country, the more likely is it that this will happen.

But this process may not be inevitable. If the small country has its own clear order of priorities, it need not accept projects or standards imposed by the donors (although there may be some trade-off between the volume of aid and the wish of a country to pursue its own development policy). Thus the ability of a country to negotiate successfully with a donor reflects the understanding and abilities of its decision-makers, and there is no clear association between this and country size.

For a small country to avoid dependence in the aid relationship, an appreciation of the motives and interests of the decision-makers in the donor countries is necessary. If these are understood, it may be possible for the small recipient country to play its cards in such a way as to keep the large country at arm's length. In this context, military aid may be considered an extreme case. It can bring with it total control over external and internal policies. But equally a major power which has committed itself to the provision of military aid to a small country (or to a particular group in a small country) may have opened itself to pressure to continue its support in almost any circumstances. The USA in South Vietnam, or Britain in South Arabia before independence, found themselves committed to military aid to governments or groups over whose policies they had very little influence or control. Again, it is generally believed that South Africa provides financial support for Lesotho's paramilitary police force, but there have been many indications of independent action by the Lesotho Government. In the last resort, the great power can overthrow a recalcitrant government; but a recipient government which plays its cards well can avoid this last resort, which may in any event be risky for the donor.

Lastly, and in many ways of most importance, there is the relationship between small countries and multinational corporations. Much has been written about situations of dominance and dependence in this area. Disparities in relative economic strength and bargaining power as between the corporations and the small country in which they operate can act as a major constraint on local decision-making. But can the international firm be 'domesticated' — that is, can it be persuaded to accommodate its operations to local interests? The foreign sector may indeed not always be damaging. It is possible to distinguish between foreign firms operating in peripheral areas of the economy and whose activities are harmless, and those in key decision areas. The former can be left alone; the problem is how to obtain control over the latter. Can the corporations be brought into the planning process and made to harmonise their interests with local development needs? This may not be impossible, although we would not underestimate the difficulty of the task. In the last resort, as Demas points out, it is possible to nationalise enterprises which are unwilling to cooperate with local development objectives.

There is a good deal of evidence from recent history that small countries can and do exploit these areas for manoeuvre, and that a few at least have done so with some success. But there is also no doubt that decision-makers in many small countries do not play their cards as well as they might, and do not fully exploit the opportunities open to them. Why should this be so? Or, as it was expressed at the conference, why do controllers of policy variables in many small countries feel caught up in constraints?

Various reasons emerged in discussion. These may be summarised as the lack of sufficient national feeling combined with psychological dependence, weaknesses in political leadership, lack of information, and mere inertia. All these are interrelated, but it is useful to discuss them seriatim.

Small countries will inevitably be open to foreign influences of various kinds. The lack of sufficient national feeling may reflect the existence of an elite whose attitudes and interests are centred on a metropolitan area. Wealthier people may have been educated abroad. They will share the middle-class attitudes described in another context as 'cosmopolitanism'. Moreover, in a small country these attitudes may not be confined to a small group. It was argued that countries in the Caribbean do not have foreign enclaves; the whole country may be such an enclave. Metropolitan values and attitudes may permeate the whole structure of society through the school system and communications media. Various participants referred to the spread in the Caribbean region of middle-class attitudes imported from abroad, especially from North America and Britain.

Psychological dependence, or poor national morale, may reflect the problems faced by decision-makers. A small country which is entirely dependent on imports for even the most basic articles of consumption, where virtually all investment and possibly even the budget are financed from abroad, and where major resources are owned and controlled by foreigners, will have a low morale. The basis of self-confidence is lacking.

Psychological dependence may also be a hangover from colonialism. Thus, in the Caribbean, it is said that:

'. . . the most powerful legacy of economic colonialism in the Region has been the creation of a dependent, mendicant mentality towards development on the part of the people of the Region. Such dependent attitudes are to be found among persons in the national private sector, the public sector, the Trade Union movement and among the unemployed. They have never been aware that by a combination of individual, national and regional efforts they can earn their own way in the world.'

(Commonwealth Caribbean Regional Secretariat, 1972.)

All these are clearly important. Decision-makers will not examine all their possible room for manoeuvre, will not consider what cards they have to play and how best to play them, unless they feel that the game is worth playing and that they have some chance of winning. If they are convinced neither of the value of the game nor of their chances, they are defeated before they start. Thus there is a need for a basic minimum of national feeling and self-confidence before room for manoeuvre can be studied and exploited. Some dependence theories give the impression that developing countries — and especially small developing countries — are the inevitable victims of a total world system about which they can do little. It has been argued that fatalistic religious systems act as a barrier to enterprise; it is not impossible that similarly deterministic world systems inhibit the search for what dependence theorists might regard as irrelevant and minor adjustments to the situation.

Some participants referred to weaknesses in political leadership, and to failures to take what appeared to be urgently needed action. Thus in one small country 20 per cent of the labour force was unemployed, but costs were so high that it did not pay to produce either foodstuffs or basic manufactures for local consumption. The cost structure was also affecting the export sector, and one major export industry was already threatened. Although a clear implication of this situation was that the currency was overvalued, the government refused to devalue, ostensibly because of the damage to the national 'honour'. A more probable reason was the immediate effect devaluation would have had on the cost of living and hence on wage demands. Government could not contain such a situation because of its heavy dependence on the trade unions. As Brookfield points out, governments of poor small countries tend to be risk-avoiders — necessarily so because of their extreme dependence — and frequently the least risky course of action may appear to be to do nothing.

It is difficult to judge such arguments. Many large countries have had poor political leadership, and examples of refusals to devalue overvalued currencies are not confined to small countries. But the quality of government may be more critical in a small poor country than in a large rich one. The large rich country may have many centres of decision which continue to operate whatever the deficiencies of government; the small poor country may have very few, and the role of government may be decisive. Therefore the quality of its political leadership is a central issue. One line of thought which emerged in the conference was that the quality of political leadership would be improved if groups of the population, who at present are excluded from the political arena, were brought into it. Thus in the foregoing example, devaluation would be against the immediate interests of those with jobs (as represented by politically powerful trade unions) but would help those without jobs (who have little political influence). If the voice of those without jobs were made more effective, better decisions would be made. But it was not clear how these groups were to be brought in, or who was to bring them.

Lack of information is undoubtedly a central reason for failure to exploit possibilities. To negotiate successfully with a great power, a multinational firm or an aid agency requires information on how they operate, what their interests are, and what alternatives are open. None of these is easy for a small country – and especially an isolated small country – to acquire. Certainly small countries should invest far more in information. We were told of countries whose economy and public revenue were almost entirely dependent on the activities of one major company, but where the affairs of that company were the concern of only one official in government, and occupied only a quarter of his time. But even if substantially increased resources were invested in information-gathering, this might not be sufficient. The resources available to the multinational corporation, for example, are such that there may well be an inevitable asymmetry between its ability to obtain information concerning the country in which it operates and that country's ability to obtain information about the corporation. This shows itself in various ways. We were told of a negotiation between a government and a major international corporation, in which one local official had received government-financed training which enabled him to understand how the corporation operated. The official was approached privately by the corporation, and was offered a job with them at three times his existing salary. The ability of the multinational corporation to block off sources of information may well be out of all proportion to the country's ability to obtain access to information.

Possibly the answer will be found in international or regional action. UN agencies might be able to provide expert information in such areas; regional organisations could more economically hire the expertise needed. But how is a small country to judge the value and accuracy of the information it obtains through such channels? There may well be no universally satisfactory answer to this problem.

Lastly there is inertia – the continued use of systems, policies, attitudes, habits of work for years after they have become obsolete and irrelevant. Examples in the field of administration are given in Jacobs' paper. But it may be doubted whether there is more inertia in small countries' administrations than in those of large countries. As Schaffer and Corbett (1965) put it:

'Decision-making, particularly of what might be called a policy making type . . . is not something which on the whole is sought for; it does tend, for the great part, to be avoided. There is an inertia here . . . a "lag".'

But although the existence of inertia may be a general feature of decision-making institutions, the effects may be more serious in a small country with little surplus administrative capacity and a need for very flexible responses to external and internal situations.

In all, the main requirement for the most fruitful use of small countries' room for manoeuvre may be summarised as national feeling plus information. Neither is sufficient without the other. But if both exist, small countries can explore new alternatives, and break out of apparently determined situations of dependence. But the sheer isolation of many small countries as well as the presence of ruling groups who identify less with their own people than with an international political and economic system are severe constraints on what is possible. Dependence is thus not simply a relation between a small country and the external world; it is a problem internal to the small country itself. Breaking out of conditions of dependence and exploring possible areas of manoeuvre involve not only a particular set of policies towards the outside world; they also involve internal changes.

But national feeling itself may be self-defeating, if it acts as a barrier in the way of regional cooperation. It was noticeable that whenever regional issues were raised at the conference they aroused little interest. However, the regional approach is important for two reasons – first, because any adequate analysis of many small country problems must take into account the regional dimension, and secondly because solutions to such problems may involve regional cooperation.

The regional dimension is more important in the understanding of small country problems than in that of large country problems. It is virtually impossible to appreciate Lesotho's situation except in the context of its spatial position in Southern Africa; an analysis of Chinese or Indian problems could largely ignore the impact of these countries' neighbours. A large country is likely to include economic regions; a small country may well be part of an economic region. This is another aspect of the increased openness of small country economies. If (as is frequently the case) a small country is part of a nuclear region, it may be either the nucleus of such a region or on the periphery. It may be part of a system of increasing and cumulative spatial inequality, involving the movement of people and resources into the nuclear country, and the decay and depopulation of the periphery. These dynamic factors are an essential element in the analysis of the problems of individual countries (although *exclusively* spatial and regional analyses may be as partial and misleading as those limited to small countries as such).

Thus studies of small countries as entities are likely to be partial and misleading. Equally, many small country problems could, at least in theory, usefully be approached on a regional level. If, as Jacobs' paper suggests, the limited clientele for specialised services makes it uneconomic for small countries to provide them, they could possibly be supplied regionally. Again, regional integration systems such as common markets can create inter-industry linkages and economies of scale, and lead to the production of a wider range of manufactures than is possible on the basis of individual country markets. If, as the papers by Ally and de Vries suggest, small countries find it difficult to develop certain desirable types of monetary and financial institutions, these could be organised on a regional basis. The bargaining power of a region with multinational corporations or foreign governments may be far greater than that of its individual members. Where individual small countries lack the resources needed to obtain information or to develop techniques relevant to their needs, these might be provided regionally.

These appear formidable arguments, and it is therefore necessary to explain the apparently limited interest in the regional approach to small country problems and in regional solutions to them. There appear to be various reasons. First, the existence of nation states as areas of decision-making means that those involved in policy formulation and implementation will have their view of the problems facing them bounded by the limits of their own country; they are not usually required to take foreign countries into account in coming to decisions. Abbott argues that nationalism is a necessary half-way house on the way to regionalism; it could equally be argued that nationalism is a major barrier in the way of regionalism. This view of problems in national terms is reinforced by the operations of foreign experts who are brought in to advise individual governments. The terms of reference of such experts will normally concern particular country problems and situations, and their analysis and recommendations may be equally so bounded.

Moreover, the history of many regional integration systems has been disappointing. First, and best known, is the uneven distribution of costs and benefits inside regional trading arrangements. Indeed, it was emphasised that no such arrangement is viable unless it incorporates some system of compensation for those members who gain little if anything from it. Secondly, the process of decision-making in regional cooperation systems may be complex and slow. The example of the Eastern Caribbean Currency Board was quoted: any decision involves the agreement of 13 governments. It is hardly surprising that the exchange rate for the Eastern Caribbean currency vis-à-vis sterling is never altered. Lastly the actual benefits obtained – and in particular from the establishment of regional trading groups among small countries – may be limited, for the reasons Ward suggests.

Many of these difficulties may be lessened if a pragmatic approach is taken to regional arrangements. The principal need is to identify the appropriate unit for specific functions. There is nothin sacrosanct about any particular grouping: the 'region' might well be of a different size for different functions. Different levels or orders might be appropriate for different types of decision. Many of us were impressed by the practical and cautious approach which has been taken by CARIFTA, and its avoidance of rigid, predetermined frameworks for regional action.

What conclusions can we draw from all this? First, when looking at small countries, our first need is to define the problem with which we are concerned. Are we concerned about problems of size as such, or about problems of poverty and backwardness as aggravated by small size? Most of us would prefer to think of small size as a constraint in tackling other problems, rather than as a problem in itself. Certainly we saw no virtue in bigness as such except as a means for achieving particular social goals.

Secondly, how weak are the policy instruments at the disposal of small countries? If they are weak, is there nothing to be done? or is there nevertheless an agenda for action? Which elements in dependence are structural and which are contingent on policies and decisions? Even those who were most impressed by the weakness of autonomous decision-making capacity in small countries believed that there were *some* areas of possible action; the argument was about the extent of that range. If there is room for manoeuvre, how can it best be exploited and what are the constraints on its exploitation? But merely to pose these questions brings out the limitations of the different disciplines. The exploitation of room for manoeuvre may involve political action in an area of economic decision-making profoundly influenced by social structures and attitudes. A full understanding of what is possible cannot be achieved by either the political scientist or the economist or the sociologist. The narrowness of the scope for action imposes the need for a multidisciplinary approach to the problem, so as to exploit all possible insights and possibilities.

All these considerations suggest further areas of study. Possibly of most importance is more detailed work on the mutual interaction of groups inside the small countries and the external organisations and systems on which they are dependent. As the conference suggested, this need not necessarily be a one-sided relationship. Internal policies in small countries may affect the nature and organisation of aid; there have been various reactions to the multinational corporation, ranging from outright nationalisation as in Guyana, to attempts to bring the activities of the corporation into line with local policies, as in Botswana and other countries. More empirical work needs to be done on the range of options open to small countries in their relations with external sources of decision-making, and on the implications of these options for internal policies and structures.

In all this, we must continuously be aware of the broader environment and problems of the post-colonial era. The colonial past both imposes constraints and creates possibilities. As Brookfield (1973) says about Melanesia:—

'The colonial process is a revolutionary transformation of a society through invasion by agents of another society. If the invasion is to have been worthwhile it must have led to the creation of new indigenous institutions capable of taking over a part of its role in maintaining and developing the new external linkages. This does not mean the "taming" of that system . . . . The measure of success or failure is thus the progress towards creation of a mixed economy which can retain and widen the external linkages created by colonialism but in a more equal partnership with the external world. This is a long process, and the ending of political colonialism is only one stage along it, albeit an essential one.'

The other principal area of study has already been suggested. Some countries appear to have succeeded — at least in part — in overcoming the constraints imposed by small size. How has this been done, and how far is their experience reproducible? Have such countries achieved industrial growth and social transformation at the expense of increasing internal inequality? Is this the kind of development which people in small countries want; and if not, what alternatives do they have?

REFERENCES

G. Beckford:	*Persistent Poverty: Underdevelopment in Plantation Economies of the Third World* (London, OUP, 1972).
B. Benedict (ed.):	*Problems of Smaller Countries* (University of London, Institute of Commonwealth Studies, Paper No. 10, 1967).
L. Best:	'Size and Survival' (New World Quarterly, Vol. 2, No. 3, 1966).
H.C. Brookfield:	*Colonialism, Development and Independence* (Cambridge University Press, 1972).
H.B. Chenery and L. Taylor:	'Development Patterns: Among Countries and Over Time' (The Review of Economics and Statistics, Vol. 1. No. 4, November 1968).
Commonwealth Caribbean Regional Secretariat:	*From CARIFTA to Caribbean Community* (Georgetown, 1972).
W. Demas:	*The Economics of Development of Small Countries with Special Reference to the Caribbean* (McGill, 1965).
G.F. Erb and S. Schiavo-Campo:	'Export Stability, Level of Development and Economic Size of Less Developed Countries' (Bulletin of Oxford University Institute of Economics and Statistics, Vol. 31, No. 4, November 1969).
I.L.O.:	*Towards Full Employment: A Programme for Colombia* (Geneva, I.L.O., 1970); *Matching Employment Opportunities and Expectations: A Programme of Action for Ceylon* (Geneva, I.L.O., 1971);

23

	Employment, Incomes and Equality: A strategy for increasing productive employment in Kenya (Geneva, I.L.O., 1972).
C. Kennedy:	'Keynesian Theory in an Open Economy' (Social and Economic Studies, Vol. 15, No. 1, March 1966).
S. Kuznets:	*Economic Growth of Nations* (Cambridge, Harvard University Press, 1971).
E.A.G. Robinson (ed.):	*Economic Consequences of the Size of Nations* (London, Macmillan, 1960).
B.B. Schaffer and D.C. Corbett:	*Decisions: Case Studies in Australian Administration* (Melbourne and Canberra, F.W. Cheshire, 1965).
D. Seers:	'The Mechanism of an Open Petroleum Economy' (Social and Economic Studies, June 1964).
P. Selwyn:	'The Least Developed Countries at Santiago' (Bulletin of the Institute of Development Studies, Vol. 5, No. 1, January 1973).
Osvaldo Sunkel:	'National Development Policy and External Dependence in Latin America' (Journal of Development Studies, Vol. 6, No. 1, October 1969).
United Nations:	*Trade Expansion and Economic Integration Among Developing Countries* (TD/B/85 Rev. 1, 1967); *Committee for Development Planning: Report on the Seventh Session* (E/4990, New York, United Nations, 1971).

1. THE POLITICS OF DEPENDENCE

Bernard Schaffer

Summary

Relative political dependence is defined in terms of a 'score' by which
countries may be ordered — a country's actual score depending on a
variety of factors such as size, poverty, remoteness, ethnicity. But
although countries are at different levels of dependence, independent
countries have a formally equal status. The formal status of
independence tends to be maintained by the ideology of 'extantism' —
the support for already existing nation states; while formal
independence itself helps to improve a country's score on the
dependence/independence scale. An example of the interaction of
these elements and the small country's room for manoeuvre is given
from the area of defence policy.

I. Introduction

The process of decolonisation has created the phenomenon of many
small independent countries. Although there is no clear association
between country size and other measures (such as income per head)
by which countries may be ordered, many small countries are in fact
poor, isolated or remote. This situation raises a number of questions.
How far are such countries more or less vulnerable? In what sense
may we describe them as dependent or independent? What room do
they have to move in, granted the apparent if varying restrictions which
comparative degrees of smallness impose?

This paper distinguishes between the formal status of independence
and a scale of dependence/independence. According to the formal
status (e.g. in United Nations voting), all independent countries appear
equal; there is no question of greater or lesser degrees of independence.
But in practice certain countries have more discretion or room to
manoeuvre than others. Countries may thus be ordered, or assigned a
'score', along an independence/dependence scale. A country's score
along such a scale will be affected by many factors, of which size is
only one. There are internal factors such as ethnicity and particularistic
divisions; there are external questions such as the various alternative
international strategies that may be available. Score is also governed
by the skill with which a country handles its internal and external
problems. A small country can achieve a higher score by the exercise
of Machiavellian 'virtù'.

What is the relation between this score and the formal status of
independence? It will be argued that these relations are in fact quite
complex, and that in particular the existence of the formal status of

independence helps a country's score through the operation of what is described as the ideology of 'extantism'. This is the ideological support given by the international community to existing international frontiers.

The paper argues that on certain conditions the small country's room for manoeuvre can be increased. Some of the apparent limitations on political discretion are contingent rather than structural. The small country has certain opportunities, if it will use them.

II. Dependence as a score

The formal status of political independence seems to be completely and astonishingly egalitarian, as with United Nations voting rights. Informal status is another thing. It can be taken to be a sort of score along a scale of dependence/independence. The score reflects three elements. The first is inegalitarian and linear, a pecking-order of states. This is a matter of international stratification (Nettl, 1967). Secondly, there is a tendency to move towards or away from the condition of the client state dependent on its patron. Thirdly, there is the factor of institutional reiteration. This operates in instances of inheritance after colonial preparatory processes (Schaffer, 1965).

Reiteration of inheritance of this sort is one of the ways in which decolonialisation is of peculiar importance in the study of small countries. Action in territory A is a result of action in territory B. This can apply in domestic administration, legislation, justice, technology. Thus Irish public administration and welfare and political institutions are not the same as those of Britain. They could not be, and there is much from the United States (as in judicial review), France and so forth. There were attempts in the past to do something different: proportional representation; the O'Higgins experiment with 'extern' ministers. Southern Ireland operated proprotionate representation, where Northern Ireland gave it up. Yet the reiterative effect in public administration and in social welfare is clear enough: the basic parliamentary, ministerial, administrative and other systems.

There is a close relationship between this sort of reiterative factor and international stratification. Internal qualities like the nature of the independence movement and the post-independence political class, will partly determine the nature of the reference groups effective for the particular small country – whom they are comparing themselves with or feel ambivalently inferior to, and hence how they feel themselves placed in the pecking-order. It follows that the way in which international stratification affects the score is related to many internal cultural factors, a psychology of dependence and the aftermath of decolonialisation. The aftermath may be more severe in small countries, because of the limitations and dependence of educational systems, the brain drain, or the uncomfortable position of some ethnic groups. The

26

small country will tend to occupy a peripheral rather than a metropolitan place, having branch rather than head offices. This can be very irritating. In brief, the formalities of decolonialisation have created smallness. Smallness exacerbates some resultant problems – the domination of smaller budgets by public service costs has not been eased by the colonial inheritance. This narrows the range of policy choices and increases the problems of political leadership in small countries as they search for more adequate sources of independent support and expertise.

These are never the problems of smallness alone, but of smallness combined with poverty and isolation. A low score occurs with isolation, poverty, dispersal, sparseness or 'congestion' in the old Scottish and Irish sense, working with smallness. The British Solomon Islands Protectorate is a classic case of isolation and smallness associated with extreme dependence (Schaffer, 1966). Even here, internal and other comparisons remain possible: unevenness within the islands affects the overall situation. There are 47 Gilbert and Ellice Islands spread over 2 million square miles of ocean with only 369 square miles of dry land, of which only 141 square miles would bear tree crops. The Solomon Islands, on the other hand, have 11,500 square miles of land mostly concentrated in 6 islands or groups spread along a chain 900 miles long. The population of 160,000 is big in comparison with the Gilbert and Ellice Islands, small by any other standard, but again very unevenly distributed, about 14 per square mile compared with approximately 800 on Nupani or 1 on Vanikovo.

The concepts we are looking at here are then comparative, and subject to indefinite disaggregation as we apply them to any particular territory: is it really small; in what way is it isolated; is its population sparse, scattered, congested? But when a number of low scores are registered on population, poverty and certain sorts of isolation and area scales, then other features do tend to occur again and again, such as a tendency towards an over-specialised or mono-culture and market dependence. In particular, isolation is often reinforced by budgetary dependence, inflexible and difficult taxation situations, and the problems of minimum institutional size.

All the characteristics associated with poverty, isolation and smallness are present in the Solomons situation – a market dependence on the British, Australian and Japanese markets, with some movement between them; with one export, copra, worth ten to twenty times as much as the next most important export, timber. But we also note three other things. There is isolationism which expresses itself in hostility towards its nearest neighbours, the Gilbert and Ellice Islands, particularly when the Gilbertese present themselves for resettlement on the Solomons. This is a sort of infinite recession since there is a similar isolation between the Gilbert and Ellice islanders and the Ocean islanders. This might presumably go down to the smallest of inhabited islands, and might be called the Easter Island syndrome. Secondly, the Solomons have been heavily dependent on a budget deficit grant-in-aid from the UK, supplemented by OSAS and schemes under the Colonial Development and Welfare Acts, and on export/import taxation. They are a marked example of this key factor. The size of constituencies, electorates and legislative council are reduced about as far as they can be.[1] Thus the factor of isolationism with group hostilities, of budgetary dependence as part of decolonialisation and minimum institutional size clearly relate to dependence/independence scores for small countries.

Papua New Guinea with nearly 2½ million people is much bigger than these examples, but is still a very small country by most standards. Something like the same characteristics tending towards dependence reveal themselves. The gross monetary sector product is currently running at about 353 million Australian dollars. The Australian Government grant-in-aid is about 134 million dollars, and the contribution to the GMSP of one single enterprise (the Bougainville Copper Project) is about 55 million dollars rising to 120 million dollars over the next decade. The budgetary contribution of the BCP has been much emphasised.

Secondly, the problems of isolation and of particularistic relations in small countries are shown by process of change here and elsewhere. The case of the Seychelles shows how these factors react on each other. Here the attempt to redress a foreign trade dependence on the export of copra and cinnamon through growth in the tourist industry is to some extent limited by geographical isolation. It is also divisive. Some people benefit sharply by the change in land values, others benefit a little by employment, and others suffer severly through radical price changes and the supply effects on basic foodstuffs. This differential distribution of benefits happens to be ethnic (the grands blancs benefit, and others suffer), so ethnicity and emergent stratification go together. Similarly, any attempt to move out of political isolation (by continuing association with Europe or by a movement towards Africa and the OAU) is itself divisive along similar lines.

The multiplex nature of interactions in a small country may reinforce the tendency of movements in one sector to aggravate the situation in another. In other words a coincidence of smallness, isolation and poverty sets up time and again certain features tending to reinforce dependence. They weaken the policy variables, strengthen the possibilities of intervention by metropolitan powers and diminish the usefulness of some formal arrangements. This is exacerbated by problems of political institutionalisation. Attempts to reduce this tendency towards dependence have costs, meet constraints, and create divisions.

The dependence of small countries is also reinforced by emerging ethnicities and stratification patterns. They limit the room for manoeuvre (the political discretion) of the small country. This can be countered by other factors, the single Catholic religion of the Seychellois, for example, homogeneity and the possibilities of integration and mobilisation. This is one thesis about dependence and the small country. Dependence is associated with smallness, poverty and isolation. This is related to institutional as well as market features, to budgets and perhaps to isolationism, ethnic problems, stratification and divisive effects of change. But dependence is a score, not a category, and the score can be changed.

III. The formal status of independence

A second thesis about the politics of dependence is the contrast between the egalitarianism of formal political independence and those actual tendencies to dependence, or to a low score on the dependence/independence scale. There is some relationship between extremities of smallness and the movement from formal dependence to independence. The dependent status or very lately acquired independence of most of the territories we have already mentioned, or of the Bahamas, are cases in point. But it was not until the number of extremely small isolated territories applying for equal country membership of the United Nations had gone on increasing for twenty years, to include the Maldives by September 1965, that the United Nations General Assembly began to search for some sort of halt or escape. It was this problem of multiplicity in conjunction with what has been called 'the significant factor of remoteness' (Benedict, p.54), rather than mere smallness itself which created a sense of difficulty. It was the large number of small countries, often remote, which added something new to the situation.

The effective ideology which dominated the participants in the United Nations for twenty years was best expressed in General Assembly Resolution 1514 (XV) of 14 December 1960: there was to be a movement forthwith from dependence to independence without reference to any conditions at all. This was in marked contrast with the League of Nations. The League's first assembly had recommended certain conditions to be met by applicants for membership, including ' . . . what are its size and population?' Yet it was from the First World War and the Wilsonian Six Points that the ideology of self-determination was developed. This had been to satisfy Slavophiles and the hostility of liberals and American voters to the prostrate Austro-Hungarian Empire (one of the great buttresses of all time against the small country), and to create a whole tradition in favour of independence in spite of smallness (Fisher).

This ideology of self-determination allowed a creation of smallness within a land continent, not merely the later use of the oceanic principle for the break-up of imperial and federal relationships. It was a principle which found expression in the multiplication of Scandinavian states, the creation of many small Slav states, the persistence of Switzerland, and the disintegration of the Czarist frontier with the Baltic and of the last vestiges of the Holy Roman Empire itself.

Many states were certainly created in this way. But this was a limited multiplicity, affected to only a limited degree by poverty and indeed smallness itself. It was scarcely affected at all by the third factor, isolation (despite Chamberlain's contemptuous words about Czechoslovakia). It was an attempt to solve ethnic divisions. It was too liberal to be troubled about class: its failures there were, precisely, what destroyed the formal independence of its small members. Ironically enough, this was in conjunction with the isolationism of others.

But the situation now (using a criterion of extreme smallness, less than 1 million population) shows something like 100 distinct countries of which more than one half are not (in 1972) self-governing. Most of the non-self-governing territories are clearly recognised as such. There are two remaining trust territories, two for which no information is transmitted to the United Nations, eight whose status is in dispute, six associated and seven protected states.

The United Nations, then, has some very small members and recognises many others as separate countries. There remains a small majority of these very small countries which are still either formally dependent or non-self-governing. But even if we accepted a dichotomy of formal dependence and independence, we would see a complex set of formal statuses and some special categories, particularly with association and protection. Formal statuses cannot be ignored in explaining actual patterns. There are three points here. First, it is a matter of approaching self-government and independence. There is no clear dichotomy even here, as the whole experience of decolonisation and preparation made quite clear (Schaffer, 1965). Secondly, many in each category are very small. A narrow majority of the very small are not formally independent. Relatively few are yet United Nations members. So the full force of this multiplicity of small, poor and isolated countries seeking and having to be granted membership has by no means yet hit the United Nations. It may have got to the Maldives and the Gambia but there are others waiting in the lobbies.[2] The third point follows: the status of formal independence may, we shall see, be worthwhile for the dependence/independence score of small countries. But it may become less easy to acquire in the future.

The large non-self-governing group recognised by the United Nations includes something like 28 countries which are subject to annual examination by the Committee of 24 or submit information to it. For the most part they are what most participants would recognise as 'colonies'. Many of them have been so described in United Nations

30

resolutions, like General Assembly Resolution 2354 (XXII), 1967. Ifni and the Spanish Sahara is a typical case in point. To the metropolitan country, Spain, it ranks as a province and to two other member nations (Morocco and Mauritania) it might rank as rightly a part of their own territory, though there may well be dispute between them. To various members some of this group of 28 are independent or self-governing or well on the way to it, a protectorate of some metropolitan power, part of some other federation or a separated part of another member. A case in point is the status of British Honduras (Belize) as seen by itself, the United Nations, Britain or Guatemala.

Many of the other categories of formal status include little other than extremely small, isolated and scattered islands in the Atlantic or Caribbean. In the past some other formal statuses like trusteeship have mattered considerably. Nothing is left there other than the 'strategic trust territory' of the US Trust Territory of the Pacific and the northern part of Papua New Guinea, all of which is now well on the way to independence. There are also some statuses which barely matter at all, for example, 'dependent, non-self-governing territories for which no information under chapter XI is asked for or sent'. The Christmas and Norfolk Islands are examples.

There are other statuses along the formal line from dependence to independence which do indicate important political facts. These include countries where there is a dispute between the United Nations and the administering power. These are all instances of Portuguese administration (save the French Territory of the Afars and Issas, and Namibia) and they are mainly small: Timor, Cape Verde and Guinea-Bissau. Secondly, there are states with various sorts of association or protected relationship with some metropolitan power. An important case here is the Cook Islands and their association with New Zealand, itself a small country. Elections were held in the Cook Islands in April 1965; they led to a formula with New Zealand in August 1965 which the United Nations General Assembly later approved (Resolution 2065 XX) on 16 December 1967. It recognised it as a form of self-government and accepted that the islands could be granted independence if they wished. There are similar arrangements with western Samoa. A formula of association was then used after the collapse of federation for some countries within the former British West Indies in February and March 1967. (West Indies Act, 1967.) The protected state formula used by India for Bhutan and Sikkim and by the UK for Tonga and for Muscat and Oman is distinct from association. So are some recent federal arrangements. British treaty arrangements in imperial days are, of course, a poor guide to the contemporary possibilities of special associations.

In addition to disputed status and these forms there are types of integration which move beyond association or federation. In one sense they involve the disappearance of the small countries. They are an integration of overseas countries with a metropolitan state. But the countries still exist as a sort of actual geographical and therefore under the oceanic principle, potentially political separation. All the examples, save two, are French, and are in the Caribbean and Pacific. France has forwarded no information about them under Chapter XI since 1947. One exception is Denmark and the Faroes. The other is Northern Ireland.

There are special arrangements, as for the Ryukus between the US and Japan; or for the canal zone between the US and Panama; or partial integration, as for the Isle of Man and the Channel Islands and the United Kingdom. There is also the important case of Irian Barat. This could have been regarded as either a small country, one part of another small country (New Guinea), or a separated part of a very large one (Indonesia). At any rate, it involved a long dispute which the United Nations settled (Lijphart, 1966). The dispute was followed by a provisional integration of Irian Barat with Indonesia between 1963 and 1969, followed now by a full integration (Hastings, 1970). There will be no formal independence here.

IV. The ideology of independence

The movement through complexities of formal status matters to the United Nations. It matters in many other ways: as creating prizes to be sought; as provoking types of political dispute; as a factor in national or other habits; and as exposing the inconsistencies of international politics. The main prize is in fact a special sort of ideological support for formal independence, presumably lessening the actual dependence (improving the dependence/independence score) of small countries. What are these factors of support and of dependence?

As far as support is concerned, we remark the confusion with which the political debate, particularly in the General Assembly, has been conducted. What, for example, are the entities which are to be moved, to be made separate, formally independent, given membership, and so forth? The United Nations has spoken variously of 'peoples', 'territory', 'territorial integrity of the country'. The United Nations talks mainly in relation to membership of 'state . . .', the World Bank of 'countries', and the FAO of 'nations'.

The emerging law of the United Nations helps to indicate when a country is a state rather than a people, territory or so forth. It must have a population and a territory but also a government and a capacity to conduct relations predominantly with the other United Nations members (Higgins). United Nations practice might also indicate a neglected but worthwhile criterion for extreme smallness, at any rate for UN members: those entitled to pay subscriptions at a minimum percentage level. Not to be represented in these arenas is a real example of dependence.[3] This is perhaps a critical group of small countries and an indication of one relation of coincidence of smallness and recognised poverty.

Political practice, again particularly in the United Nations General Assembly, has been astonishingly inconsistent between like cases, and the ideologies have scarcely been subject to examination. Thus on 19 December 1967 the United Nations General Assembly under Resolution 2348 (XXII) demanded universal (etcetera) elections for Papua in that year, despite the fact that such elections had already taken place in 1964 and were being prepared again for 1968. At the same time it had granted an 'act of choice' to the people of Irian Barat in 1963. This took place in 1969 and was accepted by the United Nations. It was totally different from the electoral process which was being demanded by the same body at the same time for this other part of the same island. On the same day the Assembly passed a resolution condemning electoral or referendum processes for Gibraltar (Resolution 2353 [XXII]). In the referendum, 12,138 opted for the UK link and 44 for Spanish sovereignty. In December 1967 the Cook Islands Association formula had been approved by the Assembly; in October 1967 the Committee of 24 had reconfirmed its Resolution 1514 demanding unconditional independence for all at once; and in February of that year the association agreement for Antigua etc. had been opposed.

It is not surprising that practices within an international arena should be discontinuous with ideologies. This may indicate the function of the United Nations (C.C. O'Brien). But the degree of inconsistency in this case is exceptional. The United Nations inherited an ideology of self-determination from the League and from decolonialisation. It added a further concept of the virtue of territorial integrity. Under the combination of these two slogans countries of any size at all could be created. Once created they would be maintained. This set of slogans expressed the ideology of the Assembly and the international community. But the virtues of self-determination and territorial integrity had two equivalent vices: secession and fragmentation. This ideology thus contains internal contradictions only solved by the strength and resources of particular groups of actors. Secession is bad, but it becomes self-determination (good) for some groups, though not for others. And Assembly resolutions had ruled out the use of any tests of scale for distinguishing these groups, as in 1514 (XV). Furthermore, the ideology could actually be used either to invite or to condemn smallness. It invited smallness for the 'self-determination' of 'peoples' (1515, 2) but defended the 'territorial integrity' of any 'country' (1514, 6). Any people could create a country but any country once created was to be maintained: what, then, of any other people? This is one view of the UN 'colonial fork'.[4] Some existing situations were even ranked as 'dismemberment' rather than 'self-determination'.

Their continued existence was an affront to 'territorial integrity' rather than an instance of it. This was the Spanish attitude to the continued separation of Gibraltar.

The burden of the ideology was to create smallness and to maintain it: an ideology of persistence, of the virtue of the extant. Some ideologies of 'decentralisation' or 'autonomy' could be enunciated to demand or justify movements short of 'dismemberment', but the dominant ideology has been what we might call extantism. The equality of status of formal independence carried the genuine political prize of this ideological support by the international community.

Grades of actual dependence, the scores on the dependence/independence scale, are affected by other things too, including the complexities of formal status. This may limit the value of the prize granted by status. Nigerian and Pakistani experiences provide cases on either side of the argument: the prize is nevertheless genuine. How then does the formal status of independence relate to actual dependence? Look at some examples of very small countries and formal status. Some very small UN member countries are parts of European history and more or less distant from formal dependence, like Iceland, which is nevertheless an extreme example of the monoculture typical of small island economies. Luxembourg and Malta are also examples of small countries which are very much part of European history. Iceland and Malta counter their problems of potential dependence by aggressive manoeuvring and Luxembourg by the regional arrangements of the Common Market. Iceland is independent and adopts one attitude to the law of the sea. Bermuda, Bahamas and the British Solomons are not independent, and have to adopt another.

Western Samoa enjoys independence, avoids UN membership, but joins international agencies. Nauru, an extremely small island territory newly independent, does not bother with agency membership but relies on Australia. It has, however, managed to negotiate with Australia on the one topic which matters. As a phosphate island, it is the extreme example of monoculture. Andorra, a very ancient non-island territory and part of European history, bothers neither with UN nor agency membership, and even manages to avoid having its own head of state (using the co-presidency of the President of the French Republic and the Bishop of Urgei in Spain). Instances of full integration have presumably gone beyond any problems of dependence, like Saar or the former British territories of Togoland, Somaliland, North Cameroons and Zanzibar, the present American states of Hawaii and Alaska, or Goa and the former French enclaves which were transferred to India in 1950 and 1954.[5]

The existence of such a list is striking. The ideology under which small countries have been ushered into existence may be full of easily-exposed contradictions. That is the nature of ideology. Many small countries have been more or less recently subject to formal political dependence, and this tends, we shall argue, to provide an inescapable inheritance of continuing significance. The simple equalities of formal independence stand in sharp contrast to the complex scales of smallness, poverty, isolation, institutional imitation, monoculture and divisiveness all limiting the actual room for manoeuvre of the small country. Yet the dominant fact has surely been the persistence of small countries, particularly in contemporary times, once they have been created by decolonialisation. This persistence is certainly aided by the ideological prize of extantism.

Furthermore, decolonialisation has been followed not merely by this persistence of status itself, but also by the persistence of those precise borders first created by the colonial scramble. How weak the 'pan' movements have been, how persistent, even bloody the arbitrary borders of some armistice lines of latitude. Why is this? It is the most modernised groups, and in particular the political class, who are most identified with these boundaries of the small country. It is they who are the leaders and enjoy the profits; it is they at least who are most aware of, even if sometimes anguished by them. This was true of the nationalist Slav intelligentsia of the last century. The potential demarcations of the hoped-for utopias of self-determination were determined by intellectual phenomena: the politicisation of religion, culture and historical memories; folk-song and fable turned to frontier posts. Above all it was newly-educated intellectuals typically rediscovering demotic languages in rural groups. The nationalist and narodnik went together. Whether the peasant himself would actually want to go with them was quite another matter (Seton-Watson).

It was only around the concept of some visible frontier that an independence movement could be created. In the last century in Europe this was meant (as by Mazzini) to be one step on the way to some sort of world humanitarian federation. In modern anti-colonialism it was at least meant to be one step on the way to 'pan' movements. Neither has eventuated. The frontiers have become precious to those who fought for them, who now enjoy them and who are made even more aware of them by the modernising forces of international trade and international cultural exchange. In the past, the European intelligentsia created the European map of 'self-determining' frontiers; the frontiers created political roles (including exile) for former intellectuals. In more recent times, European colonialism set up a fresh set of frontiers including districts (Ballard). These created independence movements. The movements and the frontiers established a political class, a modernised elite inevitably and deeply attached to these frontiers. Extantism is a successful ideology, partly explaining the persistence of small countries, partly because it suits certain groups. The external position of small countries, their frontiers and their persistence, the discretion they have, partly has to be explained then in terms of the sorts of politics they are, their ideological resources, the favoured groups, and the unfavoured.

V. The maintenance of independence

Smallness by itself does not seem to indicate any necessary coincidence with severe and actual political dependence (a very low score, a loss of status) short of the presence of some other factors. Independence can recruit several prizes and allies. How does this work out? Bargaining processes around potential dependence (who shall be our master?) can be profitable to the small bargainer, again dependent on the presence of other conditions. The willing and attractive slave can conduct his own auction. As long as he can do so, he is not, in fact, quite a slave. Malta is a case in point. It follows that in those circumstances the dependence is not fixed. A fresh auction can be called. Persistence can be maintained and the loss of status avoided partly by trading off some features of formal independence such as bases. One condition for this strategy is the presence of willing dominants. There are other rather different though not unrelated conditions which affect the possibility of successful political bargaining, and of the exploitation of discretion by the small country.

These other factors are likely to be closely related to internal as well as international factors. The small country might have a base to sell or more frequently to proscribe or to interdict pre-emption. Despite some notable cases (Cuba, Cyprus) it is difficult to insulate the base within its perimeter wholly from the domestic conditions of the small country in which the base is offered. The 1967 Act for the West Indian association arrangements formally recognised the relations between internal problems of government and the right of Britain to interfere.[6] The regime problems of St. Vincent prevented the use of the association formula.

More frequently, there is an interplay between both the economic and the political external manoeuvring of the country and domestic conditions. In most small countries a choice of allies is restricted by potentially divisive effects on domestic ethnic, class and religious facts. Particularisms are no less expressive in small countries. Caribbean and Pacific examples come to mind. It is not that small countries do not have room for manoeuvre as a counter to political dependence. But their particularism is vivid. The domestic constraints on external manoeuvre are therefore very sharp. Extantism, we have argued, is one of the potential advantages available from formal independence. It has to be developed through mechanisms of political ideology, leadership and support. These mechanisms tend to be most available and attractive for political classes and modernised groups. The supporters are the party activists, the bureaucracy, educated groups and institutional members, the capital and the urban centres: broadly the actual or potential beneficiaries of the new state institutions, rather than peasants, subsistence food croppers or indeed professionals escaping through the brain drain. At the same time the domestic version of the ideology which most easily harmonises with extantism tends to depend on a sort of nationalising of ethnicity. The majority, the people, the country or territory, the state, the regime and the political leadership become identified.

Ethnicity or some other particularism (like religion) can easily appear as a simple and suitable basis for primary loyalties. This is certainly an understandable but dangerous tendency in small countries. There are important exceptions where there is a wider basis for ideology or a successful employment of pluralism. Otherwise this tendency in small countries can exacerbate their problems of particularism, obstruct the expression of secularism and prevent the employment of some of the vital human resources available within their limited populations.

A small country can easily move either way. It is notable how different the attitude is between one small country and another, to the whole issue of 'representative bureaucracy'. In some instances it seems vital to secure the representation of all groups in public employment. In others the issue seems unimportant. In others again it seems potentially so important that it can scarcely be discussed at all. The possibilities of political mobilisation or alienation are both perculiarly important and peculiarly high either way. The tendency of political leadership in small countries is to seek the simple way out suggested by that very ideology of extantism which their formal independence provides. But this route has dangers. In the meantime changes are afoot and their effects may be divisive.

One of the changes is that most small, poor and isolated countries have moved to formal political independence only relatively recently. Their experience of formal political dependence has had a continuing impact on their politics. These are the factors of inheritance (Nettl). Several relevant points are indicated by the case of Papua New Guinea as it moves through the last stages of preparation for independence.

The non-indigenous population is minute, 43,000 out of 2,300,000. Yet the expatriate impact has been a dominating influence in increasing the economic dependence and vulnerability of the territory. 'The pattern of economic growth reflects the dominance of expatriate enterprise and investment from outside the territory' (Epstein, Parker, Reay, p.14). Formal political preparation has not so far broken down the parochial and cargoist nature of indigenous political behaviour. Here again, dependence and vulnerability continue: 'a certain timidity' or 'a sense of helplessness'. The informalities of political dependence are reinforced by the copying of political institutions, with a resultant 'formalism' (Riggs).

Throughout the processes of preparation both at legislative and administrative levels expatriates had been dominant. The indigenous members of the House of Assembly were very silent throughout the

1964-68 House (Epstein, Parker, Reay, 25). The first development of anything like an effective party was primarily in response to the anger of indigenous public servants about salaries. In other words, it was a response by the indigenous people most in contact with the expatriates. Meanwhile political and electoral education were highly 'attenuated' at village level: the nearer the village the more attenuated, apparently (Epstein, Parker, Reay, p.46).

By, say, the 1968 elections, a New Guinea political style was emerging; prominence in that arena was still dependent on prominence in the arena of contact with expatriates. But many indigenous elements existed, like the relative mildness of electoral competition and the possibility of mutual aid between candidates. While impulses towards political change were difficult to detect, 'such as they were, they pointed away from dependence and toward autonomy' (Epstein, Parker, Reay, p.356). Yet the Papua New Guinea case at this stage indicated the significance of formal political dependence for any sort of autonomous politicism which might develop.[7] Political independence has prizes. It also has complicated relationships with other sorts of continuing dependence. One of the complications is the likely continuation into the era of formal independence of an inheritance from the era of formal political dependence. This has a lot to do with the psychology of dependence and with the reference groups of the political classes created by the process of modernisation and preparation.

There must also be many types of actual dependence (i.e. low scores) short of the disappearance of the formal independence of small countries. The status persists. Luxembourg still exists within the Community, and the Union of Arab Emirates is independent of the United Kingdom. The fact that the small countries emerged out of decolonialisation added to their prestige. But the gains in status deriving from formal independence are a stabilising force for the small countries rather than for federal arrangements. The Organisation of African Unity has been notably more effective in settling disputes about territory and frontiers between its member states than in federating them. The irony is that this sort of organisation is coming to work increasingly well, but is keeping states politically distinct. It is a further factor in the success and power of extantism. The South Pacific Commission works well enough and the Pacific Islands Producers Secretariat (Tonga, Fiji, West Samoa and Cook Islands) even better in some ways, but again in making it possible for those small countries to persist rather than making it necessary for them to federate or unite. We may see a growth of forms of association between small countries. That is not the same as a growth of formal dependence. Small countries may be dependent but not so much that they have to disappear.

The outstanding instance is the failure of federation (Etzioni, Chapter 5 and R.L. Watts). Instances are familiar.[8] But there are cases of successful federal arrangements: Surinam and the Dutch Antilles with the Netherlands in 1954, Sabah and Sarawak in Malaysia since 1963, the West Cameroons with Cameroon since 1961. These have worked and have proved acceptable to the United Nations, not without certain problems. They suggest two conditions for successful and acceptable federation. One is the absence of external political competition with any interventionist capacity, which could feed on the divisive potentialities likely to be present in the particularisms of small countries. External competition can otherwise reinforce rather than weaken federal negotiation. Secondly, these successful federations tend to be asymmetrical. This may avoid the mere addition of weaknesses. They are built on a heavy imbalance, with one dominant partner. A small country might then avoid one sort of dependence by accepting as an alternative a membership in a federation where it will have to accept another sort of dependence.

Granted these conditions, as an example, will a federation like the Union of Arab Emirates work? The Union has been created among seven sheikhly states in the Persian Gulf so as to deal with problems like tribal fighting and rivalry from non-members. The previous system was to rely on arbitration by the Trucial Oman Scouts of Muscat and Oman officered by seconded UK professionals. The new arrangement seemed to be necessary with increasing wealth and the possibilities of separate armies amongst the seven. The Union is based therefore on the Union Defence Forces. This is essentially the defence force of Abu Dhabi with the defence minister supplied from Dubai. The officers are again UK professionals, either on secondment or contract, under the former commander of the Scouts, with UK arms (2 squadrons of Saladins).

The only part of the union which so far seems to be working properly is the Ministry of Defence. It has in fact functioned very successfully, for example in crushing the 1972 coup in Sharjah (though the then ruler Sheikh Khalid was killed) and in solving tribal disputes between Sharjah and El Fujayrah on the Batinah coast with Khor Fakkan and Kalba. But what would happen if there were a dispute between Abu Dhabi and Dubai? In other words the condition of a single domanant within a federation does not seem to be present.

The effect of external competition on the dependence score of small countries or federations of them is complicated. Competition amongst external powers can lead to the continued separateness of small countries. This amounts to a reduction of dependence. It can also increase their room for manoeuvre. On the other hand, it can lead to the absorption of the small countries by third parties. Competition between France and Portugal assisted the absorption of Goa in India. Competition between Ethiopia and Somalia about Djibouti led to the continued separation of that small country under French protection and its re-emergence as the French Territory of

Afars and Issas. Most striking of all is the case of Cyprus. External relations with Greece and Turkey and their local replication in community relations have made enosis, the absorption into Greece, impossible. Cyprus continues to exist as a separate small country precisely because of competition between two of the external powers acting on the divisiveness of the two local communities.

It has seemed more important for external powers to be represented in small countries than vice versa. Taking a random list of nine small countries with less than 1 million population, they had a total of 79 representatives overseas and 311 representatives of overseas countries in their own capitals. That is an average of less than 9 representatives sent by each and more than 44 received by each. Small countries cannot afford large overseas representational systems; one of the prizes of formal independence is the receipt of more representatives from other countries.

The strength and variety of factors which enable small countries once created to persist, to maintain independence, are to do with ideology, political elites and modernisation; the failure of alternatives like federations; competition between potential rivals and masters; the difficulties of absorption. But not only do particular small countries continue to exist, but many of them seem to be smaller than necessary. The frontiers themselves get fixed. The division between American and Western Samoa is a case in point.[9]

More generally the persistence of small countries in our times is contemporary with a re-emergence of a sort of cultural pluralism and a legitimation of certain sorts of relatively small groups. The melting-pot theory is over. Hyphenated Americans look at either side of the hyphen differently. Language societies are rampant, not dormant.

The oceanic concept hastened the disintegration of empires and legitimated any small country as long as it was an island, but the land frontiers established by colonial accident seemed to become persistent and legitimate facts once they were no longer imperial.[10] The interpretation of the oceanic concept increased the number of small countries which were also isolated. The persistence of ex-colonial land frontiers aggravated their irrationality. The isolation and irrationality of the situation of many small countries scarcely seemed to affect their persistence and extantism or depreciate their formal independence. There are, in any case, several different sorts of isolation.

In a classic case it was the isolation of Australia within the geo-politics of the British Commonwealth which created its peculiar dependence on the UK or the Royal Navy in particular. But it was also that isolation which broke the dependence in 1942 with the fall of Singapore. Up to then, because Australia was physically isolated and wished to remain so (that is, not associated with its near neighbours), it was for a long time effectively dependent. But in the end that isolation made the dependent relationship too expensive for the resources of the two parties. For the last thirty years Australian policy has moved between a search for a new sort of dependence (on the United States) or alternative associations. It is not at all clear what sort of dependence any particular sort of isolation will tend to create, nor whether there are alternatives.

VI. Score and status

We can now comment on the relation between the actual dependence of small, poor or isolated countries and the real prizes of formal political independence: the score and the status. Whatever the facts of dependence may be, political independence once granted tends to be persistent: the phenomenon of extantism. The cases of extantism are manifold. Potential counters, like isolation, are uncertain in their effects. The United Nations has been an arena within which the ideology of extantism has flourished. The formal independence which has been achieved has been sufficiently flexible to survive most contingencies and to survive the failure of federations, and even the re-emergence of a fairly severe dependence as between Nauru and Australia.

In some cases, the preparation for self-government and independence has left a permanent mark on the politics of newly independent but small states — the politics of dependence, in fact. In other cases it is remarkable how quickly much of the institutional impact of formal dependence disintegrated. The extra-territorial jurisdiction of the UK crown in Bahrain having been imposed was then gradually given up and withdrawn and has now completely disappeared from institutional life: 'retroceded'.[11] But all this is conditional. Room for political manoeuvre, actual political independence, is not absolute. The status affects but does not determine the score.

A small country must feel the comparatively large impact of a relatively small number of expatriate officials either in the past or the present. Bahrain or French West Africa are alike in this respect. Extremely small countries like the Gambia will go on using overseas institutions to escape from some of the constraints of scale. The factor of inheritance itself, as a small country moves from dependent to independent political development, can work out very differently both in impact, as between Bahrain and New Guinea, and in style. The British followed two styles of preparation: where the Durham Report worked and where it did not. The Portuguese used significant differences depending on racial factors. The Spanish seem to have changed their minds. The French have experimented with metropolitan absorption, with the use of the mechanism of the overseas departmental territory, the French union or community. The Dutch have experimented with federal arrangements. Generally, small countries which have moved away from formal political dependence to independence will have a politics which expresses some sort of inheritance. This can vary a good deal as the Bahrain case indicates. Inheritance elsewhere may express an actual dependence which may increase the prizes of formal political independence for some and depreciate them for others.

Sometimes the members of a small country can act as a single group. The Banabans of the Ocean Island (of the Gilbert and Ellice group) moved to Rabi in the Fiji group, rejected, as one man, independence as part of Fiji after 1966, and a demand from Gilbert and Ellice for re-association in 1968. On the whole small countries are deeply marked by particularism and by aggregate divisions of race, ethnicity and stratification. The relations between the small country and its colonial master or metropolitan state have been heavily dependent on racial factors. The Portuguese territories have been one instance. The Northern Territory became a part of the Australian Commonwealth whereas Papua did not simply because the Northern Territory has a majority of white people over aboriginals and Papua has not.

Inheritance is one factor which explains the fruits of independence and the actualities of dependence. The racial relations between the small country and the metropolitan explain this too.[12] How much room for maoeuvre, how much actual independence a small country has, also depends on ethnicity. Cyprus is one case; Ireland and the Lebanon are others. The Lebanon maintains an independence, indeed pluralist political culture with all its offices, enforced by constitutional convention, allocated 6 to 5 between Christians and Moslems. Ireland, on the other hand, has never been able to achieve an independence for the whole of its territory precisely because a pluralist politics has not developed. In the one instance a division between religions has been internally represented and produces external room for manoeuvre, and the polity is sustained. In the other case, the division was never properly represented, through the operation of the penal acts or in more recent times through the malfunctioning of the Westminster system. A single independence for the whole territory has never been even formally possible. The contrast is striking. In either case the realities, even the formalities, of independence for such small countries, a maintenance of territory and a room for manoeuvre, seem closely associated with the ways in which the problems of ethnicity are handled.

Thus many of these factors (preparation, colonial relationship and inheritance; relations with the metropolitan power; the handling of ethnicity and the room for manoeuvre) are dependent not so much on smallness as on particularism. This determined whether the British colonial preparation for independence would express the principles of the Durham Report or not. That determined the relationship between the various Portuguese territories and metropolitan Portugal, the distinction between the treatment of Papua and the Northern Territory, the territorial success of the Lebanon and failure of Ireland.

The way in which formal independence was secured and the variety of independence, the score on the dependence/independence scale, are affected at least as much by the presence and handling of these factors of division and pluralism as by smallness itself. But the outcomes are peculiar. The successful pluralism of the Lebanon sustains its independence. The failure of Ireland to achieve pluralism prevents its full independence. The memory of danger keeps the Lebanon stable, the presence of danger prevents the disappearance of Cyprus as a separate state.[13] This is an independence which was dependent on Greece, Turkey, the United Nations and the United Kingdom. This is very different from the convention which has worked for the enlarged Lebanon. The Irish case shows how particularism has prevented the development of political pluralism and has created two separate sorts of dependence. But that is not the whole lesson.[14] Economic dependence is real. So, to repeat, is political independence. What then of political dependence?

Degrees of political dependence — discretion, room to move — we suggested were an expression, a score, of some combination of reiteration, international stratification and, in the extreme case, client status. Together they create a pecking-order, distinct from the egalitarianism of formal political independence. We can now see some relationship between these combined meanings of dependence and the most important limitations on actual independence, defined as the existence of the sort of genuine room for manoeuvre which Ireland possessed under de Valera in the 1930s and in the Second World War. Clienthood, institutional reiteration and international stratification can express a low score on the dependence/independence scale. This is associated with a limited room for political manoeuvre. The interesting point here is the degree to which these limitations seem to be closely related to the operation of particularisms both between small countries and metropolitan states, and within small countries as in the case of Cyprus or in the comparison between Ireland and the Lebanon.

The contrast between the treatment of Ireland and of Rhodesia is interesting. Each had a close economic relationship with the same metropolitan country. The political question in Ireland in the Second World War was whether pressure would be put on her by the Allies to secure either her alliance or some control over the use of her ports. Economic pressure would have been possible in Ireland, political pressure slightly less so. The political effects of economic pressure would have been real but, as the 1930s demonstrated, limited. In the outcome economic pressure was not applied and political independence was unsullied. Rhodesia on the other hand was not formally independent to begin with. Economic pressure was difficult

and uncertain because of the number of escape routes. Political
pressure as force could have been used as a threat. In the outcome
political threat was not applied. Economic pressure was applied.
The result was an achievement of some sort of political independence.
In each case the success lay with the small, not the metropolitan,
country.[15]

Similarly striking is the way in which Bahrain, despite obvious
losses (like the idea of a university of the lower Gulf), its
comparative poverty and vulnerability, the powers against it
(Saudi Arabia, Qatar, Iraq), in the end accepted the limits of
independence. It preferred its own traditions, above all its room for
manoeuvre, to the loss of its formal political independence which
would have come with membership of the Union of Arab Emirates.
Its room for manoeuvre is real. It can gain support within the pattern
of marital enmities and alliances which oppose it to Dubai and Qatar
and therefore ally it to Abu Dhabi, which used its currency, the dinar.
It had support available from Iran, Kuwait and the UK. It has a real
choice between Saudi Arabia and Iran and therefore a possibility of
play-off, limited by the opposition between the Saudis and Abu
Dhabi (on the Burainis oasis) and the alliance of Abu Dhabi and Iran.

'From the defence point of view, Bahrainis probably feel that
they are safer on their own than if linked to the smaller gulf
sheikhdoms.' Despite the fact that its oil exports have now fallen
to less than 80,000 BPD, continued political separation looks a
perfectly worthwhile commodity. It is a classic instance of
extantism: the limits of apparent dependence and what the room
for manoeuvre of the independent actually can mean. Qatar[16]
is much the richer in oil but apparently not a whit less dependent
on the UK army and security and in other ways.[17] Degrees of actual
political dependence and lines of political decision are not precisely
correlated with different economic positions (greater or lesser oil wealth)
and dependence (like the Irish-UK market). Other factors clearly come in:
what cards the smaller country has (including threats) and how willing it is
to use them; its avoidance of permanent arrangements (like voting blocks and
clienthood) which reduce its discretion because it is taken for granted; its
negotiating expertise and actual style of representation; its own solidarity
(perhaps from an awareness of danger); and, in the end, to its actual
degree of determination, of readiness to bear certain costs for its
virtu. Defence is a crucial area for such factors.

Dependence can be expressed at three levels of defence situations.
The three situations measure degrees of freedom from the presence
of other powers, and therefore degrees of discretion. Level one is a
liability towards occupation providing for control of policy. Level
two is interstitial. The most frequent instance of this level is the
possession of bases. It is ambiguous since it can permit the expression
of either threats or support; and bases can be used for playing off

metropolitan powers. Level three is the attempt by the small country to maximise its alternatives through alliances, regional defence agreements, neutrality (like Ireland) or non-alignment. The record of regional defence as an escape from either of the first two levels is unimpressive. The basic defence problem for small countries is not that they do not have room for manoeuvre but that the first or ultimate level always exerts itself. The interstitial or second level is possible provided there are potential bases to be bargained with (like Bahrain). Amongst the third level of alternatives the least attractive, like bilateral defence agreements, work best; blocs work worst. The thing to avoid is the permanent, hierarchical and mobilised position of the client state. The thing to do is to move between the two medium positions of the second and third level (Robinson, p.234; Brenner, p.635ff).

The small country's dependence or room for manoeuvre, its point on the scale of dependence/independence, is closely related to its defence position. But defence worsens the dependence actualities of the small country. 'Given defence considerations alone, the economic burdens of safeguarding independence are proportionately far heavier in a small than in a large country *ceteris paribus*' (Robinson, pp.66-7). Defence exacerbates three of the major problems of the small country: economies of scale, secondary effects on trade and the division of labour, and non-economic limits on what in fact can be imported. But there is an extra factor in the burden of defence for the small country. What, above all, it cannot control is, as Kuznets puts it, 'the size of possible opponents'. This is the balance to our idea of the 'willing dominant'.

However, our previous qualifications about the significance of smallness and economics alone apply to defence also. There is no simple dichotomy or correlation. There are many factors allowing for the persistence of the egalitarianism of formal political independence. In defence as in other areas there is a possibility for the small country at level two. And the real problem is not smallness but smallness combined with poverty: what can be spent per capita. This is sharply true in defence. Yet it is still not the only point. It is not that large countries spend less per capita on defence than smaller ones, but precisely that they can indeed afford to spend more per capita.[18] Defence is in a special position. At any particular level of GNP and social services public services expenditure is roughly proportionate to the size of the nation, with the significant exception of defence (Vital, p.63. Compare A.M. Martin and W.A. Lewis). Defence highlights some of the special problems of small countries and of public administration in particular (compare the paper by B.L. Jacobs). Other factors come in also. For example, problems of minimum critical size are important for small countries throughout.[19] This feature is of peculiar importance in defence industry, infrastructure like transport, research and establishment and career. This is all made more difficult in defence because of the importance in flexible defence of military career development.

This is more important again through a combination of three other variables: potential opponent size; the problem of finding a willing dominant ally or federal partner from whom the small country can buy in the facilities of scale without surrendering its independence and room for manoeuvre; and the potential extra impact in small country domestic politics of quite small defence forces. Military intervention in civil politics through coups is more likely in small countries with quite small forces.

How does this work out in relation to the general problem of smallness and dependence? With good fortune about opponent and ally the small country might well retain its room for manoeuvre. It might escape some of the particular problems of smallness and defence organisation. What is much more difficult to escape is the impact of particularistic factors on its domestic civil/military relations.

Yet if these problems can be solved through fortune and *virtu* it may be that the defence problems of the small country can also be solved so as to avoid extreme instances of dependence (level one). The resources which a small country can put into its formal machinery for maintaining independence are indeed limited. One recent study shows that 'most nations participate in only a very small portion of diplomatic intercourse'. It is the big capitals and big countries which participate most ('the ranks conform to commonsense notions of the diplomatic prominence of various capitals'). And, as we have seen, small countries are not heavily represented overseas (Alger and Brams, pp.650 and 651).

At levels two and three, actual possibilities of strategic choice exist. An active strategy might appear to be the more independent. It is certainly more radical and aggressive. It can consist of a small country indulging in the organisation of subversion. This has certain practical virtues. It is difficult to counter, it is extremely economical, and granted the fortune with opponents mentioned above, it might show results. But counter-strategies might be available. It can invite intervention. It is only likely in relation to other small and on the whole isolated and divided countries. The small country can be driven back on a defensive strategy (Vital, pp.50-51).

Both in terms of defence strategies and of diplomatic representation one conclusion is that small countries do not necessarily suffer from such inevitable disadvantages as to make them heavily dependent. Rather, granted certain conditions of fortune, and particularly of internal harmony, a strategic choice and an appropriate style of diplomatic and defence organisation can be worked out. Levels two or three can be exploited. One study suggests that as far as diplomatic organisation is concerned, the most important thing for small countries is to allocate their limited resources much more to representation in international organisational arenas than in conventional inter-state representation. 'The most important conclusion that emerges from our analysis is that organisational ties provide most nations with far greater access to the outside world than do diplomatic ties' (Alger and Brams, p.662). This conclusion seems to apply particularly to inter-governmental organisations. 'These inter-governmental organisations offer the small powers in particular, which often do not exchange diplomats with each other, channels for mediating big power disputes and opportunities for peaceful change' (p.662).

Thus choices can be made, room for manoeuvre exploited and the degree and nature of dependence deeply affected. Taking Australia as a small country, its defence situation in the 1960s illustrates some of these points at a time when it was precisely the quantity and quality of its dependence that were in question. Its case shows first of all that the significance of smallness lies in a restriction of the sources of argument and of choice. This tends to express a certain sort of dependence (for example, on the dominant friend and ally from whom extra scale is being hired in). The combination of relative restriction and this sort of dependence creates a rigidity which can reinforce the limits already imposed on the small country's room for manoeuvre, a mirror image institutionalisation and a technological dependence. Secondly, and very important, there is a tendency towards vitiation of policy decision-making processes and an emergence of a decisional dependence. Thirdly, there are important costs in politics and the possibilities of change.

The fall of Singapore in 1942 at once destroyed the dependence of Australia on British defence and provided it with an expensive and electively short-term increase of independence. This was maintained throughout the Second World War, for example by Australian war cabinet decisions about the movement of its own forces in opposition to the wishes of the British high command. But it was maintained at a high, and for Australian peace-time politics unacceptable, cost. The outcome was a deliberately chosen smallness, which was embodied in a fixed and low budgetary ceiling for defence expenditure. The case shows the problem of 'defence in countries that simply cannot afford to provide adequate expenditures for a worthwhile system on their own account and yet are forced in various ways to provide some sort of show' (Schaffer 1963, p.236). Once this sort of smallness exists, and particularly in the area of defence, there will be an attempt to escape some of the restrictions of this elective smallness by transferring some of the costs to someone else's account.

Dependence will then occur. It tends to have three consequences: a removal of some of the possibilities of policy argument and change; a technological dependence and lassitude, a sort of built-in if modified obsolescence factor; and thirdly an international stratification factor:

choosing a low place in the pecking-order. 'Dependence means insulation ... delay ... and the acceptance of certain overseas doctrines' (Schaffer 1963, p.241). The central features in this cycle of dependence are a reinforcement of rigidity, an increase in the costs of change, a removal of some of the sources of change, a vitiation in that sense of policy making and political processes. 'Dependence and financial limitations produce rigidity. Rigidity once present reinforces itself' (Schaffer 1963, p.240).[20]

A dependent situation of this sort fails. It fails to 'provide not simply weapons, scientific resources, etcetera, but the immediate sources of argument and change that are currently required'. To buy technology means to get obsolescent equipment. To accept a fixed budgetary ceiling means to rule out many policy arguments. To buy defence research and science means not so much a trade-off in bases, which can well make very good sense; it means accepting the existing system of policy machinery imposed by the dominant friend. It means never being involved in policy decision-making at the central points of hierarchies at all, but to be involved in existing series of arguments and organisations: in missions, that is, rather than cabinets.

This condition of decisional dependence was exemplified very clearly in the Australian case, and ironically so. Its dependence has been created primarily by its own financial ceiling. It was precisely that limitation which was abolished once and for all not by an Australian but by an American presidential act: the insistence by Kennedy 1962-3 on Australian participation in Vietnam for the sake of the continuance of the Anzus alliance. The costs were very high in Vietnam, in Australia's China policy, in the depoliticisation of its relations with Japan, in the loss (up to 1965) of its once significant advantages in Indonesia. And this reinforcing cycle of dependence was very largely self-elected by Australia. It was a policy of the deliberate choice of a patron once a previous patron had disappeared; the policy which the then Prime Minister Menzies called 'our great and powerful friends'. It was inspired primarily by a desire for financial savings, which proved to be wasteful, expensive politically and not in the end rational even in budgetary terms.

VII. Conclusion

Small countries do not have to choose an exacerbation of restrictions and the cycle of dependence and rigidity, as through financial ceilings,[21] to a condition of decisional dependence. There are always alternatives. There is a choice of defensive and aggressive strategies. There is the successful resistance to apparent political implications of economic dependence, as in Ireland in the 1930s and 1940s.

48

The uses of regional agreements, like the OAU, mean reinforcing the efficacy of extantism. Thus in 1971 OAU assisted Chad (in reconciliation with Libya), Congo (with Zaire), Guinea and Senegal, and Sudan (north and south).

These alternatives are partly dependent on fortune. They are made more difficult by factors of isolation and poverty. They are made more difficult above all by domestic factors. There are special possibilities of political mobilisation in the small country but we see its susceptibility to the divisive particularisms of ethnicity and stratification or its liability to military coups.

Yet the politically integrated small country with willing friends, exploiting its possibilities for representation in regional organisations and inter-governmental organisations, and choosing its strategies carefully, can avoid the reinforcing cycle of restriction, dependence and rigidity. The Australian defence case illustrates this all the more vividly since the smallness was elective and alternatives were available. If quasi-federal or confederal arrangements are to be chosen, those which seem to be most viable are asymmetrical. The small country must then choose its willing dominant carefully. If room for manoeuvre is to be exploitable, the small country must solve its own pluralist possibilities. If patronage is unavoidable, the small country client might be able to conduct its own auctions and play off rival patrons. Formal independence itself can be modified through forms of association. The costs of diplomatic representation can be turned to good account, the advantages of regional and non-regional inter-governmental organisations can be exploited. If cartel or OPEC-like arrangements are to be set up by groups of small countries, any particular small country can carefully assess the comparative advantages of joining or playing the role of cartel-breaker. To join a voting bloc is likely to negate the value of one of the small country's cards. Some degree of dependence is no doubt inevitable for small countries. But dependence is an expression of clienthood, institutional reiteration or the mirror image effect, and international stratification. On certain conditions, a great deal can be done by any small country about each of these aspects. The client can play off potential patrons and keep the auction going rather than accept mobilisation into a long-term client/patron relationship. The cultural force of international stratification is no doubt more difficult to affect in the short term. But it is not exempt from change. Institutional reiteration can be affected in some areas very quickly indeed as in the dismantling of the judicial system in Bahrain, and by care in placing of contracts. Granted fortune and determination about the external condition of friends and opponents and domestic conditions affecting integration and mobilisation, the limitations on actual independence/dependence are never fixed.

NOTES

1. How small can an electoral and party system go? Gibraltar has an electorate of 15,000. With 15 seats and 8 votes for each elector a two-party contested system is not merely possible but in effect inevitable. The contest, so to speak, is for the 15th seat: one party has 8 and the other 7. It is presumably difficult to extend ingenuity beyond certain points so as to make party contest viable if a political system gets much smaller than that.

2. Cf. Roy Lewis, 'Britain's Little Anguillas of the Future', *The Times,* 28 March 1969.

3. To be allowed membership at that minimum level of 0.04 per cent there are 17 with less than 1 million population; of those, 13 are allowed membership.

4. For example, in the December 1972 independence negotiations with the Bahamas (pop. 170,000), the UK insisted that the people of Abuco (pop. 3000) could only be represented through the Bahaman government, against whom in fact they wanted to appear.

5. The smallest instance is presumably the former Portuguese enclave in Dahomey which was transferred in 1961: Saõ Joa Batista de Ajuda, with a population of 1 and an area of 0.02 square miles.

6. S. 7(2). This was the basis for the Anguilla intervention.

7. 'It emerges that in 1968 the mass of people were indeed dependent and the elections showed only the glimmerings of a move from dependence to autonomy.' *(Australian External Territories,* 12.2.1972, p.43.)

8. The failures up to now of the federation of various Arab states in connection with the UAR and between the UAR and the Yemen; the failure between the Yemen and South Yemen, and of the Federation of South Arabia before; and of Qatar and Bahrain to join the Arab Emirates Union or of former Brunei to join Malaysia; the secession of Singapore from Malaysia; the failure of the Gambia and Senegal to federate despite the efforts made since 1962. The definitive instance is the failure of the West Indies Federation in 1961; the dissolution in 1962; the subsequent withdrawal of Grenada from negotiations about new arrangements; the independence in 1965 of Antigua, in 1966 of Barbados, and so forth.

9. Western Samoa is heavily dependent on New Zealand. Its association is based on a 1963 exchange of letters and New Zealand's is the only diplomatic representation in Apia outside the South Pacific and some international organizational representatives. But the division between the two Samoas seems to be stable and persistent; a clear case of extantism. This is partly due to the sharp economic differences between the two sides of the island, and the persistence of the West Samoan mata system in the one part and Americanisation in the other. A comparison with Ireland springs to mind.

10. The oceanic and frontier principles can, of course, lead to conflicts, as in Ireland.

11. By now, nothing remains of the impact of British legislation outside special instances like workers' compensation and the law of patents, designs and trade marks. It is the Sheriah of Islam which is the major source of law in the state. The traditional system depended on sheikhs from the ruling family. It is staffed partly by Jordanian judges and reflects much more of the Egyptian system based on the Code Napoléon than the British pattern.

12. All the overseas dependencies of Portugal are counted as 'provinces', but how their status and relationship with the metropolitan country work out is determined racially, by the Portuguese view of the ethnic make-up of the particular territory. For example, in Guinea, Angola and Mozambique the native statute operated up to 1961 and political life

was determined by the cultural competition between the 'natives' and 'originarios'. In other provinces, more are treated nearly alike in as far as the colour mix is accepted as a single racial group. On Cape Verde all are accepted as 'mestico', on Macao as 'Luso-Chinese', on Timor the majority as 'Luso-Indonesian Malay'. Nevertheless the significance of ethnic, class and other distinctions in small countries still applies. In Timor there is, in practice, clear distinction between 'permanent' Portuguese, Chinese (10,000) and Timmese (700,000). Post-primary education has few non-Portuguese, Chinese, Goan or Eurasians.

13. Eighty per cent of the population is Greek, 20 per cent is Turkish. Independence was granted in 1960. The assumption of some that enosis with Greece would follow, of others that the pluralist constitution could work, of others that the pluralist constitution could work, of other that there might be a partition. None of these things has happened; yet the country as a separate state persists.

14. Both the north and south of the Irish island have been economically dependent on the British mainland. It is possible to explain the relationship between the form of catholicism which persists in Irish life and its property system, and the relationship between protestantism in the North of Ireland and the ways in which benefits, like employment, are allocated. At the same time there is no clear relationship between the economic dependence of the south on the British market and the viability, even the room for manoeuvre, available to such a small state with such an irrationality of frontiers. The irrationality has certainly been expensive. But the closeness of trading relationships did not prevent the de Valera government operating an 'economic war' against the United Kingdom throughout the 1930s. His political support was from non-trading sectors. Nor did it prevent his neutrality after 1939.

15. In 1970, 65.8 per cent of Irish exports were to Great Britain and Northern Ireland and 53 per cent of her imports were from the United Kingdom. Despite the expensive 'economic war' which lasted from July 1932 to April 1938, affecting questions of land annuities, the Irish ports, the control of imports, etc., the governing party won all the elections through the 1930s: February 1932, January 1933, July 1937.

16. Qatar has wahabi links with Saudi Arabia and family links with Rashid of Dubai. What mattered was who dominated the ruling al-Thani family. What matters there now is who controls the UK defence resources. These are now in the hands of the Khalifa faction. He is now, therefore, the ruler. Similarly, the Bahraini agreement with the UK about the Al-Muharraq airbase (nominally for transit and maintenance facilities) assists it to play off between Iran and Saudi Arabia.

17. It is also dependent on overseas educational institutions, the currency board, which it shares with Dubai, and the rial, the currency for the Union based on sterling transfers through London agents.

18. Robinson's figures in Table VII comparing the percentages of GNP spent on defence in say, the UK, France, Sweden, New Zealand and Jamaica, are very striking in this respect.

19. UN technical assistance might be much higher per capita in a smaller than average country (the average for 1967-8 worked out as 0.056 dollars, for the 37 smallest countries 0.630 dollars), but so low in total as to be insignificant in effect.

20. The details of the Australian case of defence policy-making in the 1960s illustrates these three features time and again. The case has been written up elsewhere but here we can give a few conclusions. First of all, the restrictions imposed by elective smallness are greater than the smallness itself. As we have said elsewhere the point is not that small countries spend more per capita on defence and similar areas, but less. This is not an escape from smallness and dependence, but an exacerbation of it. The US population was at that time 20 times the Australian population, its

defence expenditure was exactly 100 times as great. The result was that Australian defence equipment was simply American equipment brought in very late in the day. Dependence meant buying someone else's obsolescence. Secondly, the mirror image factor operates very powerfully. Previously Australian defence department organisation had been an attempt to copy the British institutions once laid down by the Esher report. Now Australian defence reorganisation attempted to follow American principles in considerable detail: in methods of unification; even in following the pentropic division or five battle-group system. Thirdly, a small and fixed budgetary ceiling meant the vitiation of many policy decision-making processes. There was never any absolute or professional military contribution. There was never enough in the budget to re-equip, to provide the basic technology of change; it was only possible to keep the thing going as it was.

21. In the Australian case the ceiling restricted the percentage available for new capital equipment to 16 per cent of the Budget. That ruled out the possibilities of radical re-equipment. It created the sort of dependence which exists between Marks and Spencers and the factories working for it on long-run contracts with severe quality control.

REFERENCES

C.F. Alger and S.J. Brams: 'Patterns of Representation in National Capitals and Inter-state Organisations (World Politics, July 1967, pp.646-65).

John Ballard: *Bureaucracy and Political Integration* (IDS, 1970).

D.G. Bettison, C.A. Hughes *The Papua New Guinea Elections, 1964* (Cambera, and D.W. van den Veur (eds.): ANU Press, 1965).

M.J. Brenner: 'Strategic Inter-dependence and the Politics of Inertia; (World Politics, 1970-71, pp.635ff.); *Alliances and Small Powers* (New York, 1968).

Burton Benedict (ed.): *Problems of Small Territories* (Institute of Commonwealth Studies, University of London, Athlone Press, 1967).

A.L. Epstein, R.S. Parker, *The Politics of Dependence* (Canberra, ANU Press, and M. Reay (eds.): 1971).

A. Etzioni: *Political Unification* (1965, Chapter 5).

H.A.L. Fisher: *The Value of Small States, Studies in History and Politics* (London, Arnold, 1920).

Baker Fox: *The Power of Small States,* Diplomacy in World War II (Chicago, 1959).

C. Geertz: 'The Integrative Revolution: Primordial Sentiments and Civil Politics in the New States', in C. Geertz (ed.), *Old Societies and New States* (New York, 1963).

P. Hastings: *Papua-New Guinea* (Sydney, Angus and Robertson, 1971).

Rosalyn Higgins: *The Development of International Law through the Political organisations of the United Nations,* Chapter 1, The Concept of Statement in UN practice.

A. Lijphart: *The Trauma of Decolonisation* (Yale, 1966).

Peter Lyon: *Neutralism* (Leicester, 1963).
Alison M. Martin and   'Patterns of Public Revenue and Expenditure',
W.A. Lewis: *(The Manchester School,* September, 1956).
Peter Nettl: *Political Mobilisation* (London, 1967).
C.C. O'Brien: *The United Nations: Sacred Drama* (London,
                                Hutchinson, 1968).
Lucien Pye: *Politics, Personality and National-building, Burma's
                                Search for Identity* (New Haven, 1962).
J. Rapaport and others   *Small States and Territories, Status and Problems*
(eds.):   (UNITAR, Arno Press, New York, 1971).
F.W. Riggs: *The Ecology of Public Administration* (New Delhi,
                                1961).
R. Rothstein: *Alliances and Small Powers* (New York, 1968).
C.D. Rowley: *The New Guinea Villager* (New York, 1965).
B.B. Schaffer: 'The British Solomons in New Guinea and Australia',
                                (Vol.1, No. 5, 1966, pp.34-47).
B.B. Schaffer: 'The Concept of Preparation' (World Politics,
                                October 1965, pp.42-67).
B.B. Schaffer: 'Policy and System in Defence' (World Politics,
                                January 1963, pp.236-262).
A. Schon and   *Small States in International Relations*
A.O. Brundtland (eds.):   (New York, Wiley, 1971).
Hugh Seton-Watson: *The Pattern of Communist Revolution* (London,
                                Methuen, 1960).
J. David Singer and   *Quantitative International Politics* (New York, 1968).
M. Small in J. David   D.E. Misten: 'Small Powers: a Struggle for Survival'
Singer (ed.):   (Journal of Conflict Resolution, 1969, pp.388ff.)
David Vital: *The Inequality of States* (Oxford, Clarendon Press,
                                1967).
R. L. Watts: *New Federations, Experiments in the Commonwealth.*

2. MULTUM IN PARVO: questions about diversity and diversification in small developing countries.*

H.C. Brookfield

Summary

Concentration on countries as such may give a misleading picture of the degree of specialisation or diversity in an economy; there may be risk-avoidance through diversification at the individual or company level, while a country's economy as a whole may be apparently specialised. Government policies for fiscal diversification may frustrate the process of structural diversification. Examples are given from studies of South Pacific economies.

The fundamental fact about small countries is that they are small, while small developing countries are both poor and small. There is a real sense in which these facts so dominate thinking as to paralyse understanding. The axiom that division of labour — and hence the rational allocation of resources — is limited by the size of the market is so firmly entrenched that it seems self-evident that in a world where economies of scale are being constantly enhanced, the truly small and poor countries find that their maximum levels of operation lie further and further below the optimum. Every constraint of developing countries, above all that immobility of production investments which Griffin (1969) identifies as a critical problem throughout Latin America, is reinforced by the scale constraints of smallness.

These scale constraints are real. In particular, they limit the range and volume of the 'linkages' which can develop around a growth industry such as a successful export staple. Backward linkages are most obvious in transport investments — mainly in vehicles or lines of communication which only touch the shores and border of the country. Forward linkages, most obviously expressed in the processing of the export staple, are constrained by the limited production of the small country. Final demand linkages, arising from investment in industries producing consumer goods for the factors in the export sector, are constrained by the size of the domestic market. Linkages can be observed in both physical and economic space, and in the latter dimension they may well 'jump' physical space; the multiplier effect of investment in many small countries, as measured by the linkage effects, often benefits areas far removed from the territorial jurisdiction of the small country itself.

A great many small countries have fallen into systems of regional spatial organisation centred elsewhere. On a world scale almost all

*This paper was written in 1972. Substantive revision was not possible without further research for which no opportunity has been available. With only minor changes, therefore, the paper is presented as first written.

developing countries are peripheral to a space economy structured around the countries of the North Atlantic, but at a more local level it is possible to identify regional structures in which small countries emerge as politically-separate portions of the periphery of regional economies centred beyond their borders. Selwyn (in this volume) thus interprets the constraints which confine the possibilities for industrialisation in the three African states constituted from the former High Commission Territories around South Africa. In the Caribbean, the Windward Islands are not only linked in a dependent relationship with Britain through trade and North America through finance and tourism, but also with Trinidad and Barbados through trade, migration and the provision of services. In the Pacific, as we shall see below, the New Hebrides fall more deeply into the regional orbit of Nouméa, the capital of New Caledonia. The possibilities for independent action by small countries in this situation are doubly limited, not only by their situation as open, enclave economies in a world-wide system, but also by their dependent relationships with regional centres of dominance.

This 'double-dependence' of many small countries leads directly toward a main argument of this paper. How far is it reasonable to conduct analysis of the economy of any country, a small country above all, by macro-economic methods in which the country itself is the aggregate used as basis for inquiry? Lipton's (1970) terse comment on the 'irrelevance' of macrocosms called 'countries' gains especial force when the 'macrocosms' are 'microcosms' by world standards. Countries, however small, are certainly relevant as units of policy-formation and fiscal management, but they are not necessarily relevant to all phases of discussion. Countries are also merely units within which individual small firms, farm-firms, and entrepreneurs are aggregated, and into which the separate parts of multinational organisations are disaggregated. Neither the former nor the latter are necessarily constrained in their operation by the size of the country. Structural diversity may be a major characteristic of the economy of a country — small or large — when this economy is disaggregated into its component organisational units; 'diversification' as a national policy may affect only certain parts of their operation. In what follows, therefore, I propose to part company with the nationally-aggregative approaches adopted in some earlier studies of this problem (e.g. Benedict, 1967; Demas, 1965), and pay attention to internal structures. I do this first in theoretical terms, then empirically with reference to a group of territories in the South Pacific. I hope to show that diversity and diversification are not the same thing, and that an approach based on the national balance of payments and on the import-export economy may lead to forms of 'diversification' that are positively deleterious to the structural diversification, or diversity, that is a source of strength and adaptive capacity to an open, dependent economy.

Diversification within specialisation within diversification

Specialisation and diversification are alternative strategies in the face of uncertainty. If we assume that a decision-maker knows the possibilities open to him, and is able to judge the alternative outcomes subjectively but unable to assess the probabilities of these outcomes in non-arbitrary terms, we essentially have the nature of the individual's problem. We must assume that his behaviour is intended to be rational and based on the principle of achieving a set of aims. These aims may be the maximisation of his short-term returns. They may be to maximise his long-term returns, that is to say, growth. They may be simply to achieve satisfaction of a reasonable set of needs that vary in conception through time and according to the state of his environment through time – and especially the vagaries of climate in the case of a primary producer and the unknown behaviour of other persons – which includes uncertainties over the market for his product. He uses his experience and whatever other information and forecasting tools are available to him, in order to estimate the course of these uncertain variables.

In regard to peasant farmers, my approach is parallel to that of Lipton (1968). Acceptance of peasant rationality does not imply that farmers maximise utility; risk-avoidance is of greater weight, and the consequence is a 'security-centred survival algorithm'. If one seeks to simulate behaviour in these conditions the most useful tool by far should be game theory. Davenport (1960) and Gould (1963) have demonstrated this in works that should have been seminal except that they have not sown much. Taking a simple case where the farmer has two crops and nature two strategies, Gould has shown how a mixed strategy maximises the minimum gain. Since higher expected profit also entails higher risk, a common choice is the policy which gains the best results while minimising the variance. A mixed strategy represents diversification; specialisation where it occurs at this level is thus interpreted as a propensity to take risks, and it follows that such a propensity would be most strongly developed among those most able to afford risk (Weeks, 1970).

I have elsewhere argued (Brookfield, 1970, 1972; Brookfield with Hart, 1971) that risk-minimisation is a major principle of modern economic behaviour in underdeveloped regions. At the peasant level I include not only the mix of crops on a small farm within the ambit of this theory, but also partial commitment to wage labour through circular migration (cf. Elkan and Fallers, 1960), partial involvement in entrepreneurship against a base of other activities, and in general the maintenance of security within the village society while seeking simultaneous access to the more uncertain benefits of the introduced economic system (cf. Lipton, 1968). Bedford (1973) has developed this argument on a solid base of empirical inquiry among migrants and non-migrants working in the New Hebrides. Proletarians are at greater risk than peasants from vagaries in the economic system; wherever possible, then, full commitment to wage employment is avoided. Equally, full commitment to cash production is commonly avoided; the Chimbu of New Guinea, for example, have evolved a four-fold range of choices including subsistence with participation in local exchange and reciprocity, cash production, wage employment and some local forms of entrepreneurship (Brookfield, 1968, 1973). For the understanding of peasant behaviour, the principle of maximin strategy is perhaps as important as Chayanov's (1966) trade-off between the drudgery of self-exploitation and the achievement of family demand satisfaction.

However, there is no reason to suppose that such behaviour is limited to peasants, or is tied to a static survival alogrithm. The importance of such ancillary activities as trading, local transport enterprise, partial or periodic employment and other forms of entrepreneurship to a large number of small-scale planters of expatriate origin can be widely demonstrated (e.g. Brookfield with Hart, 1971). Mr. Scrubb is the planter's prototype at least as frequently as Mr. Micawber. The specialist European planter, Asian moneylender or local entrepreneur is much more severely at risk than the man who diversifies his interests so that he may shift his inputs — or transform his production factors — between a range of activities. At the level of large companies we may observe a similar trend, especially rapid in modern times. Many companies originated with a single activity base; some still adhere to this form. However, the largest and most successful companies, in the developed as in the developing world, are usually those which have diversified into a wide range of activities, and also into a number of areas and countries — practising territorial as well as product diversification. Diversification may thus be a highly productive growth strategy, in which expansion is achieved by the addition of new enterprises employing different resources and serving different markets; profits of one may then readily be transferred to others in accordance with the best expectation of long-term profit, or the best expectation of opportunities for further growth. Successful pursuit of this strategy has led to the concentration of 'control over sources of raw materials and processing and manufacturing installation . . . in a set of very large corporations with power to allocate and reallocate resources on a world scale in accordance with the requirements of long-term corporate expansion and survival' (Levitt, 1970, 1971).

Analysis of an economy by its individual and corporate units may thus yield a picture very different from that gained by an examination of the aggregate data on external transactions of a country. We may find that at all scale levels a large proportion of the units practise forms of diversification, some for survival and some for growth. We will probably find that certain units, whose activities within the one country are specialised, are part of widely diversified multinational organisations. Other units have a single export activity, but also other activities which escape the statistical record. But there will also be some true specialists, including importantly the proletariat who are specialised in that they have only their labour to sell, and others – perhaps quite significant in number – who have selected the strategy of specialisation from a reasoned expectation of safe returns and not at all with any conscious risk-acceptance. And even though seeking to diversify their personal activities, a great many producers have adopted or gladly inherited partial specialisation in a single export crop, and may even have consciously neglected other opportunities.

Specialisation is a 'dominating' strategy, one that on reasonable evaluation of possible outcomes will seem to offer a better 'pay-off' than any alternative, whatever the 'play' made by nature and the market. Sugar production was such a strategy for many producers in many places for a long period; even under more adverse marketing conditions it remains 'safe' if the market is protected by preferential arrangements. In the South Pacific, copra production became a dominating strategy because its market proved less unstable than that of other crops, its production costs were lower, and in particular it was far more tolerant than other available activities of a very great range in input intensities (Brookfield with Hart, 1971). It is a low-yielding crop in terms of money output per hectare – indeed the lowest available – but land was relatively abundant and cheap, and a specialisation in copra within the export sector of an individual's or a company's economy thus offered the maximum solution. That is to say that while diversity of activities was the best strategy for the individual unit's 'economy' as a whole, for that sector of production which was devoted to cash sale the optimal solution was specialisation. Similarly for a large diversified corporation, the best strategy for each individual unit in the whole complex is often a pure, or 'dominating', strategy of specialisation. There can be no doubt that this has been true historically; it is probable, however, that it has become increasingly true in modern times in consequence of the growing complex of price supports, international marketing agreements and internal marketing boards, together with various other forms of price stabilisation and protection. But a dominating strategy may become very fragile if the actions of nature and the market exceed the range of 'expected' variance; then the degree to which a 'mixed' strategy has been sustained in the unit's 'economy' as a whole becomes vital to survival.[1]

'Fiscal diversification' against 'structural diversification'

Countries may thus be irrelevant macrocssms at a level of discussion which is perhaps the most important level, but there are a number of respects in which the country, its size, resources and policies, become of major importance. We noted above the stabilising role of policy at the national level in mediating the impact of market forces. But the public sector of a country is itself a source of investment, an employer, and a redistributing agent within the national economy. The role of government in these fields is of increasing importance in all countries; it is especially important in developing countries, and still more so in small developing countries where there is often no other locally-based body of any size that can allocate resources over a large part of the economy. The power of government to perform these functions, well or badly, depends on the resources at its command, and internally these are derived mainly from taxation in all its forms. A wealthy government, defined as one that is wealthy in relation to the size of the economy, can obviously achieve more than a poor one. In this respect a small country may be little worse off than a large one, if it has a strong revenue base and access to additional funds for large and 'lumpy' investments. Where a small country is inevitably weak, however, is in its dealings with foreign companies who operate within its boundaries, or which control its external linkages. It is also weak in its dealings with other and larger countries in matters where joint provision of infrastructure or services is required, or where elements of the national economy are closely tied to elements in the larger country. In any such open situation, a small country with a small economy is at a disadvantage which (unless true altruism is present) can only lead to an accentuation of dependency and loss of the power of independent decision. But in internal respects smallness is no necessary handicap, and may even have certain advantages.

It follows, however, that a government — especially in a small country — must strive to increase and secure its revenue base if it is to discharge its responsibilities and preserve a measure of independence. Growth of the national income is thus a major objective in its own right, and hardly less important is diversification of the sources of national income so as to insure against major variations in available revenue that may follow from dependence on only one or two activities. This can become an overriding consideration — even an obsession — at government level, and lead to encouragement of forms of diversification that benefit the national exchequer but produce few linkages independently of government redistribution.[2] This is what I term 'fiscal diversification'. It is often quite opposed to, and in competition for, inputs with 'structural diversification', which improves the mobility of factors of production in the economy as a whole, and widens the range of opportunity for the mass of the people. Seen in this way, the nature of diversification and its relationship to specialisation becomes a dimension of development as transformation rather than development as growth. It is a dimension in which spatial and ecological questions have an important place, and hence one that might particularly interest a geographer. Since linkages are fundamental, the introduction of a new activity in an out-of-the-way place is likely for reasons of location alone to be more fiscal than structural in its impact. New activities introduced at the centre will have a different set of linkage effects from those which are dispersed, *ab initio,* through the country. Innovations within the existing general production complex will differ in their effect from those which employ new resources, wherever these are located. These contrasts will be greater in large countries than in small, but the shape and topography of countries is also relevant. Countries that are composed of sharply contrasted ecological regions, such as a mountain chain and a plain, or which are made up of a group of islands, may respond to various forms of diversification quite differently from compact, homogeneous countries. The friction of distance is increased by such topographical discontinuities, and spread effects are thereby restricted. These difficulties can be overcome or at least reduced, but at a cost which is wholly additional and often difficult for a small country economy to bear.

Contrasted economies in the South Pacific

Most of my empirical material for this discussion will be drawn from the New Hebrides, hardly an independent nation but one which exhibits well the points that I wish to make. The material which I present arose from local inquiries in 1965[3] and remote observation since. I use this material to illustrate and amplify the arguments presented above, to which I return in conclusion. First, however, I briefly review the contrasted economies of two neighbouring territories, in order to put the discussion into perspective.

The South Pacific is *par excellence* a region of small territories which are now becoming small countries. Surveys of the regional economy in the aggregate or by specific countries (Salter, 1970; Brookfield with Hart, 1971; Fairbairn, 1971; Brookfield, 1972) all emphasise the great disparities in level and type of development, and some of these contrasts are indicated in the data summarised in Table 1. However, all are heavily dependent on a narrow range of exports; all import substantial quantities of foodstuffs and manufactured goods; all are concerned about diversification. There the similarity ends.

The Solomon Islands may be regarded as 'Pacific Basic'. From early in the century until very recently, copra has accounted for between 75 and 95 per cent of exports, but production reaches barely 25,000 tons per annum divided between a collectively static plantation sector and a growing Melanesian sector. There is one major town and port, and one major trading company — now Japanese-owned — which replaces two before World War II. One producing company, a subsidiary of Unilever, dominates copra production. Over large parts of the group there is no source of cash but wage employment, yet only 12,200 are employed and of these 1,000 are expatriates. The commercial economy is heavily concentrated in only three of the ten or twelve island groups (IBRD, 1969).

Since 1946, government has been anxious, not to say desperate, to diversify. First attempts were directed specifically at the largest concentration of Melanesian population which hitherto had provided little but labour to the general economy. Attempts were made to introduce cocoa as a major cash crop. Dispersal was excessive, research came after innovation, marketing was handled by government with hopes but no plans for private replacement, and by 1968 production had reached the 1964 target with no sign of rapid growth. The cocoa scheme was then dropped having attained an annual production of one ton per employee of the Cocoa Division. Later, when research has yielded a strain adapted to local climatic conditions, it might be resumed.

Other activities have aimed at diversification of a different order. An unusually thorough search for minerals was initiated by what became the best geological survey department in the Pacific. Discoveries were unfortunately small, but in 1972 a Japanese company began trial mining of bauxite on an outlying island. Timber resources attracted five companies producing veneer timbers for the Japanese market. All had difficulties and one has withdrawn, but timber became the second-ranking export. In 1970, a Japanese company set up a shore base for fisheries, bringing the catch to a freezer plant from which frozen fish ready for market is re-exported. Despite growing imports, these activities have already reduced the trade gap. But all are in isolated areas, all are capital-intensive and employ expatriate workers of various origins in skilled tasks with only unskilled local employment. None have any widespread direct linkage effects, and the main territorial contribution of all is to the central exchequer.

Around the capital, Honiara on Guadalcanal, there has been a set of changes of a different order. An Australian company is growing high-yield rice of IRRI origin at a cost below that of imported rice, and has even built up a small export. Chinese entrepreneurs have set up a successful biscuit factory. Development of cattle has improved the local meat supply. But the town itself is the main generator of this activity, and the chief business of the town is government, still financed largely from overseas grants. A 1972 employment survey of the Solomons shows that 40 per cent of all wage-employees are in Honiara, and 37 per cent work for the government. Only 19 per cent are now employed in agriculture. Of 2,240 workers in 'industrial' occupations, 72 per cent are engaged in construction. There is substantial linkage at the centre, including the stimulation of production for the urban market-place, and entrepreneurship in transport among the Guadalcanal people (Lasaqa, 1972). But severe tension over land has also been created.

The resulting pattern may be viewed in different ways. Even before copra prices fell catastrophically in late 1971 the export base had been widened by the inclusion of fish and timber, to which bauxite may now be added. There is a solid prospect that government, and its medical and educational services which have been supported almost wholly by grants, will in future balance its budget from local revenues and thus sustain the impetus that has made Honiara a growth centre. But the fish, timber and mining industries are enclave economies. Rural diversification away from the centre has not been successful and the linkage effects of the new industries are extremely restricted. The emerging pattern is of an active growth centre financed by national revenue, in turn financed by the enclave economies, surrounded by a large depressed periphery with very small local cash income and which includes some 80 per cent of the population.

New Caledonia, by contrast, exhibits an almost classic example of the constraints imposed on the export growth model by a skewed pattern of resources coupled with the small scale of the country as a whole. New Caledonia is rich in a range of minerals, all of which have been exploited in the past. In a sub-humid environment a low-productivity cattle industry was established in the 1860s and since 1880 has varied in scale between 90,000 and 120,000 head of stock. A coffee industry set up by convict settlers in the 1870s and expanded by free settlers until about 1910, has also been adopted since 1930 by Melanesians on the exiguous reserves — only some eight per cent of the total area — left to them by pastoral expansion. There is some production of vegetables, copra and forest products; indigenous yam and taro cultivation still survive, in a few instances with the highly skilled and intensive practices of pre-colonial time. But all these dispersed activities have been progressively compressed under the weight of nickel.

Until after 1945, the physically separate mining and agricultural sectors were also separate in terms of their access to production factors. The mines used Vietnamese labour in large quantity, at a productivity of only 0.3 ton/man/day. The coffee-growers and agriculturalists used mainly Javanese workers, while the pastoral industry relied on Melanesian stockmen. The link between the sectors lay through the companies and the one bank, rather than the government, though even at this time government was supporting the ailing pastoral industry in several ways. Nouméa, the capital, had a population of only 11,000 and was not expanding.

The abrogation of labour contracts, and the subsequent repatriation of most Asian workers after 1945, transformed the situation. The mines quickly mechanised, and expansion of the metallurgical industry was also capital-intensive. The labour force became European and Melanesian, and short supply led to a steep rise in wages through the fifties and sixties. Agriculturalists also mechanised, becoming monocultural in the process, and lost the ability to adjust supply to demand with disastrous results. The pastoral industry became starved of both labour and capital, and despite a shift to more profitable veal production worked on a more and more exiguous profit margin. The coffee and copra industries suffered worst, and after 1955 went into a sustained decline. Other mining operations ceased under the impact of steeply rising costs coupled with a resource base too small to repay capital intensification. The labour situation was eased from time to time by drawing in more Melanesians from the reserves, and by Polynesian immigration, but minimum monthly wages mounted through $100 to about $150 in the late 1960s, and by 1971 surpassed $200 in urban occupations.

As the mining industry lost its measure of separation from the rest of the economy it came to dominate the whole, but its 'spread' effect was channelled almost exclusively into Nouméa where expansions of government activity added its own multiplier to the boom in commerce and industry. Construction became a major industry; there were seven contracting firms in 1946, over 200 in the later 1960s, and by 1971 the business was of a scale to attract also Australian and New Zealand building and contracting firms. The upward pressure on wages and costs continued, and the total money supply reached $2,000 per head of the whole population by 1971. Until the later 1960s great efforts were made to retain elements of diversity in the economy especially through a massive structure of price supports, loans and grants to rural producers, transfer payments and direct government employment, so that in the northern region of the island over 40 per cent of regional income was derived from government sources (Rocheteau, 1966). By 1970 these policies were deemed not worthy of further expansion and a five-year plan proposed simply to enlarge the nickel industry, provide housing, find more workers, and develop the basic infrastructure of ports and roads. Even the twenty contractors and many more sub-contractors who mined crude ore for export to Japan found themselves squeezed by the rising pressures of company demand for ore. The new tourist industry became squeezed by rising costs and use of hotels for permanent residence. Efforts to sustain the rural economy were replaced by an acceptance of imports. Opportunities for profitable investment by smaller entrepreneurs became confined to Nouméa, but a territorial expansion of available opportunites arose through closer connexions with French Polynesia and especially the nearby New Hebrides. Nouméa and the mines have been strikingly prosperous, but the rural economy is in decay awaiting the development of new mining and metallurgical centres to provide new urban employment.[4]

The New Hebrides: diversification in a stable economy

The Anglo-French Condominium of the New Hebrides is the smallest
of these three countries in area and population, but has a much more
developed economy than the Solomons and on a per capita basis its
export income and GNP have sometimes exceeded those of nearby Fiji.
The resources base is comparable with that of the Solomons, but far
more land – 45 per cent – has been alienated. Though all Pacific
countries are different, this territory offers something of the highest-
common-factor combination of the several elements.

In 1965, when I worked in and out of Vila for several months,
the state of the New Hebridean economy was not fundamentally
different from that studied seven years earlier by Wilson (1966). The
core of the economy was the copra industry based on some 200
plantations and about 1,500 villages in about equal proportions, and
supplemented by a small production of cocoa and coffee mainly
produced from pre-war plantings. As much as 95 per cent of the
population was involved in some measure in the cash economy. While
all villagers produced their own subsistence, most had also planted all
available land in coconuts since the 1930s: on certain islands in the
central group the proportion of land under coconuts is often as high
as 70 per cent (Bedford, 1973). Two small port-towns had a combined
population, including periurban villages, of only 14,000. Industry
was limited to construction, soft drinks and repair-engineering. There
was no coconut-oil mill, and almost no tourism. Added to the
economy, however, were a manganese mine on eastern Efaté,
opened in 1962, and a Japanese fish-freezing plant on Santo,
opened in 1958. These provided 30–35 per cent of export income
but employed not more than 250 New Hebrideans; most of their
exployees were from overseas.

A majority of peasants were at once subsistence farmers, cash
farmers and periodic wage labourers. While only 18 per cent of the
population was enumerated away from island of birth in the 1967
census, Bedford (1971) found in 1969 that only eight per cent of a
sample on three outer islands had never at any time moved away.
But there was limited permanent commitment to the monetary sector.
Data obtained from Vila employers in 1965 showed that only
12 per cent of New Hebridean workers had been in their jobs five
years and longer, with 'spells' at home, while 44 per cent had been
employed less than a year. Among 38 New Hebridean men in Vila
whose life histories were obtained, a total of 181 jobs were recalled,
60 per cent lasting less than a year. It was normal to return home
between jobs. Bedford (1971) found that 73 per cent of a sample
of 1,883 moves away from home villages had lasted less than
12 months, 36 per cent less than three months. Men and families
returned home both to tend yam gardens, and also to make copra:

the latter activity constituted 'slow' but regular money available on demand, while 'fast' money could be obtained by working away from home in town, on plantations, or less commonly in the two new industries. Except in the immediate vicinity of the towns, where a wider range of opportunities included production for the market-place, daily employment and casual work such as stevedoring at up to $8 a day, the same pattern was followed throughout the country. Indeed, it is true of most territories in the Pacific.

This adaptation to uncertainty called forth corresponding adjustments from employers, who would have preferred a more permanent labour supply. Immigrant contract labour from Vietnam was used between the wars, but attempts to replace these stable workers with Gilbertese, Wallisians and others were possible as a sustained policy only for the two enclave activities: planters found the cost excessive, while labour immigration into the general economy generated strong public hostility. However, over 1,000 'other Pacific islanders' were employed in the country in 1966. Many planters have established regular arrangements with particular villages to provide work gangs. Wages increased substantially after the withdrawal of the Vietnamese, and jobs such as copra-cutting have been let out to roving gangs at piece rates. But persistent labour shortage led to partial abandonment of labour-intensive crops, and had important consequences that we shall see shortly. In general, the plantation industry adapted well. Yields were not below those of Pacific territories more bountifully endowed with labour, and low returns were often supplemented by other enterprises (Table 2).

The towns were the most active growth points within the general economy, their growth being due primarily to the growing scale and volume of government. In addition to a large 'floating' New Hebridean population, the towns were the residence of 5,000 of the 6,000 non-indigenes in the country, and of most of the few hundred New Hebrideans — mainly in the 20–29 age group — in professional and allied occupations. After government, the New Hebridean branches of the Sydney and Nouméa-based trading companies were the largest employers, followed by six construction companies. Some 65 other businesses in Vila and 30 in Santo were very small employers. In Vila, 39 private businesses of all sizes employed 530 persons of whom 43 per cent were non-New Hebridean. Among European employees, however, 41 per cent were born in the country, and the names of many plantation families were represented.

The general economy was focused into and through these two towns to a remarkable degree. Inter-island shipping comprised 113 or 168 vessels (according to two different sources) to which was added an unknown number of village-owned launches. The core fleet was provided by the trading companies and a locally-resident entrepreneur; the small airline was also locally owned, a combine of two very small companies established by resident expatriates. All services focused on Vila and Santo, carrying a large volume of passengers and goods. With the exception of the direct overseas connexions of the fish and manganese companies, virtually all other overseas trade was handled through Vila and Santo.

It was at these points of entry and exit that the economy was centralised. Almost all finance was then controlled by a single bank. Excluding the fish and manganese, 96 per cent of all exports by value were consigned abroad by only three companies, of which the two largest shared 86 per cent. One Chinese trader handled two per cent, and the remaining two per cent was handled by nine other consignors, five of whom were planters who had independent arrangements with overseas importers. The pattern of import trade was similar. Ninety-seven per cent of all foreign trade was handled by only five companies, none of which was locally owned, and all but one of which had its principal interests abroad.

The economy of the mid-sixties could thus be summarised in these terms. The village people produced their own food with a small surplus which contributed to urban and plantation supply. Their activities were diversified between subsistence, cash production and wage labour, but within cash production there was heavy specialisation in copra. The resident expatriate minority were mainly urban with a range of employments and enterprises, but also controlled the plantation production of copra. However, few individuals depended wholly on this source. Government and the larger companies integrated this structure through control of the external linkages, and penetrated the system deeply. However, both government and companies provided opportunity for local enterprise. Lastly there were the two enclave companies, contributing a third of export income and a substantial share of revenue, but with minimal linkage to the general economy.

In this not very dynamic situation, structures dominate the scene more than scale. Small-scale operators, peasant or otherwise, could fairly readily diversify their base of support and could find opportunity for limited growth. The large companies competed for a limited quantity of business, and had the power to exclude competitors, which they exercised with discretion. However, the small scale of the economy did not attract much competition, except some specialist branch-firms from Nouméa. Though the economy was small, dualistic, fragmented, lacking in capital and tightly controlled at the centre, it was none the less tolerably well adjusted through extensive internal diversification which its apparent specialisation concealed at the aggregate level. Its weakness was a dependence on foreign aid in the form of direct government grants for growth. This aid was being used mainly to finance welfare investments whose effect was to raise levels of demand and hence create an urgent need to raise the absolute level of foreign earnings.

New Hebrides: fiscal diversification and its pitfalls

Much has changed since the mid-1960s in this small country. Most important is that government spending has more than doubled, reaching $7 million in 1968 and $14 million in 1972, with heavy emphasis on education, medical services and the more sophisticated forms of communication. More than any other single factor, this has led to replacement of a normal export surplus on current account by a deficit that reached $5 million in 1971. Although the 'joint' government services are still locally funded, the two 'national' budgets now derive almost 90 per cent of their funds from metropolitan sources. In 1971 a new five-year 'development plan' was approved, covering only the 'joint' area of the public sector, and proposing an expenditure of almost $9 million, mainly in public works, communications and urban development. It is interesting to analyse this plan spatially. Eighteen per cent of expenditure cannot be located within the group, but of the balance only 16 per cent is allocated specifically to the 'outer islands'. Two per cent goes to telecommunications based on Vila and Santo; 6 per cent belongs to projects in the rural areas of the two main islands, Efaté and Espiritu Santo; no less than 59 per cent is earmarked for projects quite specifically in and around the two towns. Yet these towns have only some 20 per cent of the population, and the 'outer islands' have 69 per cent.

The manganese mine closed in 1968, following a failure to secure contracts, but was bought by a new company which reopened on a reduced scale in 1970. The fishing company has expanded its activities in response to a growing overseas market and in 1971 fish became the largest export. A timber concession on a southern island has been working since 1969. Other developments have affected or invaded the general economy, with interesting results. Cattle have been important on plantations as a substitute for scarce labour in cleaning the plantation floors since the 1920s. In the 1950s certain planters on Efaté and Espiritu Santo assisted entrepreneurs to set up as butchers in the two towns, spontaneously replacing imported meat to a large degree. In 1958 trial shipments of chilled beef were sent to New Caledonia, and in the early 1960s small freezing and canning plants were set up in both port-towns to export beef to both New Caledonia and Tahiti. Subsequent failure of the New Caledonian pastoral industry to respond to rising demand has facilitated growth of meat exports, so that even in 1965 (Table 2) there was already evidence of specialisation in cattle rather than copra on certain plantations. Cattle have a lower money yield per hectare than coconuts, but require less labour input, and since 1968 the business has expanded rapidly. Some large areas of previously undeveloped plantation land have been cleared for cattle, leading on Espiritu Santo to serious conflict with squatters. This has generated an anti-European political movement. Though there are also cattle on New Hebridean land, there is as yet only a little participation in beef production. Numbers of cattle have risen from 35,000 in 1961 to 84,000 in 1971, only 10,500 being owned by New Hebrideans. It is now proposed to establish large new abattoirs with freezing plant and processing machinery, so as to be able to extend exports more widely, even to Japan. What began as an adaptation to labour shortage became an import-replacement industry which is now becoming a new export staple. However, the combination of large land and small labour needs may generate internal problems of a severe order.

Tourism had scarcely begun in 1965, when air services were very weak and the one tourist hotel was empty much of the time. Local and New Caledonian capital were, however, invested in a large new tourist venture just outside Vila which has been strikingly successful, and is being followed by other hotel developments financed abroad. Success is based on an improvement in air connexions following takeover of the local air company by an international consortium under Australian management. It also reflects problems encountered by tourism in New Caledonia, leading to a shift of promotion effort towards the New Hebrides. As yet tourism is confined mainly to Efaté and developments elsewhere have been less successful.

Beyond this there have been some remarkable developments arising out of speculation. Beginning in 1968, a Hawaii/Hong Kong consortium bought plantations and has subdivided them, mainly on paper, for resale unseen to buyers mainly in Hawaii. Reportedly as much as $5 million was made before the New Hebrides legislated in 1971 to tax improved values and impose strict conditions on subdivision. There has been little real investment on the ground, except for one unsuccessful hotel on Espiritu Santo. This affair helped to make known the curious constitutional status of the New Hebrides, with the combined advantages of an absence of direct taxation and access to the EEC through New Caledonia. From 1970 foreign companies began to register in the country in some numbers, and by 1972 well over 500 companies had put up nameplates in Vila. This attracted trust companies, lawyers and accountants, and also banks, so that from one bank in 1965, Vila now has seven, all branches of foreign concerns. Others are to follow. All maintain that they have come to help in New Hebridean and regional development, but it has been estimated that as much as $150 million may pass through Vila in a year, barely touching ground. There will be some small fiscal benefit, and a little employment. But meanwhile land values in central Vila have reached $20 per square metre, and $6.50 per square metre in the outskirts. Local freeholders, who are principally the governments and companies, stand to benefit appreciably, as also from the accession of a small number of well-heeled immigrants.

The 'resources' employed in all this are very varied, but although the potential fiscal benefits are substantial and there may be useful spread effects if status vis-à-vis the EEC leads to the establishment of forms of light industry, the present linkage effects are small and sharply channelled. Construction has certainly benefited, and so has trade in the towns. The success of the fishing industry has enabled the minority European partner in the enterprise to set up a small shipbuilding yard at Santo. Tourism and forward linkage from the cattle industry will generate employment. But in general the new activities are capital-intensive, and their main demand for workers is specialised and best satisfied by immigration. Even a training scheme for stockmen has only just begun. There is heavy emphasis on the towns, yet even this is benefiting mainly the shops: the market-places probably had a smaller volume of trade in 1971 than in 1965, and they were not even mentioned in the town plans (Ball, 1969).[5] The growth of retail trade and services has attracted capital from Nouméa, and several new branches have been set up. Australian construction firms have shown interest. But the tight control over the points of entry into the system, already in existence before the boom began, enables the companies, and those with whom they are willing to share the benefits, to be the principal beneficiaries.

The villages and the plantations on the outer islands meanwhile have fallen on hard times. The 'dominant' strategy of copra production has failed in the face of a depression exceeded only by that of the 1930s. New Hebridean copra is of low grade, and always commanded below-average prices. In early 1971 a price of $85 per ton was regarded as marginal, but the decline did not stop until a low of $27 per ton was reached early in 1972. Created by an oversupply of vegetable oils in the edible oil market, coupled with inroads from synthetic oils in non-edible uses (Roger Williams Technical Services, 1966), this decline has now ended because the low price of coconut oil has made it competitive with other oils. Demand is therefore recovering, but with a low price ceiling determined by the ease of substitution. There is every indication that a secular price fall, comparable with the series of price drops that have affected rubber, has occurred. In 1971, before the real depression, it was at last proposed to erect a coconut oil mill at Santo and establish grading stations. This sort of forward linkage could have been established long ago: it now seems rather late.

There has however been no rural disaster, thanks to the established diversification in economic behaviour. Many planters and some New Hebrideans have accelerated their shift to cattle – or have been angered by the discouragement to speculators applied in the 1971 legislation. Villagers have their subsistence base, and have found new opportunities for wage labour in the towns, and also abroad. In 1965 two of the Nouméa-based construction companies were already moving labour between the two countries as required.[6] From 1969 onward this began to be supplemented by voluntary movement, and each vessel clearing for Nouméa was carrying upward of a hundred deck-passengers. By 1971 it was estimated that there were 3,500 New Hebrideans in Nouméa staying an average of five to six months, and employed mainly in construction and general labour, with smaller numbers — mainly of skilled men — in other activities. Average take-home pay for a month of between 200 and 240 hours was from $250 and $350, four to five times the range available at home. Even allowing for high living costs, and the costs of some high living, individual savings averaged about $55 per month. It was estimated that at least $2.5 million was being transferred or brought back to the country in 1971. In contrast to fish and copra, which earned $6.5 and $4.5 million respectively in the same year, this third ranking body of foreign income remained entirely in New Hebridean hands (Fabre and Kissane, 1971).

The results of this substantial enlargement of the New Hebridean economy are thought-provoking. Partly by design, but mainly by unforeseen chance, a substantial measure of fiscal diversification has been achieved so that the decline in the basic industry and former main export has not been accompanied by a decline in either trade or revenue. Fish has become the most important 'domestic' export. It is caught over a wide sea area in Japanese vessels employing Korean crews, slightly processed at a shore base on Santo and then re-exported in Japanese ships. Manganese and forestry production, both in company hands and separate from the main economy, remain small but useful. Tourism is bringing in new revenue (and adding to the import bill), and circular migration to Nouméa has become a major source of foreign income. A wholly non-productive business as a tax-free haven brings in some income, a surprising weight of financial services and some specialised immigrants, and has pushed land values in Vila up to the levels of Australian cities. Speculation in land has enabled some planters to unload profitless plantations, and may now bring in some revenue. Internally, a useful but problem-laden cattle business has been created by the more extensive use of land, a small shipbuilding industry has been set up and urban construction has been expanded enormously. A higher proportion of the economy than hitherto is in foreign hands, and a much higher proportion than before is dependent on the vagaries of foreign demand.

The essential structures have not been altered, and nothing has yet been done to generate growth in the outer islands, or to intensify use of the country's land resources. Internal trade and specialisation have not advanced, and only a long-established diversification of spontaneous origin has saved the rural majority of the population from economic disaster. Though new activities have been added, the economy has in structural terms became more specialised. Possibilities of further diversifying rural cropping, of — for example — expanding and commercialising old-established pig production with the use of coconuts, of developing local supply of the urban market-places, of

70

upgrading the locally-owned inter-island fleet, of developing small industries for local consumption – all these have been neglected. Until now nothing has been done to add value to the principal rural export. It is evident that entrepreneurship has not been wanting, but the best opportunities are being absorbed externally. It is also evident that scale has not been the fundamental limitation, except in dealings with the larger world.

Conclusion

The New Hebrides offer a rather extreme example of diversification of the wrong kind, which fails to take account of existing diversification within the economy. The difference is however only one of degree. One might compare present developments in Haiti, where diversification takes the form of bauxite mine on one peninsula, a major tourist development on an offlying island, and some tourism and a little manufacture in and around the capital, leaving the rural mass untouched (Boucher, 1972). Similar patterns emerge in other parts of the Caribbean where sugar dependence or banana dependence is giving way to dependence on tourism. Diversification which permits loss of control over the growth points of the economy, which evolves in isolation from the general economy so that it has few direct linkage effects, and which benefits mainly the central revenue, tends to have its 'spread' effects channelled into the central places where local control is already most eroded, and to generate sharp rural-urban differentials which create problems of a new order.

One may look at diversification in many ways. I have tried to look at several and to show their interrelation. The key to the problem is twofold: the maintenance or creation of factor mobility that remains mobile, and does not simply entail a shift from one state to another; the development of linkages throughout the economy, and not merely from the top down. The problem is scale-related in that both these are easier to achieve when the bounds of the economy are large. But there are also substantial possibilities for diversification within and among units at the very bottom of the pile. Recognition and utilisation of these often disregarded possibilities is essential if we are to have development for the many, and not simply growth for the few.

It may seem fanciful to conclude with an ecological analogy, but it follows naturally from the tenor of my argument. In nature, as well as in economy, diversity is advantageous and conducive to stability. Without diversity, an ecosystem cannot readily adapt to invasion or catastrophe – such as plant disease. The ecological argument against monoculture thus meshes rather closely with the socio-economic argument against specialisation. Diversity enables an economy to survive, as it has enabled New Hebridean rural society to survive in 1971-72, and as it enabled all Pacific rural societies to survive the great depression of the 1930s which brought ruin to so many specialists in the region. Views of development which stress the value of diversity in less developed societies are now emerging on ecological grounds (e.g. Clarke, 1973). May we not also see that the complex of institutions we have regarded as inefficient, obstructive to the course of progress, or a set of mere 'static facts' are in fact the true wealth of these small countries? And if so, maybe the closeness of government to the people in a small nation could be an invaluable asset in checking the disruption of diversity which is a product of much of the 'diversification' that we have reviewed.

Table 1 : Data on South Pacific Islands

	Solomon Islands	New Hebrides	New Caledonia	Fiji
Area (km^2)	29,800	11,860	19,103	18,270
Population (1971)	165,000	80,000	120,000	520,000
Expatriate population	10,000	4,000	50,000	10,000
Melanesian population	150,000	73,000	55,000	220,000
Population of largest towns	14,000	12,000	60,000	100,000
GDP (factor cost per capita: 1968 US $)	200	1,720	390	330
Value of exports	$6.9m (1970)	$12.8m (1971)	c.$80m (1969)	$53.2m (1969)
Value of imports	$10.0m (1970)	$17.8m (1971)	c.$90m (1969)	$77.9m (1969)

Table 2 : Some data on commercial agriculture on plantations in the New Hebrides
(Figures in brackets represent number of plantations with data on each topic)

Plantation Group	Number of Plantations	No operated by owners or lessees	Mean area of holdings where given	Mean area under coconuts where given	Mean number of cattle where given	Plantations with cocoa and coffee, as — Major crop	Minor crop	Plantations with other enterprises	Owners/lessees with other activities	Mean production copra per plantation Tonnes	Mean yield of copra per planted ha Tonnes/ha
	No.	No.	ha	ha	No.	No.	No.	No.	No.		
Efaté island	25	18 (25)	648 (17)	160 (18)	390 (18)	1	5+	9+	12+	101 (6)*	0.84 (6)*
Central islands (Epi, Malekula)	7	2 (7)	856 (5)	184 (7)	470 (4)	0	1+	2+	1+	126 (7)	0.69 (7)
Santo and nearby islands, Gp.A	15	11 (15)	1701 (5)	292 (10)	585 (11)	1	5+	No information	No information	284 (6)	1.26 (3)
Total of above plantations	47	31 (47)	880 (27)	191 (35)	466 (33)	2	11+	11+	13+	168 (19)	0.84 (16)
Santo and nearby islands, Gp. B.	7	2 (7)	2069 (5)	345 (7)	742 (6)	4	0	5	0	305 (7)	0.89 (7)
Santo and nearby islands, both groups	22	13 (22)	1874 (10)	314 (17)	640 (17)	5	5+	5+	?	296 (13)	0.94 (10)
All plantations combined	54	33 (54)	1066 (32)	217 (42)	645 (39)	6	11+	16+	13+	205 (26)	0.84 (23)

General note: Data for Efaté Island, the Central Islands, and Santo and nearby islands, Group A, are derived from short descriptions of each plantation visited by the French Commissaire-Resident during 1965 and 1966, and published in the Bulletin d'Information de la Résidence de France, Port-Vila. There are many omissions, and most figures are rounded.

Data for Santo and adjacent islands, Group B, refer entirely to plantations owned and operated, or leased to gérants libres by La Société Française des Nouvelles-Hébrides. These data are derived from Doumenge (1966, 356-57, 360).

Since the data in the second group are somewhat different in nature, though they refer to the same general period, and since they concern a group of relatively large plantations, the analysis is presented in both, separated and combined form.

* A majority of plantations on Efaté, and a few elsewhere, now have cattle-rearing for meat (and in a few cases, also dairying) as main enterprise. Data on copra production are thus subordinated to information on livestock enterprises in the descriptions published in the Bulletin d'Information.

NOTES

1. This discussion in game theoretic terms is essentially qualitative, although it is based on fairly comprehensive data on the costs of plantation production of certain crops in the south Pacific context, and on extensive observation and literature covering particular peasant communities, including my own studies in Chimbu, New Guinea. For the plantation sector, at least, it would be possible to play a series of 3-person games employing selected data from within the range available (from field research and input-output data obtained from plantation accounts) in order to test these hypothetical statements. Some of the relevant data are presented in Brookfield with Hart (1971).

2. It may be noted that such diversification also increases the power of government in the economy, for almost all benefits from the new activity are channelled through government and few reach the population directly from the innovating industry. There are some striking examples, especially in modern mining developments, and in tourism that is confined to offlying islands and similar remote corners. Among certain governments also, there is benefit for well-placed individuals in this form of diversification.

3. This work was basically a socio-economic study of the capital town, Vila, carried out by members of the Research School of Pacific Studies, Australian National University. The main results of this research have long since been published (Brookfield, Brown Glick and Hart, 1969; Brookfield and Brown Glick, 1969; Brown Glick, 1970), but much of the material presented here has not been utilised previously. I revisited the New Hebrides in 1969 and 1971.

4. In 1972, however, steeply rising costs in New Caledonia finally had an adverse effect. Following the opening of large new resources of low-grade nickel ore in Indonesia, Japanese buyers sought reductions in the proposed contract prices for New Caledonian crude ore. With continued delays in the formation of new companies, there was a decline in the rate of immigration and also in investment. But there was little evidence that this 'crisis' would lead to any fundamental redirection of development policy.

5. However, the development plan does make provision for small covered markets, to be built in 1973 and 1974.

6. Although the 1914 Anglo-French Protocol (Arts. 31-56) contains extensive provisions concerning labour, these relate almost entirely to contract engagement, which has now almost ceased. New Hebrideans may not be subjects, citizens or protected persons of either power separately (Art. 8.2). However, the activity of carriers of either power is under the jurisdiction of that power, and since the New Hebrides are a region of 'joint influence' of governments based in Nouvéa and (now) Honiara, there is no legal limitation on movement to either territory provided that the New Hebridean labour regulations are not infringed. Following objections to the loss of labour by both planters and New Hebrideans on the Advisory Council in 1971, some regulation was introduced, but this was only regulation, not in any sense prohibition. The mutual benefit — New Caledonia gets labour, and the New Hebrides get a money income — is too patent to permit an embargo.

REFERENCES

A high proportion of the more recent information derives from ephemeral sources, especially the following: *Bulletin du Commerce* (Nouméa); *Bulletin d'Information de la Résidence de France* (Vila); *British Newsletter* (Vila); *British Solomon Island News Sheet* (Honiara); *Pacific Islands Monthly* (Sydney); *Pacific Islands Trade News* (Canberra). Also important have been the *Annual Reports* of territories and their departments, and the Fiji *Current Economic Statistics*. Other principal sources and references are as follows:

D. Ball:	*Vila and Santo: Development Plans 1970-1990* (London, O.D.M., 1969 unpublished).
R.D. Bedford:	*Mobility in Transition: an Analysis of Population Movement in the New Hebrides* (Ph.D. Thesis, Canberra; A.N.U., 1971).
R.D. Bedford:	'A Transition in Circular Mobility' in H.C. Brookfield et al, *The Pacific in Transition* (London, Arnold, 1973).
B. Benedict, et al:	*Problems of Smaller Territories* (London, Athlone, 1967).
P. Boucher:	'Clair-obscur sur Haiti' *(Le Devoir* (Montreal) Vol. 63, Nos. 100-2, 1972).
H.C. Brookfield:	'The Money that Grows on Trees' (Australian Geographical Studies, Vol. 6, 97-119, 1968).
H.C. Brookfield:	'Dualism and the Geography of Developing Countries' (Presidential Address, Sect. 21, A.N.Z.A.A.S. Port Moresby [unpublished] 1970).
H.C. Brookfield:	*Colonialism, Development and Independence: the Case of the Melanesian Islands in the South Pacific* (Cambridge, University Press, 1972).
H.C. Brookfield:	'Full Circle in Chimbu' in H.C. Brookfield et al., *The Pacific in Transition* (London, Arnold, 1973).
H.C. Brookfield and Paula Brown Glick:	*The People of Vila* (Canberra, Dept. of Human Geography, A.N.U., 1969).
H.C. Brookfield: Paula Brown Glick and Doreen Hart:	'Melanesian Melange: the Market at Vila, New Hebrides' in H.C. Brookfield et al., *Pacific Market Places: a Collection of Essays* (Canberra, A.N.U. Press, 1969).
H.C. Brookfield and Doreen Hart:	*Melanesia: a Geographical Interpretation of an Island World,* (London, Methuen, 1971).
Paula Brown Glick:	'Melanesian Mosaic: the Plural Community of Vila' in L. Plotnicov et al., *Essays in Comparative Social Stratification* (Pittsburgh, University Press, 1970).
A.V. Chayanov, (ed. D. Thorner, B. Kerblay and R.E.F. Smith):	*The Theory of Peasant Economy* (Homewood, Ill., American Economic Association, 1966).
W.C. Clarke:	'The Dilemma of Development' in H.C. Brookfield et. al., *The Pacific in Transition* (London, Arnold, 1973).
W. Davenport:	'Jamaican Fishing: a Game Theory Analysis' *(Yale University Publications in Anthropology,* No. 59, 1960).

W. Demas:	*The Economics of Development in Small Countries with Special Reference to the Caribbean* (Montreal, McGill-Queens, 1965).
W. Elkan and L.A. Fallers:	'The Mobility of Labor' in W.E. Moore et al., *Labor Commitment and Social Change in Developing Areas* (New York, S.S.R.C., 1960).
J. Fabre and M.F. Kissane:	'Report on a Mission to Nouméa, Vila: British Residency' (unpublished), 1971.
I.J. Fairbairn:	'Pacific Island Economies' (Journal of the Polynesian Society, Vol. 80, 74-118, 1971).
K.B. Griffin:	*Underdevelopment in Spanish America: an Interpretation* (London, Allen & Unwin, 1969).
P.R. Gould:	'Man against his Environment: a Game Theoretic Framework' (Annals of the Association of American Geographers, Vol. 53, 290-7, 1963).
IBRD:	*The Economy of the British Solomon Islands Protectorate,* (Washington, International Bank for Reconstruction and Development, 1969).
I.Q. Lasaqa:	'Melanesians' Choice: a Geographical Study of Tadhimboko Participation in the Cash Economy' (New Guinea Research Bulletin, No. 44, 1972).
Kari Levitt:	*Silent Surrender: the Multinational Corporation in Canada* (Toronto, Macmillan, 1970).
M. Lipton:	'The Theory of the Optimalising Peasant' (Journal of Development Studies, Vol. 4, 327-51, 1968).
M. Lipton:	'Interdisciplinary Studies in Less Developed Countries' (Journal of Development Studies, Vol. 7, 5-18, 1970).
G. Rocheteau:	*Le Nord de la Nouvelle-Calédonie: Région Economique* (Nouméa: O.R.S.T.O.M., 1966).
Roger Williams Technical Services Ltd.:	*A Survey of the United States and Canadian Non-food Uses of Coconut Oil* (prepared for the Food and Agricultural Organisation of the United Nations, Princeton, N.J.: Roger Williams, 1966).
M. Salter:	'Economy of the South Pacific' *(Pacific Viewpoint,* Vol. II, 1-26, 1970).
J. Weeks:	'Uncertainty, Risk and Wealth and Income Distribution in Peasant Agriculture' (Journal of Development Studies, Vol. 7, 28-36, 1970).
J.S.G. Wilson:	*Economic Survey of the New Hebrides* (London, H.M.S.O., 1966).

3. INDUSTRIAL DEVELOPMENT IN PERIPHERAL SMALL COUNTRIES*

Percy Selwyn

Summary

This paper is concerned with the location of industry in small countries which are peripheral areas in their regions. It argues that their problems can best be understood in a regional context (and that this is so whether or not there is a formal system of regional cooperation – such as a customs union or a free trade area – in the region) but that social and political structures are also of central importance. The discussion is based on a study of the small countries of the Southern African periphery – an area of extreme and possibly atypical inequalities, but one which throws light on small country problems elsewhere.

I. National and multinational regions

A 'region' is one of the vaguest and least clearly defined of all economic terms. Indeed one recent writer has said:

'It has been suggested . . . that a region means an area that a regional economist gets a research grant to study' (Hoover, 1971).

This vagueness reflects the fact that economic regions themselves are not unambiguously delimited, and may be distinguished in different ways for different purposes. The common factor among all the ways in which the word is used is as an economic area which it makes sense to consider as a whole.

Most of the writers on regional economics have assumed that an economic 'region' (however defined) is part of a country. Indeed Lösch (1954) pointed out:

'. . . there are economic regions within political boundaries and others again that extend beyond them.'

Lösch came to the conclusion however, that economic regions would normally be limited by national boundaries rather than shared by two or more countries.

'Political frontiers are wider, so to speak, than economic boundaries. States, like oases, are separated as in a great desert by customs duties, laws, language, a sense of community, insecurity and destiny. Economic boundaries separate only through minute price differences.'

This view has been implicitly held by most writers on regional economics. Indeed many standard textbooks in this field totally ignore

*I am grateful for comments and suggestions from Gerry Helleiner, Willie Henderson and David Steele, and to my colleagues at the Small Countries Conference – and in particular to Fuat Andic, Harold Brookfield, and Salvatore Schiavo-Campo. My mistakes however are my own.

the possibility that economic regions may cross political boundaries. The principal exception to this rule has been work on regional economic associations such as economic unions, common markets and free trade areas, where there is a substantial literature, covering such problems as the distribution of costs and benefits and the polarisation of development inside common markets. (See e.g. Robson, 1968; United Nations, 1967.)

One reason why regional economists have frequently assumed that a region is smaller than a country is that the subject was developed mainly in large countries in Europe and in the United States. When we consider small developing countries, however, many of the types of argument for looking at regions primarily as parts of countries appear far weaker. The smaller a country is in economic terms, the less likely it is to be self-contained as an economic unit and the more likely it is that it can usefully be considered to be part of a region transcending its own frontiers. The various barriers referred to clearly have less importance for small poor countries. This is particularly the case in Africa, where national frontiers may be fairly open and may cut across tribal and language divisions. In general, the following features of small countries will frequently make a regional type of analysis more relevant for their circumstances:

(a) Small poor countries usually cannot afford highly protective tariff structures, and may indeed have few industries to protect. Import duties are more likely to be mainly for revenue purposes. Therefore customs barriers may be less important than in larger and more advanced countries.

(b) The smaller a country, the less likely it is to be self-contained in factors of production. Migration will be more important than in large countries; the country may be a substantial net importer or exporter of skills and enterprise; its indigenous financial institutions will be weak, and it may rely on financial centres outside its own borders.

(c) Small countries are generally more specialised than large ones, and their internal economies may therefore be very weakly integrated. Linkages with neighbouring countries may be stronger than internal linkages.

(d) The smaller a country and the narrower its market, the less likely it is that major investors such as international firms will regard it as a separate unit, and the more likely it is that they will look on it as part of a wider region. Their decisions on the location of activities will be taken on a regional level, and while such a company might regard, say, the eastern seaboard area of the United States as a region, they might equally regard the Eastern Caribbean or Francophone West Africa as a region.

We may distinguish two types of region — 'homogeneous' regions and 'nodal' regions. A homogeneous region (such as the Empty Quarter in

Arabia) may cut across national boundaries, but may be of little dynamic significance because there may be few interactions among its constituent parts. Here we are more concerned with nodal regions – those containing a nucleus and a surrounding peripheral area.

The word 'peripheral' has been applied to many countries and situations. Thus Levitt (1970) describes Canada as a 'hinterland' economy in relation to the United States. In another sense, the third world in general can be described as peripheral in relation to the rich countries; major decisions affecting poor countries' economic structure, development and welfare are taken in the rich countries, and there is little influence in the reverse direction. Here we are concerned with peripheral countries in a narrower context. In a region consisting of several countries, it frequently happens that development is polarised in one or a few countries and that this process of polarisation creates a clear distinction between 'core' or 'nuclear' areas and 'peripheral' areas. These divisions may indeed not correspond to national frontiers, but the smaller a country is, the more likely it is that the country as such can be described as either a core country or a peripheral country in a regional context. Thus a region which itself may be considered as peripheral in a world context may include countries which are also peripheral in a regional context. It is usually not difficult to identify such peripheral countries. There are a number of indications which can be used.

(a) The most obvious one is economic structure. The core country will have a greater relative development of non-primary production than the peripheral country. Thus, to take an extreme example, whereas manufacturing industry in Lesotho accounts for under 1% of the national income, the corresponding proportion in the Republic of South Africa is over 20%.

(b) This greater specialisation on the part of the peripheral country will be shown in the structure of foreign trade. Thus in the trade between Upper Volta and the Ivory Coast, 80% of Upper Volta's export exports to the Ivory Coast in 1969 consisted of live animals and animal products, and a further 15% of vegetable products. Ivory Coast's exports to Upper Volta were far more diversified, including cement (15.6%), wood and cork products (10.3%), textiles (9.6%), chemical products (9.2%), transport products (8.6%), food, drink and tobacco products (5.6%) and base metal products (4.9%). This structure clearly shows the peripheral relation of Upper Volta to the Ivory Coast economy.

(c) In so far as there is migration between the core and the periphery, it will tend to be from the periphery to the core. This is, of course, only another aspect of rural/urban migration; in this instance, the urban area which exerts a pull on migrants is in another country.

(d) Economic geographers have developed other indicators suggesting peripheral status. Thus Odell (1968), in analysing the location of economic development in Latin America, uses indicators of economic activity based on electricity generating capacity.

There will normally be dominance by the core over the peripheral country – i.e. the peripheral country will be far more dependent on events and decisions taken in the core country than the core country will be on events and decisions taken in the periphery. Dependence may be of various kinds. Thus a land-locked peripheral country will be dependent on decisions by a maritime core country on the use and development of various modes of transport. The financial institutions and potential investors may be centred in the core country. The pattern of trade may involve dependence. Indeed Friedmann (1966) describes the relation between the core and the periphery within the same country as 'colonial'; such a relation might also apply as between core and peripheral countries within a region, although its nature will be different as a result of the existence of other centres of political decision.

It will be noted that these indications do not assume the existence of machinery for regional cooperation, although such machinery could add a new dimension to the relationship. In one of the examples quoted above – the relation of Upper Volta to the Ivory Coast – there is only a weak system of regional economic cooperation, but the nucleus/periphery situation is very similar to that found in regional free trade areas and common markets.

Where a nuclear region is within national boundaries, it creates problems of a different order from those in which the region crosses national boundaries. In the first instance, although the rural/urban drift which is implied in the creation of nuclear regions may well involve serious problems of unemployment, rural decay and the cumulative growth of spatial inequalities, it could be argued that there was a national benefit in the building up of such centres. These may provide the basis for industrial growth and the source of savings which could, at least in theory, be used for the benefit of the peripheral areas. Where, however, the peripheral area is in another country such arguments clearly have less force; in such a case the periphery may receive no benefit from nuclear growth apart from the remittances of emigrant workers, and this benefit may be very small. Such peripheral areas may thus remain 'least-developed countries' (as several of them are), and may face severe difficulties in countering the forces making for spatial inequality. It is for this reason that the development of industries in peripheral countries becomes an issue of such urgency; they see in the building up of growth centres associated with industrialisation an important means for countering the forces making for polarisation in the region. But equally they may find the development of industries extremely difficult and the price which they have to pay for them very high.

II. The location of industry in multinational regions

There has traditionally been a gap between the theory of the international location of industry and that of the internal location of industry. The distinction goes back to Ricardo, whose basic assumption was that factors of production were mobile inside national frontiers but immobile as between different countries. The classical theory of international trade and the international location of industry thus took factor endowments and costs as a datum. Actual location of economic activity (i.e. position in economic space as a factor) was largely ignored. A totally different approach was developed to account for industrial concentration inside countries. Thus whereas the classical theory of international trade was based on the theory of comparative advantage and even many modern theories (such as the Product Cycle theory) are essentially variations on this basic approach, the theory of the internal or regional location of industry is concerned with differences in absolute costs, such as production and transfer costs, external economies, market location, the economies of urbanisation and so on.

But, as is recognised, the 'least-cost' answer formulated by Weber (1929) is an inadequate explanation of the regional location of industry. Other important elements are the location of decision-making and control over the use of investible funds, the extent of monopoly, the flow of information and associated uncertainties, and political structures. Also we may be less concerned about the location of individual industries than about the prospects for the growth of an industrial complex (Isard, Schooler and Vietorisz, 1959).

The theory also used the notion of cumulative causation developed by Myrdal (1957) and Hirschman (1958). Much empirical work has shown that, at least in certain stages of development, spatial inequality is not self-correcting but cumulative, and that an area which (for any reason) gets a head start in industrial growth, tends to stay ahead, and indeed increases its lead (Williamson, 1965). Thus the main reason for the location of a new industry in a particular area may be that industries are there already. A general statement of the theory is in Smith (1971). But we are not merely concerned with the actual location of industry; equally important are where and to whom the benefits of industrial growth accrue. Thus it may be argued that even where peripheral countries do obtain industries the local benefit is small.

The kind of theory we need to explain the location of industry in peripheral small countries in a regional context is not very different from that needed to do so within countries. As Sutcliffe (1971) says:

'... the pattern of growth in one country depends very much upon its relationship with other countries. The nation defined by a political boundary is often an inappropriate unit for the study of economic change. The mainspring of industrialisation in one country may be found in another . . . On the other hand the failure of a country to industrialise may also be attributable to its relations with another country or other countries in the international economy. Just as within a country some areas industrialise faster than others, often at the cost of the de-industrialisation of other areas, so in the international economy some countries industrialise faster than others'. . . (p.32).

But political boundaries do make a difference. However open the economy of the peripheral country, there are still powers of local political decision-making which are not available to regions within large countries. The boundary may mark a difference in political or social structures and attitudes, and may also have an influence on flows of information and resources. A theory of location of industry in peripheral small countries cannot therefore be based simply on a regional/spatial model; the complications introduced by the existence of national borders must be taken into account.

III. The peripheral countries in Southern Africa

The question with which we are concerned is why the peripheral countries in Southern Africa experience such difficulties in attracting or promoting industrial development. The following discussion draws on material collected in a study of industrial development in Botswana, Lesotho and Swaziland.[1] It might be thought that these countries represent an extreme case in view both of their extreme weakness vis-à-vis the Republic of South Africa and of the peculiar and possibly unique political and social structure of South Africa itself. But although their situation is extreme, their experience throws some light on the problems in other peripheral small countries. The hypotheses underlying the study are in Selwyn (1972).

Here a little background information will be useful. Table 1 shows the basic statistics of the Southern African region in so far as they relate to our present concerns. The 'region' as shown here omits other countries which might be considered more or less peripheral to the Southern African economy — such as Malawi and Rhodesia — and is confined solely to Botswana, Lesotho, Swaziland and the Republic of South Africa. The figures in Table 1 are not strictly comparable since they relate to different dates, but here we are concerned only with orders of magnitude; these are not substantially affected by the internal inconsistencies in the table.

The following points emerge from Table 1:—

(a) The population of the Republic of South Africa is roughly ten times as great as that of all three of the peripheral countries together.

(b) GDP per head in the Republic is some ten times the level in

82

Table 1 : Basic Statistics of the Southern African Region

	Botswana	Lesotho	Swaziland	Republic of South Africa
Population (thousand)	626 (1971)	968 (1966)	451 (1971)	21,448 (1970)
Area (sq. miles)	220,000	11,716	6,705	471,455
GDP at factor cost (R million)	46.0 (1968/69)	46.3 (1967/68)	50.6 (1967/68)	9,641 (1968)
GDP per head (R)	73.5	47.8	118.2	450
Industrial production per head of population (R)	4.5	0.3	14.9	93.2
Industrial production as proportion of GDP (per cent)	6.1	0.6	13.2	21.1
Employment in manufacturing industry (thousand)	2 (1971)	0.5	5 (1969)	1,164 (1970)
Absentees as proportion of de jure population (per cent)	N/A	11.9 (1966)	6.5 (1971)	N/A

Sources   South Africa Statistics 1970   )   Pretoria Department
             Bulletin of Statistics March 1972)   of Statistics

             Republic of Botswana: Statistical Abstract 1971 (Central
                                                  Statistics Office, Ministry of
                                                  Development Planning).

             Kingdom of Lesotho: Annual Statistical Bulletin)
                                           1970.   )Maseru:
)Bureau
                                           Census of Population 1968,) of
                                           1969.   )Statistics
                                           National Accounts 1967/68)

             Swaziland: Annual Statistical Bulletin 1971
                                           (Mbabane: Central Statistical office).

Lesotho, seven times that in Botswana and three times that in Swaziland. In terms of GNP, the discrepancy between South Africa and Swaziland would be greater because of the important part played by foreign investment in the Swazi economy; net factor income paid abroad in 1967/68 was R7.9 million, or 14.8 per cent of GDP. On the other hand, the difference between Lesotho and South Africa would be reduced on such a basis because of the importance of the earnings of emigrant workers from Lesotho in the Republic.

(c) Total GDP in all three countries together is less than 2 per cent of the value of the South African GDP.

(d) Value added in manufacturing industry in all three countries together is equivalent to about 0.5 per cent of value added in South African industry.

(e) Industrial production per head of population in South Africa is about 20 times that in Botswana, over 300 times that in Lesotho and over 6 times that in Swaziland. In both Botswana and Swaziland by far the greater part of value added in industry is in the processing of local primary products (meat-processing in Botswana and sugar-refining, fruit-canning, woodpulp production and meat-packing in Swaziland). The difference between the apparent level of industrialisation in Lesotho and that in the other two peripheral countries is largely accounted for by such industries, which are virtually absent in Lesotho.

(f) Total industrial employment in all three countries is some 0.6 per cent of the level of industrial employment in South Africa.

(g) All three countries are areas of emigration – primarily to South Africa. The most extreme situation is in Lesotho, where some 40 per cent of the labour force at any time is employed in the Republic. On the other hand (as the tables do not show) all three countries are importers of skilled manpower.

This information is sufficient to show the extreme inequalities between South Africa, *taken as a whole*, and these peripheral countries. But this gives a misleading picture because there are also extreme inequalities inside South Africa, both socially and spatially, and some parts of the Republic are just as much peripheral areas as are the countries with which we are concerned. Many of the same types of analysis which we would use to understand the process of industrial development (or non-development) in the peripheral countries would be equally applicable to a consideration of the problem of, say, the Transkei. The common factors are strengthened by the existence of a customs union and a common currency between the four countries.

In many ways the nature of the problem, as well as its importance, varies between the three countries. Thus, to take Friedmann's classification (1966), we might describe Lesotho as a downward-transitional area, whereas in both Botswana and Swaziland there are elements of resource frontiers. Industrial development is a far more urgent need in Lesotho than in the other two countries. But in this paper we are more concerned with their common problems than with their differences.

The investigation was concerned with the problems of industrial development in these countries as influenced by their peripheral situation. It was concerned with costs – and in particular labour costs, the availability of capital, management and enterprise, and access to markets. Some explanation was also sought for the weakness of the internal linkage effects arising from the existing industries. But attention was also paid to social and political factors as far as these could be assessed.

(a) Costs

Here we were concerned with labour costs, the costs arising from the absence of economies of agglomeration, and transport costs. An attempt was made to compare these elements in costs with what they would be if the industries were located in the nuclear areas of the region such as the Southern Transvaal. Of these, labour costs are possibly the most important, in view of the interest of all three countries in the promotion of labour-intensive industries.

(i) Labour: Peripheral countries normally look to labour-oriented industries, i.e. industries where labour costs are an important element in total costs. There are various reasons for this. First, there is usually a shortage of local employment opportunities, and industrialisation may be looked on as one means of providing jobs. This is a major consideration in Lesotho, where the lack of local jobs is most acute. Secondly, there may be a shortage of capital available for starting industries, and a desire to get the maximum impact in terms of jobs for a given level of investment. Lastly, it may be considered that the main locational advantage such countries have for industry is a supply of cheap labour, and that labour-oriented industries are therefore the ones most likely to be attracted in the first place and to be successfully established.

This approach is realistic only on the assumption that the peripheral country genuinely has an advantage in wage-costs over the nuclear area in the region – i.e. that efficiency-wages are lower in the periphery than in the core area. Indeed, as Robinson (1969) points out in respect of backward areas in advanced countries:

'There is no *a priori* reason for thinking that a solution can always be found to the problem of creating in an unfavourable location a comparative advantage for the production of some new product on the basis of the payment of the same efficiency-wages to labour as are paid in other more favourable locations. There is, on the contrary, a likelihood that the problem cannot be solved in these terms.'

Thus the level of efficiency-wages is likely to be a key locational factor for industries other than those which have a special local advantage (e.g. those based on the exploitation of a local resource, or small-scale industries catering for the local market where economies of scale are insufficient to overcome the transport cost-disadvantage of foreign suppliers). It was therefore necessary to examine how far these peripheral countries in fact had an advantage in terms of the level of efficiency-wages.

One would expect wage rates to be lower in peripheral than in core areas — although it does not follow that efficiency-wages are necessarily any lower. Workers in peripheral countries will be willing to accept lower wages because the local job opportunities are more limited and living costs are usually less. There will however be a lower limit to wage rates in the peripheral area which will be determined not only by the local opportunity cost to the worker of accepting employment but also by the worker's access to employment in the core area. The greater the ease of access to the labour market in the core area, the smaller will be the gap between wages in the core and the periphery. This is illustrated in Fig. 1.

Figure 1: Labour Offer Curves in Peripheral Small Countries

OA is the going wage rate in the nuclear area; this is assumed to be exogenously determined, and to be unaffected by the supply of labour coming from the periphery. PQ is the labour offer curve in the peripheral country. The shape of the curve is determined by the preference that citizens of the peripheral country have for staying at home, the cost of moving, relative living costs in the peripheral and core areas and the attitude of the workers concerned to the risk of moving. The curve crosses the core area wage-rate line at R, and the angle PRA is less than 90 degrees. This implies that there are some workers with an absolute preference for going to the core area even if wages there are lower — possibly because they see more opportunities for jobs and advancement in the nuclear country. P^1Q^1 is the labour offer curve under conditions of restricted mobility and limited access by citizens of the peripheral country to jobs in the core country. P^1Q^1 is consistently lower than PQ. Where it crosses the core area wage-rate line at S, it is nearly vertical — signifying that a wage rate substantially lower than the wage rate in the core area will attract virtually all the local supply of workers. This approach will be found particularly relevant when we come to consider the problem of skilled labour.

It is difficult to generalise about the degree to which efficiency-wages were in fact lower in these countries than in the nuclear area; there were wide variations from firm to firm, and several enterprises were unable to give very clear information. The following account is therefore more impressionistic than quantitative. Generally speaking, unskilled and semi-skilled wage rates were lower in these countries than in the nuclear areas of the Republic — sometimes substantially so. But certain firms — especially large companies exploiting a local natural resource — said that they paid wages roughly equivalent to those they would pay in a similar enterprise in the Republic. (Since resource-based industries in South Africa might also be located in peripheral areas, it is not surprising that wage rates were comparable.)

Many firms said however that labour productivity was substantially lower than they would expect in the nuclear area. Several reasons were given for this, but basically it appears to have reflected the lack of an industrial tradition. Since peripheral countries lack industries, they lack the experience of working in industry. Apart from the lack of specific skills (which may not be a major handicap in industries such as assembly plants where work is mainly repetitive), people without an industrial background have to acquire the general rhythm and speed of industrial work. Other factors may also have been of importance. It was difficult to resist the impression that some of the firms which complained of poor labour productivity suffered from poor management — a point on which more will be said later. Moreover, labour productivity suffered where there were frequent changes in the work to be performed. Thus a firm making a variety of products in short runs would suffer from high wage costs; this would clearly be of importance in import-substitution industries where the local market is too small to permit much specialisation. Lastly, where capacity utilisation was low because of market limitations, labour and capital costs would tend to be high.

A further element in labour costs was the cost of training. Virtually every firm had to train its own labour force (although in certain instances the amount of training given appears to have been minimal). This is a cost which has to be met by any industrial enterprise in a peripheral country without an industrial base, and is the other side of the coin to the economies of agglomeration which a firm might expect to obtain in an already established industrial complex.

In all, it was difficult to judge whether unskilled and semi-skilled wage costs were genuinely lower in these peripheral countries than in the core area; in certain instances it appeared that they were actually higher. The situation is complicated by the fact that unskilled and semi-skilled work in the nuclear area of South Africa is done by people with neither political nor industrial rights — and who lack in particular the right to organise effective trade unions. Thus unskilled and semi-skilled wages in the core area are kept artificially low (i.e. the line AB in Fig. 1 is lowered for unskilled and semi-skilled workers), and the potential advantage of the peripheral areas in terms of lower efficiency-wages is relatively reduced.

Much skilled labour for industry in these countries is imported, and enterprises therefore have to pay at least the equivalent rate to that in the Republic. Apart from this, one would in principle expect that the margin between skilled wage rates in the nucleus and the periphery would be less than that for unskilled and semi-skilled labour. The skilled man is more mobile; many studies of migration show that migrants have a higher average level of education than the general population from which they come. A man with skills is more likely to compare what he can earn in his own country with what he could earn if he migrated; this comparison will raise the level of PQ in relation to AB in Fig. 1.

There is however one element in this calculation which is of central importance in the Southern African region — and where the situation is particularly atypical. As we have shown, the degree to which the skilled labour offer function is affected by the going wage rate in the nuclear area will be determined by the ease of access to skilled jobs in the nucleus. The greater the barriers to effective mobility, the greater will be the gap between skilled labour wages in the core and the periphery. In Southern Africa the barriers to mobility are very powerful. Skilled jobs in the nuclear area are mainly 'white' jobs, and Africans have only limited access to employment above the semi-skilled level. Where they do occupy such jobs, they are paid substantially less than are white people doing the same work. At the same time, these restrictions on access to skilled jobs have forced (white) skilled wage rates up to monopolistic levels. In these circumstances the gap between skilled labour wage rates in the nucleus and in the periphery should in theory be greater than in situations where there are fewer restrictions on mobility – i.e. the skilled labour offer curve is more likely to follow $P^1 Q^1$ than PQ.

Such a situation should in theory provide competitive advantage to the peripheral countries in skilled-labour intensive industries. The difficulty is that the actual supply of skilled labour is so small. Not only are industrial training facilities limited, but effective training in industrial skills can be given only in industrial enterprises; where such enterprises are very scarce, the supply of skills will be equally limited. As long as indigenous skills remain scarce in the peripheral countries, any theoretical advantage they might obtain from such a wage gap will hardly be realised. Moreover, there appeared to be pressure in some firms for the 'rate' to be paid for the job – that is, that where a black worker was employed in a previously white job, he should be given the same pay (less any special expatriate allowance the white worker may have received). Since the rate so determined is based on the monopolistic wage structure of South African white workers, such a policy will reduce any competitive advantage peripheral industries might obtain through the local employment of black skilled workers, when they are available.

(ii) Economies of agglomeration: The second element in costs where differences might be expected between the nuclear and the peripheral areas is the agglomerative economies to be found in nuclear areas and lacking in peripheral areas. We have already noted one example of this: an enterprise in a nuclear area can normally rely on the existence of a labour force with a range of relevant skills. An enterprise in a peripheral country can have no such reliance. Apart from this, the investigation yielded many examples of the higher costs of operating in peripheral countries arising from the lack of such external economies. Maintenance facilities were either not available or were said to be expensive and poor. Many managers had to maintain their own machinery and other equipment. Major faults might involve flying in a mechanic at high cost and possibly a complete shut-down of operations. Many enterprises had to carry a larger stock of spare parts than they would need in a nuclear area where specialist firms holding stocks of such parts would be readily available. Enterprises in remote areas would also have to hold larger stock of raw materials and other industrial inputs; transport services for such inputs were not thought to be reliable and in any event some enterprises wished to be in a position to meet unexpected demands for their products, and could do so only if their stocks of the relevant inputs were adequate. With high interest rates, such levels of stocks were

expensive to maintain. Moreover, power supplies and other public utilities which are produced under conditions of decreasing costs tend to be very expensive in peripheral countries; some enterprises claimed that electricity cost three times as much as it would have cost in Transvaal. Then there are the more intangible factors, such as the readier availability of information and suitable contacts in nuclear areas, which add to relative costs in the periphery.

As against this, it is possible that there are also diseconomies of agglomeration which could give some advantage to peripheral countries. Thus land is more expensive in urban sites. But actual construction costs may be less in nuclear areas, and there was little evidence to suggest that lower rents in the peripheral countries were an important locational factor. Indeed some firms had experienced difficulties in obtaining suitable land. Where public utilities are provided under conditions of increasing cost (e.g. water in many countries) a peripheral country may be at some competitive advantage (although in much of Botswana water is far more expensive than in the South African industrial areas).

(iii) Transfer costs: Transfer costs are usually a major locational factor in a small peripheral country. Since such countries by definition have a limited local market and frequently a narrow resource base, they will depend heavily on transportation facilities with the outside world – and in particular with the nuclear country of their region – both for industrial inputs and for marketing industrial outputs. This dependence is of special importance in land-locked countries, which may have little choice of transportation modes with the nuclear country of their region or with third countries. In Southern Africa the situation is complicated by the position of South African Railways. Although Botswana and Swaziland have transport links with the outside world, all three peripheral countries depend heavily on their transport links with South Africa. Long-distance transport for many products inside South Africa is virtually monopolised by South African Railways, and permission to use alternative modes of transport is frequently refused. Although in principle such arrangements should not place the peripheral countries at a comparative disadvantage vis-à-vis enterprises in South Africa (since they are equally subject to the same restrictions), in practice the system does add disproportionately to transfer costs in the peripheral countries. All three have poor connections with the South African railway system. Botswana is traversed by Rhodesia Railways, which meets the South African railway system at Mafeking – a notorious bottle-neck. The only railway in Lesotho is a minor branch line whose employment involves frequent handling of goods. Swaziland has no direct contact with South African Railways; goods are transported by road to nearby stations on the railway – a process which again involves changes in the transport mode and therefore additional costs. On the other hand, enterprises in the

90

nuclear area are likely to be more favourably located in relation to the structure of the railway system. Moreover, the South African railway tariff structure favours foodstuffs and raw materials over finished manufactures. This provides a locational advantage for regions with a large market for manufactures, and therefore favours the nuclear over the peripheral areas.

As a general rule we can take it that restrictions on transportation modes that have the effect of raising transport costs make peripheral small countries even more unattractive locations for certain types of industry than they would normally be. Here we can distinguish between input-oriented, output-oriented and footloose industries. If the price of products of input-oriented or resource-based industries is determined on world markets, the effect of high transport costs is to reduce the return to the producer. Unless this acts as a deterrent to production of the primary product itself, it is unlikely to affect the location of the initial processing industry; this is usually determined by the relative cost of transport of the unprocessed and processed goods as affected by such factors as losses or gains of weight, bulk, perishability and so on. An increase in transport cost for the processed product is unlikely to affect substantially the margin between the cost or practicability of transporting the processed and unprocessed product, and is thus unlikely to influence the location of the processing activity as such. Equally, transport costs may have little impact on market-oriented industries, except in so far as the margin between the cost of transport of the finished product and the inputs for the industry is increased.

The most damaging effect is likely to be on footloose industries. Several such industries in the peripheral countries studied clearly found it difficult to compete on the South African market as a result of high transport costs both for inputs and for their products. Not only were the rates themselves high, but there were also losses through damage and delay. It is noticeable that none of these countries has attracted assembly industries established by international firms to take account of low labour costs. Apart from the possibility already mentioned above that labour costs may not be low in relation to such costs in the nuclear area, transport costs are undoubtedly a major factor making against location of such industries in these peripheral countries. This might be a less important factor in a small peripheral island with reasonable sea communications, but it may be an important reason for the lack of success of small land-locked peripheral countries in attracting assembly-type footloose industries.

Thus it seems likely that overall costs of operation are frequently greater in peripheral countries than in nuclear areas, and that the apparently lower costs in such countries – and in particular lower labour costs – may well be illusory. The implications of this situation will vary according to the nature of the enterprise. Large resource-based industries may be able to internalise the higher costs resulting from operating in peripheral countries or, where they are in a monopoly position, may be able to compel their suppliers to carry the additional costs. Again, an industry whose product has a low price elasticity and high income elasticity of demand may be able to pass any additional costs on to the consumers. Both these situations obtained in the countries studied. The most successful and competitive industries appeared to be the resource-based industries, but certain industries producing for the tourist market or for the luxury market in South Africa also appeared to be operating competitively. Those industries which appeared to be operating under most difficulty were those making standard consumer goods in direct competition with imports, where it was impossible to pass these additional costs on to the consumer.

(b) Capital, enterprise and management

Peripheral countries will normally lack enterprise, capital and good management. If they did not, they would probably not be peripheral countries. But put in this way the statement is misleading. Frequently peripheral countries are exporters of capital and enterprise – that is to say, savings are exported and people with enterprise leave. At the same time, entrepreneurs in the modern industrial sector are usually foreigners who bring in capital with the enterprise. Management is usually imported with the enterprise. The whole process increases the small country's dependence and increases the cost (or reduces the benefit) of industrial development. One implication of this process is that industrial development in such countries depends heavily on the views of foreigners (individuals or companies) on the potential profitability of operations there. But the large international firms which are responsible for much industrial investment in the Third World may not even be aware of the existence of such peripheral countries, unless these are a source of some raw material of interest to them. As we have already suggested, the world-view of the international firm may well be regionally structured rather than country-structured, and this is more likely in the case of regions including small countries. Where this is so, the company's attention is more likely to be attracted to the core than to the peripheral countries of the region. Neither the threats to such firms' positions arising from the imposition of tariffs nor the potential advantages of such countries as a base for cheap-labour based industries are likely to be sufficient to attract the companies' interest to the peripheral countries. Moreover, as Kilby (1969) points out:

> ' . . . competitive pressures, generated by a rapidly growing demand, have constituted the catalyst (for a majority of cases) in transforming ample market opportunities and fiscal incentives into actual investments . . .' (p.54).

But such competitive pressures are likely to be very weak in peripheral small countries, mainly because the grow+h of demand is so slow.

In the peripheral countries of Southern Africa, the industries in which international firms were mainly concerned were resource-based industries such as fruit-canning and woodpulp. Most of the purely manufacturing industries were started by people (mainly Europeans) and companies centred on the Southern African region – mainly in South Africa. Industrial growth thus depends substantially on the perceptions and opinions of a comparatively small group of people – mainly expatriate and nearly all non-African. There are various ways in which these perceptions and opinions affect the rate of industrial investment. First, there is the general question of perspective. Most Southern African enterprise and capital is centred and controlled in the nuclear area of South Africa. To them, the peripheral countries are not in their central field of perception (unless there are special reasons for their interest). It is *a priori* probable that a firm in the Southern Transvaal thinking of expansion will consider the Southern Transvaal as a location rather than anywhere else. This is part of the process of polarisation of industries. (We are ignoring here South African Government policies for the decentralisation of industry, since these are not to the benefit of the peripheral countries.) Secondly there is the question of risk. Many white South Africans consider that the peripheral countries in the region are places of high risk merely because they have black governments. This view is held despite the fact that all the governments concerned are conservative in their economic policies and have shown no leanings towards nationalisation, expropriation or any of the other activities that are disliked by foreign investors. This view of risk is not of course universal; one international firm actually said that they thought these countries were areas of low risk – but this may have reflected as much the company's power relative to that of the governments concerned and its ability to put effective pressure on them, as any lack of prejudice on its part. This perception of risk will increase the risk premium – i.e. the return which will be expected from an investment over and above what would be expected at home – and will reduce the rate of industrial investment by altering the cut-off point beyond which investment decisions are not taken.

As we have pointed out, management will usually be imported. Peripheral small countries may normally be expected to lack managerial skills for industry. Industrial management is learned within industry; where there is no industry, managers will be scarce. Thus peripheral small countries wishing to establish industries will normally have to import managers. This may be difficult and costly. There are moreover special difficulties in developing local management. In large concerns, management is specialised. Thus there are production managers, sales managers, export managers, financial managers and so on. Management in a small concern is less specialised, and the managers in the type of enterprise likely to be prominent in small peripheral countries may have to carry out all managerial functions — and may indeed have to do jobs which are not normally thought of as management functions. Thus we have already noted that managers may have to service the machinery and other equipment of the enterprise. It was noticeable that the managers of industrial enterprises in the peripheral countries of Southern Africa had to bear heavier individual responsibilities than the more specialised managers in larger concerns in nuclear areas. A potential manager in these countries should ideally have had experience in a range of industrial jobs; such experience may well be difficult to acquire — especially for Africans, who are barred from skilled and responsible jobs in South African industry. It is therefore hardly surprising that these countries are so heavily dependent on imported management or that this management is frequently inadequate.

Thus such peripheral countries may both lack local enterprise and management and receive only very limited benefit from the activities of foreign companies. There remains the possibility that government itself should act as entrepreneur and establish industries. This would normally be done through the creation of an industrial development corporation or a similar body whose general functions might include not only the promotion of industrial investment in the private sector but also the direct establishment of industries. All three governments of the small countries in Southern Africa have adopted this policy, but results have generally not been encouraging. The governments lack business and industrial expertise. The management of industrial development corporations is necessarily imported, and the international machinery for providing suitable management is unsatisfactory. The relations between such corporations and governments have been far from happy. If the management is powerful, it may become a centre of authority in opposition to government; if it is weak, it may be ineffective. In Hirschman's term (1967), such managers can either be trait takers (in which case they do very little) or trait makers (in which case they are necessarily a source of conflict with important elements in the local society). Two of the three corporations have suffered from a rapid turnover of staff, and the manager of the third was provided by a large South African firm — a situation which was felt by many people in the country to involve increased dependence on South Africa.

(c) Markets

A small peripheral country without access to external markets has very little prospect for industrial development. But access to external markets may usually be obtained only in exchange for some degree of access by foreign producers to one's own market. This may take the form of a regional economic association of some kind, or more limited arrangements covering a range of reciprocal concessions. In the negotiations for such arrangements, small peripheral countries may well find that they have little bargaining power, and that such central issues as the level of any common tariff are determined by the interests of the nuclear countries of the region.

The three peripheral countries of Southern Africa have had a customs union agreement with South Africa since 1910. This was renegotiated in 1969, and the present agreement incorporates a number of concessions by the South African government to the peripheral countries, including a more favourable share in customs receipts and the right to protect their own industries against South African industry for limited periods. Moreover, arrangements for consultation are written into the agreement (although the principal decisions in matters affecting the customs union as a whole are inevitably taken by the South African Government to meet the perceived interests of South African enterprises). There is little doubt that the main motive for these concessions was political – that is to say, they were not based primarily on an assessment of the economic costs and benefits of these concessions to the Republic, but were intended to serve South African purposes in other fields.

Thus manufacturers in the peripheral countries theoretically have access to the whole of the customs union market. But they have had little success in this wider market, and many industries were clearly finding it difficult to compete even in their local market. There are no statistics of intercountry trade, but even the most cursory observation is sufficient to demonstrate that South Africa has an overwhelming surplus in trade in manufactures with the peripheral countries. Thus the free movement of goods within the customs union has been far more to the benefit of South African manufacturers than to that of manufacturers in the peripheral countries. This is of course a normal feature of core/periphery relations. In the Southern African situation there are several specific reasons for this pattern.

The local markets are completely open to South African exports. A firm producing primarily for the local market will inevitably be small and, where there are economies of scale, will produce at higher cost than the larger South African firm. This may be counteracted by high transport costs for manufactures, and it is noticeable that some of the most widespread industries are those producing such articles as cheap furniture or building materials which are far bulkier and more expensive to transport than the intermediate products or raw materials of which they are made. Industries which were apparently competing most successfully on the local market were those producing inputs required by a local resource-based export industry (e.g. packaging materials) or those with some advantage in factor proportions (e.g. skilled-labour intensive industries such as printing).

One difficulty which some manufacturers faced in their local market was that of communications. In a nuclear region, the pattern of communications (including the communication of information) is usually centred on the nuclear area; communications between different parts of the periphery may be very poor. Thus consumers in these peripheral countries may be better informed about South African products than about the products of their own country. The information media are mainly South African and publicise South African products. The local press and other media are very weak in all three peripheral countries; there is no local trade paper, and frequently the only means of getting products known is through personal contacts.

Thus many industries face difficulties in competing in their local market. There has however been very little demand for the protection of local industries against South African products, and no such protection has been afforded in spite of the provision in the customs union agreement. Since local industries are so weak, they do not form an effective pressure group. The only industrial enterprises which might be powerful enough to put effective pressure on governments for protection are the large foreign firms. But these are mainly involved in resource-based export industries, and therefore have no interest in protecting the local market. Indeed, in so far as a protective policy would increase local price and cost levels, they would be opposed to it. There is another consideration which may weigh with governments. A policy of protection means transferring resources from consumers to producers of manufacturers. But consumers in all three countries are very poor; a policy of subsidising the industrial sector at the expense of the agricultural sector presupposes that there is some surplus available in the agricultural sector. This is hardly true of any of these countries apart from the mainly white-owned commercialised farming sectors of Botswana and Swasiland. It is true that such transfers already happen under the customs agreement as a result of South Africa's protective policies. But a policy of special protection of local manufactures would add still further to the burden on consumers. None of the three governments accord any preference to local manufactures in their public purchasing policies (because possibly of budgetary difficulties) although there are no restrictions under the customs union agreement on the right to grant such preferences.

So far manufacturers in the peripheral countries have made little impact on the South African market. In principle, access to the South African market should be a means of overcoming the disadvantage of small-scale production but, with the exceptions noted above, few manufactured products from the peripheral countries have competed successfully in the nuclear areas of the region. Several industries do indeed export to neighbouring areas of the Republic, but those parts of the Republic bordering on all three of the peripheral countries are themselves peripheral areas — thinly populated and with a limited market for manufactures. The industries which have made furthest inroads in the South African market are of the following types:

(i) Luxury products and goods designed for tourists. The demand
for these products reflects the inequality in income distribution in
South Africa. Here, as we have pointed out, the low price elasticity
of demand has meant that high transfer costs have been less damaging.

(ii) Resource-based products, such as meat from Botswana and
Swaziland. One industry is located in a peripheral country by a large
company in the Republic because of arrangements whereby it has
access to a cheap source of its raw material.

There are various reasons, many of which we have already touched on,
why industries in these countries find it difficult to compete in the
South African market. Basically they amount to the fact that labour
costs, if at all lower, are not sufficiently low to compensate for the
higher transfer costs and lack of external economies involved in a
peripheral location. There may be other factors, such as the
monopolistic structure of much of South African industry and the
resistance it is said to place in the way of competition from these
countries. Where there are market-sharing arrangements among a few
firms, these tend to strengthen the position of the areas which
are already industrialised, and thus help in the process of polarisation.
But even without such arrangements the experience of many
peripheral countries suggests that breaking into the markets
of the nuclear area from the peripheral country is extremely
difficult.

(d) Linkages

One of the arguments for industrial development in peripheral countries
is that it is desirable to strengthen the local integration of the economy
and to help reduce dependence. One means by which industries increase
local integration is through inter-industry linkages, and industrial policy
in such countries is very centrally concerned both with encouraging
the kind of industry likely to have local linkage effects and with
developing linkages from existing industries. We are therefore concerned
to examine how far existing industries in these countries have had
linkage effects.

There is no statistical information on inter-industry linkages in any
of the peripheral countries, and even in South Africa the latest
such published information dates from the 1950s. However, since
there are so few industries in the peripheral countries, it is possible to
give a non-statistical account of linkage effects which is not too
misleading. We consider first backward linkages and secondly forward
linkages.

Apart from Swaziland, where there has been some development of a
light engineering and a packaging industry, there are few apparent
backward linkage effects of any of the industries so far established
in these countries. There appear to be various reasons for this. First,
there are so few industries that the market for such backward linkage

industries would be small. Secondly, some of the large resource-based industries are located in isolated places where no services are available. They were thus compelled to establish their own ancillary industries as part of their operations; if they had not done so, they would have been unable to operate at all. Since these linkages have been internalised, they have not involved the establishment of new activities separate from the industries themselves. Lastly, apart from bulky products (packaging) or market-oriented services (engineering), there is no particular locational advantage in establishing linkage industries in the peripheral countries. Linkages are more likely to have been established with South African industry – i.e. with industries located in the nuclear area. The same factors which have made the peripheral countries unfavourable locations for industry have meant that backward linkage effects have tended to be outside the peripheral countries.

Other factors are relevant when we consider forward linkages. It is noticeable that very few of the resource-based industries take their products beyond the earliest and most essential processing stages – i.e. those stages which are necessary if the product is to be exported at all. The companies give various reasons for this. Frequently later processes are said to be market-oriented; the cost of transporting the product in its more finished state is said to be greater than that of the initially processed product. One company pointed out that the 'local' market for the product would have to be in South Africa, where the product in question was under the control of a large group and where entry would be expensive and difficult. Again, in a small country the actual scale of production of a natural resource may be too small to justify investment in a stage of processing where there are substantial scale economies. In once case, it is known that a particular mineral resource is limited in extent, and the amount available would not be sufficient and the probability of finding new deposits would be too small to justify investment in processing facilities. This is the type of difficulty that is of importance in a country which is of small area, and where the chances of finding new natural resources are necessarily limited. It is of course less relevant in a country like Botswana, which although small in terms of population has a large land area and substantial prospects for further resource discoveries.

These arguments do not include the barriers created by rich countries against the entry of the products of later stages of processing. Thus Swaziland does not produce refined sugar because of the working of the British import regime for sugar. But this is not a factor peculiar to small peripheral countries. It is important only in so far as larger and nuclear developing countries may have internal markets which will

permit the profitable operation of such industries, whereas small
peripheral countries are totally dependent on exports of these products.

IV. Some policy issues

Here we consider two areas of policy choice open to governments.
First we consider policies designed to increase competitiveness by
reductions in costs. Secondly we consider policies concerned with
access to markets.

(a) Costs

We have noted that many costs of operation are greater in peripheral
countries than in nuclear countries, and that in the main area — that of
labour — where costs may be lower the margin may be insufficient to
attract industries. Policies designed to lower costs to industry are roughly
of two kinds — those involving some kind of government subsidy
(through for example cheap factories or subsidised public utilities) and
those where whatever help is given to industry is paid for by some other
means. These latter might include policies designed to keep wage costs
down to competitive levels.

The difficulty with any policy of subsidies is the lack of governmental
resources in small peripheral countries. As we have already emphasised
in reference to tariff protection, any policy of transferring resources
to industry assumes the existence of a surplus elsewhere in the economy.
In the case of the peripheral countries in Southern Africa, such
subsidies also have to be competitive with those given to South African
industry as part of that government's industrial decentralisation policies.
It is virtually impossible for the peripheral countries to grant subsidies
of a comparable amount.

One form of subsidy which does not directly reduce costs is income
tax concessions such as tax holidays or accelerated depreciation
allowances. They are popular with governments because they apparently
cost so little (since the alternative to giving the concession may be not
to have the industry at all). Both Lesotho and Swaziland give such
concessions, partly in competition with similar concessions given to
so-called 'border' industries in South Africa. Very few of the firms
interviewed considered that such concessions were a major element in
their location decision. The reason is clear; such concessions are weak
because they do not affect costs, and thus do not make an industry
profitable if it would have been unprofitable without them. Any such
concession which does directly help to reduce costs (e.g. an employment
or a training subsidy) must involve a transfer from government to the
industry and hence will involve government in a direct choice between
using its budgetary resources in this or in other sectors.

Since wages are a major element in costs, especially in labour-
intensive industries, wage restraint policies may be an important

element in government policies for encouraging industry. Thus Ghai (1971) has argued strongly for such a policy in Botswana, and the Botswana government has issued a white paper supporting his proposals (Government Paper No. 2, 1972). There are however two problems to be faced in this area. First, these policies are concerned with wage rates and not wage costs. This is probably necessary for administrative reasons but, as we have seen, wage costs in peripheral countries may be high not because wage rates are high but because productivity is low. The reduction in wage costs may be more effectively carried out by improvements in labour productivity (e.g. by suitable training) than by wage restraint. (This is not of course to question the desirability of preventing the large international firms operating in these countries from paying wages greatly out of line with what other enterprises can afford; these however are a special case.) The Botswana government white paper refers to the need to improve efficiency through training, but by its emphasis on wage rates may give a misleading picture of the problem. Secondly, such wage restraint policies are in danger of ignoring the peripheral country's situation in relation to the core area of the region. If local wages in the peripheral country are kept artificially low, people with the opportunity of getting jobs in the core area will leave. As we have already emphasised, there is thus a substantial constraint on possible wage policies in such peripheral countries, and the force of this constraint will depend on the barriers to labour mobility imposed in the core area.

One final policy area relevant to the reduction of costs is measures designed to provide external or agglomerative economies. Such economies are lacking because there are so few industries. If there were more industries each would operate more cheaply. Therefore it is possible that measures designed to promote or attract a group of industries stand more chance of success than efforts to attract individual industries. Thus it might be worth subsidising a group of industries in the hope that they would form a self-reinforcing structure and rapidly be able to dispense with such assistance. This would be the 'balanced growth' approach to peripheral development. But to carry out such a policy would involve a complex process of identifying industries where such external economies would make a substantial difference to costs, and which would become viable if this initial assistance were given. If the wrong decisions were taken, government might find itself faced with the need to provide subsidies for an indefinite period. Governments of small peripheral countries normally lack the expertise needed for such a critical job of evaluation, and the experience of bringing in experts from abroad to do the job is hardly encouraging. This is thus a very high risk strategy.

(b) Markets
Internal markets in peripheral small countries are small, and although

governments can take measures to widen them (through for example government purchase policies or the improvement of communications media) such measures can never be of more than marginal assistance. Production for the small local market is frequently high cost production, and as we have argued, the protection needed to make such industries viable may impose heavy burdens on the rest of the local community. The question of markets is therefore essentially one of external markets, and in most cases of regional markets. Regional arrangements for market access are therefore central to a consideration of industrial prospects in small peripheral countries.

The traditional approach to the problem is through the establishment of free trade areas or customs unions. These have frequently proved disappointing to peripheral countries; unless specific measures are taken to locate industries in such countries, the polarising tendencies at work in the region will mean that industries continue to be located in the core country. Thus peripheral countries will have to pay the costs of such arrangements (e.g. in trade diversion) but will receive little of the dynamic benefit which they are intended to bring. These countries may therefore consider that not only do they receive little benefit from regional economic cooperation, but they actually lose from it. They may therefore prefer to leave the association, as Chad (another peripheral small country) left UDEAC in 1969.

It is however clear from our analysis that polarisation of industrial development is likely whether or not there is a customs union or a free trade area, and that the peripheral small countries may be blaming the regional trading arrangement for a trend for which it is not responsible. Following Robson (1968) in his discussion of the gains and losses of the East African Common Market, we would suggest that there are two practical questions to be considered by small peripheral countries which are members of a common market or free trade area. First, what gains or losses would be involved in leaving the association on comparative static assumptions? Secondly, what would be the long-term gains or losses in leaving the arrangement? Of these the latter is the more important; the gains of a regional trading arrangement are essentially long-term, and it is by long-term trends that they must be judged. If in the short run there is inequality in relative benefit between the nuclear and peripheral countries in the region, as long as there is any benefit at all to the nuclear country it is theoretically possible for some bargain to be entered into whereby the core country compensates the peripheral country (as happens under the Southern African customs union). The basic policy question then is what are the long-term prospects for industrial development in the peripheral country inside or outside a regional trading arrangement?

These long-term prospects can be improved — at least in theory — through regional trading agreements. First, as we have implied, they may involve a transfer of resources from the core to the peripheral countries which may permit investment in infrastructure and other services in the periphery. Secondly, deliberate policies may be adopted to encourage and assist industrial growth in the peripheral countries (although, as Brewster [1971] points out, such policies do not have a very impressive record of success). Lastly, regional trading arrangements may be associated with or lead to cooperation in other areas relevant to industrial growth in the periphery. For example, there could be consultation over regional transport policies, so that these were more helpful to the peripheral countries.

Whether or not such policies are agreed is essentially a political question. Where there is a strong feeling for and interest in regional cooperation, or where for any reason the peripheral countries have a strong influence in the regional decision-making process, the core countries will be more willing to transfer resources to the peripheral countries and take account of their interests in regional policies. An extreme situation would be one in which the nuclear and peripheral countries abandoned their sovereignty altogether and formed some kind of political union or federation. Here too there would be the theoretical possibility of transfers of resources from the core to the periphery; how much this actually happened would of course depend on the power which the periphery had in decision-making at the centre. If it had little influence, a sacrifice of sovereignty would leave the peripheral country worse off (as appears to have happened to southern Italy and Sicily as a result of the unification of Italy). It would have given up the limited range of choices open to it in exchange for a situation in which it had no choice at all.

IV. Conclusion

The not very original conclusion from the evidence on Southern Africa is that the prospects for industrial development in the peripheral countries can only be understood in a regional context. But a simple 'least-cost' model is clearly inadequate. We need to take account of the economic and social structure of the area with its effects on attitudes, mobility and access to resources, as well as of the political relations between the nuclear country and its neighbours. The situation of peripheral countries in a multinational region in many ways resembles that of peripheral regions within a country, but there are significant differences. Political boundaries may affect (favourably or otherwise) access to resources and mobility; decision-makers with command over resources will be influenced both in their access to information and in their interpretation of it by the existence of the border; there will be a local element in decision-making which is absent in peripheral regions.

Although these conclusions may appear obvious, it is surprising how many analyses of small peripheral country industrialisation problems ignore the regional dimension. Certainly none of the studies undertaken in the peripheral countries of Southern Africa have made more than a passing reference to the influence of peripheral status on industrial prospects. Possibly the reason for this gap is that such countries will normally depend for these studies on visitors from large countries, who naturally take the area surrounded by a national boundary as the appropriate unit for consideration. It was noticeable in the course of the investigation that all these actually involved in encouraging or running industries were strongly aware of the regional dimension. There is here (as probably in other areas) a strong advantage in building up local expertise which is more likely to be aware of the real nature of the problem.

NOTE

1. The study is financed by the Nuffield Foundation. A fuller account of the results of the research is in my *Industries of The Southern African Periphery* (London, Croom Helm, 1975).

REFERENCES

Havelock Brewster:	*Industrial Integration Systems* (UNCTAD, TD/B/345, July 1971).
John Friedmann:	*Regional Development Policy: A Case Study of Venezuela* (Cambridge, Mass. and London M.I.T. Press, 1966).
D.P. Ghai:	*Labour and Economic Development in Botswana* (1971).
Albert O. Hirschman:	*Development Projects Observed* (Washington D.C., The Brookings Institutions, 1967).
Albert O. Hirschman:	*The Strategy of Economic Development* (New Haven and London, Yale University Press, 1958).
Edgar M. Hoover:	*An Introduction to Regional Economics* (New York, Alfred A. Knopf, 1971).
W. Isard, E.W. Schooler, and T. Vietorisz:	*Industrial Complex Analysis and Regional Development,* (Cambridge, Mass., M.I.T. Press, 1959).
Peter Kilby:	*Industrialisation in an Open Economy* (Cambridge Univ. Press, 1969).
Kari Levitt:	*The Old Mercantilism and the New* (Social and Economic Studies, Vol. 19, No. 4, 1970).
August Lösch:	*The Economics of Location* (New Haven, Yale University Press, 1954).
Gunnar Mydral:	*Economic Theory and Underdeveloped Regions* (London, Gerald Ducksworth, 1957).
Peter R. Odell	*Economic Integration and Spatial Pattern of Economic Development in Latin America* (Journal of Common Market Studies, Vol. VI, No. 3, March 1968).
E.A.G. Robinson (ed.):	*Location Theory and Regional Economics in Backward Areas in Advanced Countries* (London, Macmillan, 1969).

Peter Robson:	*Economic Integration in Africa* (London, George Allen and Unwin, 1968).
Percy Selwyn:	*The Dual Economy Transcending National Frontiers: The Case of Industrial Development in Lesotho* (Institute of Development Studies Communication No. 105).
David M. Smith:	*Industrial Location: An Economic Geographical Analysis* (John Wiley and Sons, 1971).
R.B. Sutcliffe:	*Industry and Underdevelopment* (Addison-Wesley Publishing Company, 1971).
United Nations:	*Trade Expansion and Economic Integration Among Developing Countries: Report by the Secretariat of UNCTAD* (United Nations Publication, Sale No. 67 II D. 27).
A. Weber:	*Theory of the Location of Industries* (University of Chicago Press, 1929).
J.G. Williamson:	*Regional Inequality and the Process of National Development: A Description of the Patterns* (Economic Development and Cultural Change, 13: supplement).

4. SMALL STATES – THE PARADOX OF THEIR EXISTENCE

George C. Abbott

Summary

The notion of viability as justifying the separate existence of small states is questioned. Not only is viability an ambiguous and in many ways an irrelevant concept, but small states accord independence a higher priority than viability. Attempts to achieve regional interdependence which go against the principle of national independence are likely to fail. Not only can small states exist as such, but they can play a responsible part in the international community.

Very little serious or systematic analysis has so far been undertaken on the concept and existence of small states. Consequently, after more than two decades of decolonisation and the emergence of an impressive number of new nations, one is still unable to answer such basic questions as, why do small states exist? Attention appears rather to have been concentrated primarily on the question of their viability, whether or not they could exist as separate and independent economic entities and also meet all the international obligations and responsibilities of statehood. By concentrating on these questions, attention was diverted from the important issues, i.e. the why and wherefore of separate existence.

Thus the debate about independence and self-government has been conducted against the background of a series of misconceptions, contradictions and irrelevancies. For example, the new post-war states were assumed to be microcosms of the larger metropolitan industrial nations. Their performance and potential were thus assessed in terms of conventional economic analysis, which regarded the vast majority of them as either too poor or too small to exist on their own. But as the history of decolonisation shows, the size of new nations has become progressively smaller over the years.

Similarly, viability, or lack of it, being identified as the basic problem of these new nations, solutions have not unnaturally followed the conventional prescriptions of integration and cooperation. Many of them have, however, defied the rules. They prefer to exist separately, or to go it alone. And one asks, why is it that in the face of the many obvious and substantial advantages to be gained, do these states behave so irrationally?

The purpose of this paper is to suggest that we rethink our attitudes and opinions of these states, and try to understand the forces which make for separate existence. It also attempts to assess the role and function of small states in the present international context of expanding political and economic units. Why, for example, in spite of the obvious pressures and present trends towards larger and more efficient units is there a proliferation of small states? Is this a contradiction? Are there values which compensate for the constraints arising out of small size?

During the last century, size in the sense of geographical area was considered the most important single determinant of a country's economic wealth, political power, and international prestige. The bigger the country, the richer, more powerful, and internationally influential it was. Overseas expansion and territorial aggrandisement were considered the ideal, if not the only, solution for a country's economic problems. They were also the most obvious means by which to achieve one's political and international aspirations.

But there was another side to imperialism. The scramble for Africa and the establishment of empires were as much the outward manifestations of might and majesty as of economic forces. Colonies, however they were come by, increased the geographical size as well as the political power and influence of the imperial power, in addition to constituting a new source of economic wealth. Given these motivating forces, it made sense to expand overseas as far and as fast as possible, and without much regard for the shape, size or economic characteristics, not to mention the political sensibilities and wishes of the territories being colonised. They were colonised not only because they were needed, but because they were there to be colonised. The process was total. Anything and everything that could be, was colonised. The larger ones were colonised because of their size and resource base, and the smaller ones in spite of their size and obvious lack of resources. How else can one explain the acquisition of the many rocks, cays and small islands which are now ungraciously referred to as 'the remnants of Empire'?

Obviously, in such an international environment, a country's size was both its most vulnerable and its most variable resource. Countries gained as well as lost part or all of their territory. The present new nations were all on the losing side. They lost the ownership of their respective countries and with it the right to determine their own political and economic future. They lost their identity both as a people and a country. Vast areas of the globe disappeared as separate units, only to reappear as extensions of larger and more powerful nations. Expansionism and absorption into Empire were at one and the same time the accepted milieu and purpose of international relations.

Nowadays, the international situation is very different. The whole concept of national boundaries is more firmly established. Countries have come to recognise and respect each other's national rights and territorial integrity.

A country's size is now regarded as its most specific and inviolable factor, even though there are a number which, secretly or otherwise, harbour territorial ambitions against their neighbours. Every so often, too, there are territorial disputes which break out into open warfare.

The possibilities of conflict and aggression are therefore still very real. There are, however, differences between the two situations. First the scope for hostile and unfriendly activities is circumscribed by the strength of international opinion and reaction, thereby making it more difficult for would-be aggressors to realise their international and territorial ambitions. Secondly, and this is perhaps the more important difference, size *per se* is not now as crucial to a country's national existence as a hundred years ago.[1] Short of war and other hostile activities, there is not much that the new nations can do to increase their national boundaries. There is thus a certain finality about size. They start with it, and will probably finish with it. They accept it as a fact of life and operate within the national and geographical constraints which it imposes on them.

But given their limited resources and extreme vulnerability to world economic forces, one automatically questions their viability. What exactly does this term mean? Does it mean, for example, a country's ability to balance its budget? Does it mean the ability to bring about political stability, economic development and social transformation? Or, does it mean that in addition to all of these things, a small state should be able to maintain certain specified levels of public services, international representation, military establishment and so on — in short, all the paraphernalia of a modern industrial state?

The fact that viability can mean all of these is evidence enough of the elasticity of the concept. Not only is it subject to various interpretations at any one point in time, but the criteria of viability have themselves changed markedly over the years. During early colonial days, viability was determined principally on the basis of commercial criteria. Colonies were viable if they earned a profit. Viability was thus equated with profitability. Later, it was re-interpreted to mean ability to provide basic economic and social needs from their own resources. When they finally began to demand political independence and self-government, viability was equated with full financial and economic independence. To quote a former Colonial Secretary, 'political responsibility goes ill with financial dependence'. Since independence there has been a further 'raising of sights'. Viability is now defined in terms of the minimum criteria necessary for supporting a modern industrial state.

However, very few of the developing countries, regardless of their size, can claim to be viable in this sense. This suggests two things. First we have been using the wrong criteria. We have been applying standards and criteria set by political, social and economic developments taking place in the developed countries, to a group of countries whose underlying social and economic structures have hardly changed since independence. Further, the new nations find themselves continually confronted with fresh standards of viability, before the majority of them have even satisfied what were considered to be the basic economic and social preconditions of political independence. In other words, viability has the 'ratchet effect' of continually raising the stakes of viability.

Secondly, and this is an extension of the first point, the concept of viability, as thus interpreted, is not only unattainable but also quite unnecessary for most small states. Their goals are more immediate and mundane. They want to transform and modernise their societies, not necessarily to conform to Western concepts and ways of life, but rather in keeping with their own cultures, mores and value systems.

This idea of viability is quite different from that of the developed countries, which measure success and viability in terms of material wealth and possessions, economic efficiency, productivity, profit margins and so on. Many of these states never have been and probably never will be as concerned about their economic viability as the developed countries except, perhaps, in a perverse way. At one stage of their historical development they lost their independence and identity because of their lack of economic viability, and at a later stage, they had to give proof of viability in order to regain their independence and self-respect. It is not, therefore, a concept to which they take kindly. It has always conflicted with and compromised their right of self-determination.

As colonies, there was not much they could do about this conflict. The situation is different today and there is no doubt that they would all choose independence rather than viability. Not only is it their most recent and cherished achievement, but having fought for it, they are unlikely to surrender it almost immediately to a concept as vague as viability, the very concept which denied them it in the first place. There is therefore one point on which all the new nations agree, regardless of their size, perspectives or priorities, and that is that independence must be maintained. Economic viability and all else take second place to the right of self-determination.

But how far are small states in a position to enforce this principle? Given the economic and political disadvantages which they face, would it not make more sense for them to integrate, in order to preserve their independence and to achieve a greater degree of self-sufficiency? When the question is posed in this manner, the answer seems clear. One suspects however that the matter is not quite so simple.

The arguments making for integration are familiar enough. By pooling their resources, small states can share the cost of administrative, foreign and consular services, international representation and military establishments. They can cut the duplication and waste of effort, as well as develop proper political and administrative institutions, thereby promoting stability and order. On the economic

108

front, they stand to gain from the expansion and enlargement of markets, mass-production and economies of scale, increased investment as well as planned development. They can also benefit by sharing regional and advisory services. These are substantial advantages.

On the face of it, therefore, more can be achieved through integration than by remaining independent. Yet states have often refused to be integrated, or if integrated, have opted out at the first opportunity. This suggests, first, that the benefits of integration are long-term and theoretical, rather than tangible and immediate.[2] Secondly, that integration does not necessarily make small states more efficient. Thirdly, that the greater viability which is induced does not compensate for the loss of independence.

The West Indies offer themselves as the ideal case study. They are small in size and limited in resources. They also experience all the social tensions and pressures of development. Integration of one form or another has always been advocated as the appropriate solution for the many political, social and economic problems facing these small islands. The idea of 'closer association', which gave rise to the ill-fated Federation, was originally conceived as the most appropriate means by which to implement the declared aim of British colonial policy of quickening 'the progress of all colonial peoples to the ultimate goal of self-government'. However, as the pre-federal discussions got underway it became apparent that integration was a *sine qua non* of independence and self-government. By the time Federation became a reality, both the nature and purpose of integration had changed again. It was now a substitute for independence. What the islands achieved was not independence, but interdependence, which is a completely different proposition, and certainly not what they had been bargaining for.

Although they were at different stages of political and constitutional development, their demands broadly speaking conformed to the conventional pattern of seeking the replacement of the nominated and official elements by elected representatives, and the extension of the franchise. Full adult suffrage would lead to representative government, and eventually to self-government and independence, according to the classical Whitehall pattern. But the customary constitutional processes were never allowed to work themselves out. Questions of economic viability entered the discussions at an early stage and succeeded in shunting them onto different lines. Viability, in fact, replaced independence as the major issue.

This re-ordering of priorities was itself largely responsible for the failure of the Federation. There was no evidence to suggest either that the West Indian colonies would be more viable as a group or that individually none of them could make a go of independence. We know differently now.[3] By emphasising integration and uniformity the United Kingdom Government compromised the principle of the right to independence and self-government. This was an attempt to replace colonialism with internationalism, without first passing through the necessary stage of nationalism. The West Indian colonies were being asked to substitute federation, a form of internationalism, for the more potent and natural force of nationalism and independence.

The importance of having a national identity does not appear to have been generally recognised when federal independence became a live issue. Consequently, no attempt was made to understand and accommodate the strong motive force of nationalism which lay behind the demands for independence. The larger units seceded principally because Federation did not allow adequate scope and expression for individual island nationalism. Nor did it give each island state a meaningful political identity in the eyes of its own subjects. Jamaicans, for example, were urged to think of themselves as West Indians first and Jamaicans after; similarly with Trinidadians and Barbadians. The first occasion on which nationalism had an opportunity to assert itself heralded the break-up of the Federation. The Jamaican Referendum, involving the choice 'Jamaica-Yes, Federation-No', was essentially a play-off between nationalism and internationalism.

Political independence is the *sine qua non* of economic independence, and not the other way round. Unless a country is free and independent it cannot properly take decisions affecting its political and economic life — whether to join a customs union or a free trade area, whether to federate or 'go it alone'.

This is why integration or federal independence was regarded as a denial of basic freedoms. It denied the units the freedom of decision and identity. It sought, in fact, to perpetuate the relationship against which the struggle for independence was waged. This is why, too, such questions as political immaturity and economic viability were irrelevant. Independence is an end in itself. It is only after a state enjoys it, that it can decide whether it wants to compromise it for greater economic viability, or even to opt out of the whole international viability scene.

Federal independence was an uneasy yoking of disparate elements, each with its own individualistic preferences, prejudices and priorities. It originated with an attempt to replace one form of colonial tutelage by an ineffectual substitute, under the overall control and supervision of the Colonial Office. Once this was removed, the whole brittle fabric was bound to collapse. In other words, internationalism is not a viable substitute for nationalism, and federal independence failed precisely because it attempted to ignore the strength of basic loyalties and group identities. The fight for political independence and self-government was the outward and visible sign of a desire for a sense of identity, self-respect and national pride.

These aspirations are all embodied in the term nationalism. Viewed in its more constructive role, nationalism is the unifying force serving to give people a sense of their own identity and existence, of oneness

110

and of belonging. It does not depend on such questionable concepts as viability for its justification. In the context of colonialism it was the rallying cry of all colonial peoples seeking a lost heritage. It was the call of the native against the expatriate. It was the cohesive force which sustained the march to independence. It was the answer to colonialism.

There are of course, other cohesive elements, such as homogeneity of language, religion, and culture, all of which may sustain and cement small states. However, while these attributes of statehood do play an important role, the most compelling reason for their separate existence is their sense of the right to exist, and to decide their future freely. One certainly does not question this right in respect of large states. To do so for small ones is both illogical and invidious.

Anguilla's decision to break away from St. Kitts, to which it has been historically, as well as traditionally, linked, is perhaps the classic vindication of the right of any state, community, or group of people to decide their own future, as they see fit. The island is very small and very poor. Until the Royal Engineers went there, it had none of the basic economic, social and political infrastructure which is essential for development. It has no major resources beyond a few good beaches, suitable for tourist development. Theoretically, therefore, if ever there were a community which stood to gain from integration, it was Anguilla. Yet this was precisely the one that opted out, vowing in the process 'never to return to St. Kitts' under any conditions. Whether or not the break is final and irrevocable, only time will tell. But the point which the Anguillans established was their right to decide their own future.[4]

Anguilla's decision to break with St. Kitts adds a new dimension to the process of disintegration or secession as an expression of national identity. Formerly, it was the larger units in the Caribbean which refused to be integrated with the smaller ones. Now the process has turned full circle, and it is the smaller units which are refusing to remain with the larger ones. This has far-reaching implications not only for the West Indies, which is essentially an area of potential Anguillas, but also for a number of other states which have themselves entered independence with an uncomfortable amalgam of fissiparous elements. The Anguilla experience is just as likely to repeat itself in any situation in which sizeable minorities are either persecuted or deprived of the ordinary rights of citizenship and the respect of their fellow-citizens; when people experience a feeling of non-participation and alienation, of not belonging; when their own culture and way of life is in danger of disappearing, or of being supressed. Any of these emotions is strong enough in itself to give rise to separatist movements, and eventually to secession in order to assert the right to exist. In such a situation one does not raise questions about economic viability and efficiency. Any form of freedom and independence is better than none. This is why the emphasis which is being placed on the ability of small states to 'go it alone' is largely misplaced. Often there are no alternatives.

But what good is it insisting on the rights of statehood, if a state is too small or poor to provide for the ordinary needs of its citizens, let alone meet all the international obligations and responsibilities of statehood? What future is there for small states in an age of ever-widening political and economic unions? These questions touch the very paradox of their existence. On the one hand, the hard practical realities of international power politics, economics and finance are continually forcing the governments and the business corporations of most large states into alliances, mergers and the like. Yet this global movement seems to have had surprisingly little effect upon small states. Alongside the trend towards larger and more powerful units are equally strong forces making for the emergence of small states. In other words, there seem to be two major contradictory world movements in operation. The first is making for fewer, but bigger and richer international political and economic entities, while the second gives rise to an increasing number of smaller and poorer states.

How is it, then, that small states of questionable viability can exist in a world tailor-made, so to speak, for and by the large international corporations, or political and economic unions? Perhaps the simplest answer, apart from the obvious facts of geography and history, is that they act as a safety valve. If the pressures and strains of large international unions get too much for any member, it can opt out, and join the ranks of the small states.

It is not, however, being suggested that states will, or even that they should, pursue an intractable policy of independence at all costs. Such a position is neither sensible nor feasible. There are obviously areas and activities in which cooperation will be both desirable and possible. These will be explored and developed, perhaps tentatively at first. One already sees evidence of this in the case of the West Indies. The institution of CARIFTA, the Caribbean Development Bank, and the Caribbean Secretariat are examples of the sorts of efforts which will eventually bring about re-integration and closer cooperation. One can look forward to a period of gradual but limited cooperation among small states. This trend is not likely, though, to duplicate the pattern set by large states. Military alliances, for example, one of the major pursuits of large states, seem to have low priority among small states.

Finally, the role of small states must be assessed in the context of the international community, and the contribution which they make towards world peace and stability. Can they, for example, influence the course of international events? Or have they the capacity to honour international obligations? Taking the first question: as members of the UN and its several specialised and regional agencies, this is precisely what they hope to achieve. One has only to read the record, or to attend any of the major international conferences. They are there in great numbers, and they express their views frequently, and with great candour. They are usually the severest critics of large states, serving either to restrain them or to bring about reforms. One can point to a number of shifts in international opinion for which small states can claim their fair share of credit. For example, the whole ethos of international cooperation and development which gave rise to the Development Decades was due as much to the small developing nations as to the developed countries.

As far as international obligations are concerned the new nations show a respect for international law and morality which often transcends that of the older nations. They are certainly not as prone to flout international opinion and conventions. In fact, they often appear to place them above their own national obligations. For example, although many of them are crippled with rising international debt burdens, they continue to honour their debt service payments, much to the detriment of their own development. In some instances, indebtedness has replaced development as their major preoccupation.[5]

Not only do they take their international obligations seriously, they go to great lengths to honour them. But the conventional obligations of nationhood were themselves evolved to suit another international environment. It is possible, therefore, that those who question the capacity of small states to make treaties and so on, may in fact be using the wrong criteria to assess their role in the international community.

In summary, the paradox of small states is not so much the fact that they exist as separate entities, but rather that the experts have persisted in judging them by conventional criteria which have consistently been proved wrong.

NOTES

1. Considering the absolute range in size of the earlier new nations, for example India and some of the more recent ones like Barbados, post-war trends seem to represent a complete reversal of the 19th century doctrine of expansionism and enlargement of national and geographical boundaries. It is as if there had been a complete reversal of the role of size, and to be big were a national perversity.

2. There is of course nothing new about this suggestion, as anyone who has been following the debate over Britain's entry into the European Economic Community will realise.

3. See my article 'What's Happening in the West Indies', published in *Co-Existence*, Vol. 8, pp.227-40, Maclehose, Glasgow, 1971.

4. This was recognised by the British Government, as well as guaranteed by them. Having sent troops in 'to end intimidation' and 'to restore peace and stability to the island', they ended up guaranteeing the people of Anguilla 'never to return them to an administration which they did not want'. For a fuller analysis of the Anguilla crisis, see my article 'Political

Disintegration: The Lessons of Anguilla', *Government and Opposition,* Vol. 6, No. 1. (1971).

5. See my recent article 'Aid and Indebtedness – A Proposal', National Westminster Bank, Quarterly Review, May 1972, pp.55-67.

5. DEPENDENT DEVELOPMENT – problems of economic planning in small developing countries

Michael Ward

Summary

The constraints facing planners in small countries are examined with the use of a neo-classical framework. On the supply side, there are limitations on the availability of land and other natural resources, skilled labour, capital and enterprise. On the demand side, the local market is limited and there are difficulties in the expansion of production for export. The influence of the public sector is considered, especially in the context of the control of recurrent expenditure, the implementation of a prices and incomes policy, and the extent of government influence generally over the economy.

Introduction

The importance of size

In the following paper size is assumed to be important in a real, practical sense. In the medium term, existing institutions and possible social and political decisions connected with medium-term economic planning, and certain economic variables associated with size are taken as given and limited. Although economic linkages clearly jump physical space, for the purposes of economic planning the national frontier is regarded as the main frame of reference and size is therefore defined essentially in physical terms. The size typology of countries given in the appendix is useful because it represents a similar typology of problems. These problems arise not only out of small size *per se,* but also from those issues generally connected with poverty and underdevelopment which tend to be aggravated by small size. The size of countries is thus considered to be important both in relation to the process of development and in the actual practical planning of the development process.

This paper, whilst drawing attention to the contingent factors of size that can be circumvented, tends to lay greater stress on the significance of natural or structural variables that cannot so easily be ignored within the scope of a traditional development plan or as planning has been conventionally implemented. It gives much less emphasis to the policy variables theoretically amenable to change where, in a utopian situation, an almost infinite number of permutations are feasible. The latter approach is rejected on the grounds that the solutions proposed are often unrealistic because they are bounded by physical or institutional constraints. Furthermore, these natural variables are probably more important than the instruments of control, not least because the latter — in attempting to change the institutions and framework of organisation — are frequently self-defeating. Indeed, a decision to try and change the structure of 'dependence' may make very little difference to the actual situation because the existing institutions and economic organisations are often as much a *reflection of size* and geographical location as of political and economic history. In this respect the problems of small countries are little different from those facing certain regions in larger countries. An economy or region is small when it is unable to devise techniques of organisation, production and marketing free from reliance on foreign or metropolitan institutions.

The discussion which follows is based on a simple neo-classical framework and it attempts to demonstrate the limited possibilities of generating increases in total income. To a large extent the same factors determine a country's ability to reduce distributional inequalities and to create additional employment. The model essentially compares the narrow natural resource base and the limited and unbalanced stock of other resources which influence total income generation with the existing demands on these factors of production and the absorption of the economic flows to which these resources give rise. The alternatives for development are more narrowly circumscribed in a small country because the available resources or means of production are distorted and restricted whereas the wants are diversified and quantitatively small.

Subsequent paragraphs underline the significance of national 'political' size and show that it has essentially two dimensions: first, in relation to the larger and mainly richer, large countries, and secondly, in relation to large international firms. It emphasises the weakness of the policy variables which often amount to little more than an affirmation of resolve rather than feasible, positive action.

The critical factor in policy is the relative importance of the basic determinants of development rather than the operational mechanism underlying present conditions; a solution to small countries' problems primarily must be founded on means of circumventing these fundamental economic constraints. But the degree of freedom of operation in small countries is more limited, not only in a theoretical sense because it is bounded by natural factor constraints and limited markets, but also in a practical sense because the scope of economic control possessed by a small country is narrowly and strictly defined within the context of the international economic environment.

The international economic environment
The Third World is the two-third's world. Two-thirds of the world's population are poor and approximately two-thirds of the poor countries

116

are small, All but one of the 25 UNCTAD 'least developed' countries have small populations and the majority of the 'Group of 77' countries, so identified because they have special development problems, are both poor and small. There is, therefore, considerable *a priori* evidence that the problems of under-development and of achieving self-sustained growth cannot be considered in isolation from the size of a country, although small size *per se* is not an insuperable obstacle to growth and the improvement of general living standards, as the experience of Switzerland, Luxembourg and Hong Kong has shown. In practice, it is difficult to draw any hard and fast line between large and small countries (or between 'closed' and 'open' economies) without reference to structural and institutional features as well as GNP per capita, population, geographical size and cultivable land area, but a very simple scheme is suggested in Table 1 of the Appendix. The disadvantages of smallness assume greater significance when many of the larger countries are industrially advanced and control dominant trading positions. The estimated degree of 'international concentration' of income in 1971 is shown in Table 2. Many of the countries falling into groups (1) – (3) are large.[1] Furthermore, the organisation of international business enterprise and the modes and complexity of production adopted (i.e. the use of modern capital-intensive technology) are geared to the needs and capabilities of rich countries (both as producers and consumers) and are generally unsuitable to the poorer smaller nations. This growing 'technological gap' makes almost inevitable the perpetual tightening of conglomerate business hegemony over the world economic scene. Thus, of the 100 largest economic units in the world, only 50 are nation states; the other 50 are multinational companies, the largest of which has a total turnover which exceeds the national incomes of all but a dozen countries.[2]

The nature of development planning in small developing countries
Not so long ago it was fashionable for economists to draw a broad distinction between a loosely defined form of policy favoured by Western countries and known as 'indicative' planning (which showed basically what was possible under certain assumptions and conditions), and the more rigorous, formal and centrally controlled type of programmed planning (based on the need to achieve prescribed 'targets' for output, etc.) that characterised the official economic procedures adopted by most communist countries.[3] These forms of planning and methods of carrying out policy are not, in practice, mutually exclusive. But, regardless of their political structures, given the framework of the international economy, small developing countries cannot expect to implement either style of planning and retain any real prospects of achieving their main goals. The success and indeed the very structure of their development plans depend so much on the unpredictable actions and unknown objectives of both internal and external

organisations over which they have little or no control. Thus their problem is essentially one of 'dependent planning', where the successful attainment of desired economic and social welfare objectives hinges on the explicit support and sympathetic cooperation of other economically significant (and invariably non-indigenous) organisations. The plan objectives can only be achieved if these organisations decide to pursue policies consistent with official aims. Since social returns differ, sometimes quite significantly, from private returns they may in many cases be in basic conflict — particularly where the control over raw material supplies is concerned.

Although there is an extensive agenda for direct public action in the fields of capital development, expenditure control (particularly of salaries) and the provision of economic and social infrastructural services, the governments of most small developing countries now wish to progress beyond the stage where planning is merely regarded as the preparation of a public capital expenditure programme. They recognise that planning is more the formulation and execution of a consistent set of interrelated policy measures which are designed to achieve specific economic and social goals for the nation. This usually involves a desire to transform the whole structure of production and consumption in the economy. But such structural changes invariably imply major shifts in the composition of output, labour, domestic savings, etc., over a comparatively short period of time. Occasionally this would also mean a substantial dislocation which the country would be unable to survive either economically or politically. In practice, therefore, a development plan tends to assume more the character of a government manifesto expressing an affirmation of resolve than of a policy blueprint with a deliberate and coherent framework of policy directed towards the achievement of certain goals. Of course, the plan may incorporate some informed guesses or optimistic prophecies about the future, but in attempting not only to predict outcomes but also to shape actual development governments of small countries possess little power for manoeuvre. The scope of their plans must lie within the bounds of possibility. So much can go wrong because so much lies outside the sphere of their direct control or influence. At best, in pursuing the aims of their development plan, these governments can seek to ensure that the general economic environment is favourable to growth and that their policies will facilitate rather than hinder the achievement of their other main objectives. Thus, although the limited ability of the government to control affairs and the force of circumstances would in any event confine the role of planning to areas under fairly strict direct official control, it follows that the government should devote much of its attention to the detailed planning and close scrutiny of public expenditure (and revenues) to ensure that adequate priority is accorded to the development of economic and environmental infrastructural services. The government could extend its role to the operation of industrial and commercial enterprises, but these would have to be established on an autonomous basis to avoid the risk of their being run along political lines with little regard to the efficiency of the price-wage structure.

Basic constraints

The general economic, social, structural and institutional difficulties experienced by most developing countries when formulating and implementing their development plans are shared in greater measure by the small countries. All developing countries are characterised by large gaps in productivity levels between different parts of the economy, but the respective isolation and imbalance between the 'advanced monetary' and predominantly 'foreign enclave' sectors and the 'rural household' sector is often more marked in a small country where there may be no intermediate sectors and few other industries. Partly as a consequence, domestic agricultural production for home consumption tends to lag behind the demand for food. Furthermore, because of industrial diversification difficulties and economic compartmentalisation, the unfavourable ratio between population and capital stock also assumes greater importance in smaller countries.

These features, together with the more specific constraints that restrict the basic development prospects of smaller countries, are best examined in traditional demand and supply terms. This type of analysis not only throws into sharp focus the fundamental problems to be overcome – the limited factors of production and markets – but also reflects the basic underlying methodology of development planning.

Fundamental supply problems

Small countries are comparatively less well endowed with the basic natural resources of land, labour and capital and this imposes, in the first instance, a basic limit on what is possible.

Land: Not only is land limited in area, but often the inherent physical properties of the land as well as its variety of resources are limited. The basic mineral, animal and vegetable properties, including the actual soil fertility, the availability of water, natural sports, etc., restrict the potential use of land. Although the actual available quantities of any particular given resource may not be so limited, the existence of large amounts of any one natural asset virtually precludes the existence of others. Thus, in the exploitation of natural resources, small countries tend to be typically less diversified with a comparatively high proportion of output and productive factors concentrated on a few sectors dominated by one or two primary commodities. Furthermore, such concentration will be encouraged not only by the comparative

119

advantage the small country has over larger countries in this particular resource use but also because these sectors tend to be the advanced ones controlled by foreign firms anxious to improve or preserve their relative position in the economy. The dependence is — in theory — doubly compounded. Indeed, strict adherence to the principle of comparative advantage in the present framework of the international economy simply implies that the rich ought to stay rich and grow richer whilst the poor ought to stay poor and grow poorer. Even in the absence of other practical drawbacks, the application of such a limited and static theory leads inevitably to the ossification of the economic structure.

Insofar as many small developing countries are tropical islands and desirable for tourist and residential expatriate development, there may also be problems of controlling real estate speculation and land price rises.

Labour: In terms of the land area available for habitation and use, small countries may suffer to a proportionately greater extent from the problems of total population pressure and the related problems posed by an age and sex structure imbalance. The importance of population control and official planned parenthood policies in such circumstances hardly needs to be stressed.

A small country is also likely to possess a narrower spread of labour skills as well as a comparatively less effective manpower capability even though the proportion of people in the labour force may be the same as in a larger developing country. The country will probably be more affected by imbalance in its demographic structure, particularly in the age structure and sex composition of the population, and by rural-urban differences. In the past such problems were partly solved but more often aggravated by emigration since this tended to apply mainly to skilled and semi-skilled adult males. Racial differences will tend to aggravate the problem of smallness by encouraging an often unnecessary economic and social fragmentation. The latter already tends to occur in relation to particular economic activities, e.g. in the Pacific Islands there is a fairly clearly defined social and racial stratification of economic functions in cash agriculture, commerce and peasant farming.

The presence of expatriates in favoured commercial and sometimes official posts serves only to emphasise feelings of domination and subservience, especially when this divine right of privilege is made manifest by racial differences. The fragmentation of activities is thus compounded by the social differences that exist within activities. This also occurs in larger developing countries but — because of the smaller variety of economic operations and relatively greater scarcity of opportunities and narrower range of skills — the impact is often much greater in smaller territories.

Capital: In a small developing country a relatively large proportion of the capital may be owned and controlled by foreign organisations. In the public sector also, the government has to rely heavily on outside grants and loans. The borrower is therefore small in relation to both actual and potential lenders and the country becomes increasingly dependent on the policies pursued by outside companies and overseas governments. Normally, because of the burden of both private interest and dividend payments and public interest and loan repayments, the country's GNP, i.e. the value of goods and services becoming available from economic activity that can be disbursed amongst residents, will be less than the GDP, the total value of goods and services actually produced during the same period in that country. There are, however, one or two notable exceptions where the inflow of migrant workers' remittances contribute to an increased value of GDP. In such cases, e.g. Lesotho, it is even more true to say that the country's well-being is dependent upon foreign capital. In these instances the capital is non-resident and outside the government's sphere of influence.

(i) Private capital: Perhaps three-quarters to four-fifths of all domestic private capital formation will normally be carried out by foreign firms, and the share of total turnover taken by foreign firms will be of a similar order.[4] These firms will be the most efficient means of exporting technology where the capacity of local entrepreneurship to absorb technology and new methods of production is much less than the capacity of the firm to utilise it. The faster the technological progress, the lower the level of real wage costs and the faster the rate of capital accumulation. If labour costs per unit of output are low in the first place and productivity growth exceeds wage rate increases (because wage rates are contractually fixed and only respond to change with a time lag under the established collective bargaining process) then the country will become a progressively cheaper labour cost economy and attract increased as well as more varied flows of capital. For a small country with very limited import-substitution possibilities and a trainable low-cost unskilled labour force, these factors represent the necessary (but not sufficient) preconditions for the establishment and development of export-oriented industries.

Historically, the establishment of manufacturing industry in the developing countries was led by old-fashioned industries like cotton textiles. But the most successful development has occurred with modern advanced technology industries like electronics, i.e. medium-size, mobile and flexible industries requiring relatively low levels of skill and training and involving the manufacture of products for which there is a high income and price elasticity of demand. Part of the sluggishness in the export growth of many small developing countries has occurred not so much for structural reasons, as is often suggested, but because of a failure to exploit export potential. Although the economic and political policies of the industrialised developed nations act as a barrier to export expansion, some of the failure is due to the basic inability of small developing countries to become sufficiently cost competitive. (It should be recognised, however, that this may also be a reflection of an overvalued exchange rate.) The principal constraint has been plant size, and the problem of exploiting potential economies of scale. There is a basic discrepancy in most small countries between, on the supply side, a maximum plant size dictated by the technically most efficient scale of operations and, on the demand side, a minimum plant size determined by the optimum size of the (principally domestic) market. In many small developing countries, a significant amount of new foreign investment in manufacturing activities has been on a comparatively small scale and invariably the mode of production has been far more capital-intensive than the average for the country as a whole. The foreign firms do, however, provide scope for the training of local management; when the overseas subsidiary of a foreign enterprise becomes fully localised and managed, some of the criticisms that such firms operate against domestic interests lose much of their substance.

The objectives and requirements of the international firms and the government are sometimes, however, in basic conflict (private benefits and social costs v. social benefits). The main business activities in small countries are dominated by multinational corporations which form an integral part of a wider international system of resource allocation. 'Harmonisation' in the advanced industrial enclave tends to be primarily metropolitan-based and is not dictated by any local need either to integrate domestic industries or to achieve a better industrial base. The small economy is a locus of production made up of fragmented compartments of economic activity of varying importance and size.

It is argued that heavy economic dependence on the policies of foreign companies dominating operations in the one, or in all, leading sectors (including entirely 'domestic' industries like construction and transport) not only limits the power to act *positively* for the general benefit of the country but also affects policies and decisions *negatively* through the extension of a metropolis-satellite relationship to the sphere of government activities. It is most unlikely that desirable developments will be directly opposed or stifled. What is more important is that if the level of savings, rate of growth and balance of payments deteriorate with increased inflows of foreign investment, then the country becomes increasingly dependent and less capable of self-sustained growth. Furthermore, if foreign firms reinvest their profits in local enterprises and expand their sphere of operations to improve the vertical, horizontal and locational integration of their activities, then this merely increases the government's dependence on foreign firms and restricts its ability to adopt its own line of policy. An appropriate development strategy necessarily implies the adoption of official methods (and greater consultation) to ensure that, as far as possible, the decisions of large multinational corporations are in harmony with the overall national interest. The direct income and capital leakages from the foreign enclave invariably become larger with time and there are further indirect effects arising from the higher marginal propensity of foreign companies, both to consume and to import. Their tendency in many cases to produce inessential goods for personal consumption and the ability of such firms to pay higher than average wage rates (occasionally forced on them by politically backed T.U. pressure) also undermines the capacity of less efficient firms (in many cases, locally owned enterprises) to become economically viable and employ more labour. Criticism of overseas companies is attributable to the growing realisation that private foreign investment, as it is conventionally given, is not conducive to the sustenance of permanent growth, not least because of its import-consuming rather than import-substituting bias. [5] [6]

(ii) Public aid: It is generally recognised that the public aid policies of donor countries are geared to some extent to political as well as economic considerations both internally and internationally. A political dependence is superimposed on an economic dependence, with the smaller developing countries feeling more duty-bound in their allegiance because of their comparatively high receipts of aid per head from the advanced industrial nations or special relationships with certain 'groups'.[7] The largest share of public aid from Britain, for example, goes to the Commonwealth; the smaller developing Commonwealth countries may thus tend to feel some moral obligation to Britain to 'toe the line' over wider international economic issues (e.g. exchange rates and reserves) even if this does not apply to political issues. This perhaps operates more in a negative way in the sense that if a country 'steps out of line' the aid flow may be cut.

The real impact of aid – in terms of the actual projects approved and financed – can also significantly affect the very fabric of a small country's development.

Entrepreneurship: Although the extent of local entrepreneurship has been limited both by the lack of skilled people and by the lack of available capital, there has been a significant increase in the number of local businessmen in many small developing countries in recent years. Whilst this trend is partly a reflection of general economic growth, it is mainly in response to the increasing pressures of official 'localisation' policies. The evolution of such entrepreneurship, although on a small scale, has in fact taken place in the fundamentally different environments of both the rural sector and the large urban areas. But even a fairly large increase in the number of local businessmen will not automatically result in any general rise in the living standards of the local population. These developments may however be seen as a move towards partially redressing the inequalities of property ownership whilst also facilitating the acquisition of organisational skills. Independent local businessmen have to contend with many obstacles; the local entrepreneur's preference for trading and similar activities is more a reflection of the basic impediments in the economic environment than any result of alleged 'culturally determined pre-conditioning' or basic inability and unwillingness to accept production risks. Various forms of assistance and extensive protection now exist for local businessmen in many developing countries to help stimulate domestic enterprises (particularly in cash agriculture). There may, however, still be stringent financial restrictions inhibiting local private enterprises in the more advanced monetary sector where a much wider variety of business opportunities exist. The unfavourable economic environment, including the problem of securing freehold tenure for industrial activities, together with the still inadequate level and supply of local entrepreneurial ability, is probably far more important in determining the growth potential of domestic enterprises than the acquisition of capital *per se*. This inherent 'hostility' of economic conditions is clearly greater and thus more restricting in small developing countries.

Demand constraints

The domestic market: Perhaps the overriding problem facing small developing countries is the limited size and narrowness of the domestic market. This basic problem is sometimes further complicated by demographic characteristics which serve to increase the diversification of the pattern of demand and lead to an even greater fragmentation of an already limited market, e.g. Fiji. In any event, the structure of the domestic market, or sector outputs, will usually differ quite significantly from the domestic composition of final demand. But a policy of import substitution – favoured by the larger economies with potential home markets to exploit the advantages of scale offered – is extremely expensive (in terms of the efficient use of the scarce resources available) as well as difficult to implement, primarily because it has to rely on the willingness of foreign investors to initiate production. The maximum, let alone optimum, technically efficient scale of plant that can be introduced renders some productive activities completely uneconomical in a small developing country unless a substantial export potential in terms of total output also exists. The alternative – import substitution behind prohibitive tariff barriers – is rarely a viable long-term solution, especially if costs are also underwritten by generous tax and investment incentives. This is particularly true of the production of capital goods. But the heavy reliance on overseas markets for manufactures is not always a sound basis for development. This imbalance tends to reinforce a position of weak inter-industry relations;

this not only reduces potential external economies but also increases dependence on a few industries. On the other hand, there is usually very little home demand for the main commodities produced; these are primarily for export and are usually produced with very much greater efficiency than most other goods produced in the economy. Although it is possible to operate production at different efficiency levels of output and plant size, the size of an economic unit is at least partially a function of market sales. The scale of output and basic imbalance in the structure of most small developing countries' economies invariably restricts the volume, nature and variety of inter-industry transactions. These relations will increase as the objectives of development policies are achieved, but the expansion of output either in terms of volume or variety is unlikely to be achieved simply by depending on the development of the home market.

Although, therefore, the economy may be less complex and in theory it should be easy to prepare and formulate a development plan, in practice it is far more difficult to ensure its effective implementation. The size and growth prospects of the home market impose an important limit on the scope of a development plan which aims to diversify the economy and reduce economic openness.

External markets: As a result of the limitations of the domestic market, the rate of growth of the economy (GDP) tends to be primarily a function of the rate of growth of exports of goods and services. Thus the rate of growth of external demand has been mainly responsible for the more general development of Singapore (manufactured goods), Hong Kong (goods and services) and Fiji (services). For most small countries, the major brake on the growth of the economy and the improvement of living standards is the difficulty of raising exports sufficiently (either in terms of output or prices) to pay for the additional imports of capital and intermediate goods for development and the imports of consumption goods on which a higher standard of living depends.

Foreign trade thus assumes a comparatively greater importance in small countries. There is, in fact, clear evidence of an inverse relationship between population size and the ratio of foreign trade to GDP. But the problem goes beyond this; exports are highly concentrated on one or two products. These are usually sold to a relatively small number of overseas markets — normally to advanced industrial nations and sometimes just to a few select customers (who thus, potentially, hold strong monopsonist positions) — whilst domestic demand for these products is negligible. By contrast, because of the narrowness of the domestic economic base, imports are very diverse. But, like exports, mainly for historical and institutional reasons (e.g. established trading links), most of these imports tend to come from only a small range of industrialised countries and sometimes involve only one or two trading companies. This is particularly the case where there has been (or still is) a continuation of a previous economic and political metropolis-satellite relationship.

This dependence on external goods and the continued importance of only a few domestic products in international trade raises three main problems:

First, a small country may be able to exert no influence over the international market because the sales of its major exports are entirely dependent on predetermined world prices and quotas fixed by 'mutual' agreement of purchasers and suppliers. These must be accepted as given in the short run. Net export revenue thus depends on the country's ability to reduce production costs – a problem aggravated by declining terms of trade and rising labour costs.

The second problem arises where the country cannot (because of its size) determine or influence price but where it can, to some extent, raise output without causing a disproportionate drop in price. In these circumstances, the problem has both financial and physical aspects. Export revenues can be increased if costs can be reduced and output expanded. But the country may possess only limited supplies of skilled labour and capital; thus important physical constraints on output expansion may exist. Moreover, output may be more determined by natural conditions and limitations and cannot be increased very easily. Lastly, because of the structure of some international markets (with 'spot' and 'forward' sales and speculative pressure operating within a restricted market) expectations of increased outputs from even small countries may tend to depress prices. These difficulties would not be so acute if there were either a domestic demand for the country's main exports or some alternative exports to spread the load and reduce the domestic income effects of external cyclical fluctuations. Hence the growing desire amongst small developing countries – particularly tropical island economies – to promote tourism as a major industry (although this too has its attendant economic and social problems).

Thirdly, there are difficulties in improving export performance in a competitive environment where the goods concerned are not primary commodities but manufactured articles. Whereas very little can be done by a Planning Office in such circumstances to encourage exports directly, domestic policies – by acting on prices and costs (wages and raw materials imports) or by providing indirect incentives to industry – can improve the prospects of foreign sales of manufactured goods. The difficulty is that the domestic production of these export goods (which also have a home demand) requires the import of machinery and equipment and usually working capital as well.* Furthermore, it is normally the larger

* And, of course, favourable international tariff policies.

126

foreign companies* (or the subsidiaries of overseas concerns) that have the financial and productive capacity which are able to secure appropriate tariff concessions (high domestic protection plus concessions on imported inputs) as well as obtain the full range of direct tax benefits, e.g. tax holidays, accelerated depreciation and investment allowances and subsidies. The aid they receive from the government is also usually supported by preferential treatment from the commercial banking sector and other loan agencies. This all tends to raise local prices and value added, and the enhanced profits will tend to be remitted overseas to the detriment of the balance of payments.

Official policies in this sector may also have adverse indirect effects on both exports and imports, as well as on the prospects of other sectors, particularly agriculture. The government cannot counteract such effects and depress the demand for imports without affecting the efficiency and productivity of the growing sectors in the economy. Credit restrictions (assuming that the financial system allows them to be effective) and higher taxes involve increased costs and tend to reduce both investment and consumption. The loss of reserves which occurs as a result of pursuing fairly 'free' industrial international promotion policies without adequate exchange control regulations may eventually require the imposition of more and higher import tariffs, the establishment of import quotas and priorities, foreign exchange restrictions, and licences, all of which are in conflict with increased economic development. High tariff protection is a valid means of encouraging greater import substitution in a small country only if it results in a change in the economic structure, and then only when it is limited to a specific time period. The costs of import substitution in a small country are high and mistakes are expensive. The opportunities for broadening the economic base are more limited and the various possibilities for establishing import-substituting industries are more difficult to select. Thus major development planning problems exist.

The adoption of a set of consistent and related stimulative economic measures designed to ensure the creation of a general economic environment favourable to internal development and export growth may therefore not achieve its objectives. Its success will depend on whether management and labour respond in the right way and foreign companies support the main objectives of the government development plan. New forms of working relationships may be needed to deal with the locally established foreign sector within the international context of decisions. Governments should also seek to establish a formula that will satisfy both the international strategy of a foreign based firm and their national objectives.

*Who, for strategic or political reasons, may not wish to expand exports to particular markets (already only supplied from home-based subsidiaries).

The public sector

Recurrent expenditure: In a small developing country the above problems tend to impart a bias to the structure and pattern of public finance. Actual expenditure and 'indirect' expenditure (in terms of revenue foregone through the granting of concessions) on the newly expanding industrial or tourist sector tend to be comparatively high. The effective administration of these policies is also costly; it would be almost out of the question to have a detailed official plan and method of control for each industry, since to do so would require an army of civil servants. Such policies have to be integrated with general planning procedures so as to avoid some of the high costs of preparing programmes, enforcing necessary controls, etc.

Experience suggests that although small countries need to spend less on such matters as defence and foreign representation they do not usually take advantage of the opportunites presented. The price of preserving a national identity is high. With the comparatively high costs of the social services and administration, the problems presented by diseconomies of scale have also to be faced by the government. But since the public sector plays a more important role in the economy there is some scope for positive planning policies with respect to both recurrent expenditure (and in particular the scale of wages and salaries) and capital development expenditure, especially where the latter involves the domestic construction industry and the supply of productive skilled labour.

Prices, incomes and employment: Both the private and public sectors would benefit considerably from the establishment of an official prices and incomes policy. Although clearly important in themselves, the problems of a rising domestic price level and the granting of inflationary wage awards cannot be considered in isolation from the wider question of creating more employment opportunities.

Prices in general are mainly determined by import prices (and tariff policy) and fluctuations in output in the agricultural sector – over both of which the government usually has very little control. The government can however exert considerable influence over the level of wages, particularly in the dominant public sector. Yet even in a completely planned economy, the wage rate can never be fully under control. Wages tend to be governed by custom, trade union pressure (based on western systems of free collective bargaining), geographical and particularly occupational immobility, incentives, the scale of social services and international pressures; and they are not, in practice, so amenable to control as a policy variable. But the government can take a lead with its own employees. It can also decline to support those workers in industries and firms controlled by foreign firms (whose ability to pay higher wages is rarely open to doubt) who are trying to raise their levels of remuneration. Given current levels of industrial wages and productivity, increased wages can only be at the expense of other sectors, employment and future development prospects. Nevertheless, it should be added that any programme of restricting wage levels in the externally controlled sector must be accompanied by relevant taxation measures, if it is not merely to lead to an increased outflow of profits.

The extent of government influence: Thus the government of a small developing country is faced by a number of extremely difficult economic planning and development policy questions to which no satisfactory answers have yet been found. It is difficult to predict development in the external sector and the economy is highly dependent on foreign investment and aid. Government may lack sufficient control over its own monetary − and to some extent fiscal − system and over the foreign private sector which tends to be a separate financial system in itself. Where a small country is a recipient of grant aid which forms a major element of its current revenue receipts, the government becomes dependent on the goodwill of an external government. Moreover international policies of monetary and fiscal stabilisation often lead to decreased overseas and domestic demand and credit, and adversely affect trade prospects.

The scope of development policy and the power of decision of the government sector are thus very narrow. This sometimes imposes severe planning limitations. Because it is difficult for the government to exercise proper controls, it has to adopt an open economic strategy. The economy thus tends to follow a 'forced' rather than a natural path of development with decisions affecting key areas of the economy being taken outside the country. One of the fundamental questions a small developing country therefore has to answer is not how can it best integrate foreign direct investment and capital into the proposed development plan, but how can the plan itself best fit into the foreign investment to serve its principal objectives?

Conclusions

Small developing countries have often remained underdeveloped because of the distortions and rigidities built into their economies as a result of their integration into a world market from a position of profound and basic weakness. Their imports and exports and general economic operations are more determined by the needs of the developed countries than by their own. This weakness is emphasised by the large element of foreign control over their domestic economies and by the conduct of business operations geared more to the needs of the overseas companies than to those of the country itself. Any development effort within this distorted pattern of economic relationships implies an increase in the degree of dependence and the development of underdevelopment.

Many of the problems identified and described in this paper are indeed shared by all developing countries and not merely by small ones with their limited resources, fewer opportunities for domestic industry, and restricted markets. But the difficulties of planning in small countries are compounded by the greater importance of structural and institutional factors over which the government may have virtually no control. Predictions of capital information, consumption and imports cannot be accurately based even in the short run; moreover these variables are so closely interconnected by a series of unknown and essentially unquantifiable dynamic relationships that original assumptions and estimates are sometimes subject to dramatic revision. Within the general context of development planning and the limitations to the effective coverage of the plan, as well as the specific economic problems and constraints faced by small developing countries, the best that most governments can hope to achieve is the maintenance of a stable policy favourable to continued expansion. This would be no mean achievement. It requires recognition of the urgent need not only to keep costs down and to maintain an equitable incomes policy but also to develop a viable agricultural sector. Measures such as these would enhance the prospects of establishing and maintaining potentially prosperous and fast-growing export-oriented industries on which the main hopes for future progress must be based.

NOTES

1. The existing comparative advantage enjoyed by the advanced industrial countries in industrial products and services (other than unskilled migrant labour) is an acquired advantage due to huge stocks of capital, large-scale production units, superior technology and skills, advanced infrastructure and high-level managerial experience and capacity. The assumption underlying this doctrine is that factor endowments are fixed. Whilst this may not be generally true, in the Third World countries the possibility of manoeuvre may be severely restricted for institutional, structural and social reasons.
2. Fewer than 200 firms (each of which has established operations in 6 or more countries) based in the U.S.A. and W. Europe own more than 2,000 manufacturing subsidiaries abroad. This small number of multinational companies includes all the main producers of raw materials as well as the principal manufacturers and users of them.
3. Some critics of British economic planning, commenting on its evident lack of success, added a third category, viz. 'subjunctive' planning; i.e. a particular objective *might have been* attained *if* only a particular growth rate (or surplus on the balance of payments, etc.) had been achieved.
4. It has been said that the subsidiaries of foreign-based companies will be established in developing countries so that these companies can manufacture goods where labour is cheapest and channel their profits

to another country where taxation is the lowest or non-existent. More generally, the objects of these companies will include:

(a) The need to capture new markets and get close to customers.
(b) The desire to control raw material supplies.
(c) The wish to utilise cheap labour.
(d) The desire to take advantage of producing behind a high protective tariff.
(e) The desire to maximise tax planning advantages and to minimise or avoid exchange rate risks.

5. More common but less profound economic criticisms centre on the traditional form of foreign investment and its association with the exploitation and exhaustion of a country's irreplaceable natural resources (mineral deposits, soil, etc.) and cheap labour. Unfortunately, the recent tourist investment, like mining, drilling and plantation activities, similarly creates just the wrong sort of social and political attitudes and conditions.

6. Many small developing countries have operated on the philosophy that if they cannot change the fact of dependence, they can at least control it. But the nationalisation of (certain selected) foreign firms and the localisation of their staff merely reflects a desire to buy back the past and it invariably represents a serious misallocation of the limited resources at the disposal of the government.

7. The higher aid proportion going to small countries is probably a reflection of the higher costs of achieving the same objectives of development as larger less developed countries. It may also be a recognition of the possible diseconomies of institutional structure and the existence of infrastructural indivisibilities because aid tends to be associated with activities rather than numbers of people (although there may be an institutional constraint on the maximum amount of aid that can be granted per capita). It is also argued, however, that the status of having an international loan for a project will mean that the firms (which invariably come from the advanced industrial countries) submitting tenders will inflate their prices and that the small countries will lack the expertise to discern where costs have been overestimated.

Table 1 : A Simple Classification for Identifying Small Developing Countries

Type	(1) Population Size	(2) Cultivable Land Area	(3) GNP per Capita	(4) Share of Trade in GNP	(5) Main Development Possibilities
I	Small	Large	High	Low	—
II	Small	Large	Low	Low	Development of Natural Resources and Domestic Market
III	Small	Small	High	High	} Development of External Markets
IV	Small	Small	Low	High	}

Notes:

(1) Type IV countries constitute the small, open, dependent developing countries which are faced with special problems in planning development.

(2) Type IV countries may be of two types:–
   (a) Island economies. These face problems of relative isolation, costly transport and difficult access to larger markets; but government customs duties and indirect tax revenue (the main source of government local revenue) can be more readily assessed and assured.
   (b) Land-locked territories. Potentially they have access to a much wider range of neighbouring markets without incurring excessive transport costs, but government indirect tax revenues cannot be so easily estimated or calculated in formulating development plans.

(3) Regional economic integration of either island economies or neighbouring land-locked territories has so far achieved very little in terms of more rapid economic progress because of their similar structures and common anxieties to increase their individual country's trade in almost identical products, i.e. they all tend to want to produce and sell the same goods.

Table 2 : The International Concentration of Income and Wealth

Country Group	Number	Population (million)	GNP (£ billion)	GNP per head (£)	Recent Annual Percentage Growth in GNP	Annual Percentage Population Growth
1. United States	1	200	400	2,000	4	1
2. Rich	17	500	500	1,000	6	1
3. Middle Class	22	600	450	750	7.5	2.0
4. Poor	112	2,300	200	85	5	2.6
TOTAL	152	3,600	1,550	430	5	2.3

Source: The Economist, 22 January 1972, Barclays International Atlas (Based on World Bank data).

6. ADMINISTRATIVE PROBLEMS OF SMALL COUNTRIES

B.L. Jacobs *

Summary

The paper is mainly concerned with the administrative problems of small countries which have recently been colonies. A number of such problems are identified, including small manpower resources, possible diseconomies of small scale, the limited clientele for administrative services, an inadequate concern with the economics of administration, the real or assumed need to provide new or expanded services (including foreign services), difficulties created by the distribution of population or limited natural resources, the personal relations between administrators, politicians and the public, limited career opportunities, lack of spare capacity – especially in relation to training needs – the difficulties involved in decentralisation, limited capacity to use technical assistance effectively, and the frequent absence of key people abroad. Emphasis is placed on the need for a tough approach to administrative issues.

I.

This paper does not concern itself with the marginal advantages which derive from the size of small states: it is concerned more with their problems. It defines small states as states or territories of less than 5 million population. No attempt is made to distinguish problems of small self-governing states from those of small states which have still retained some formal dependence on a metropolitan power, but some of the points made are of direct and immediate relevance only to independent states (e.g. when there are references to the maintenance of foreign services or diplomatic missions). Much of this paper is concerned with countries which have only recently emerged from colonial status.

In 1966, the United Nations Institute for Training and Research (UNITAR) commissioned a study on the Status and Problems of Very Small States and Territories. In 1968, the Public Administration Division (UNPAD) of the Economic and Social Affairs Department of the United Nations undertook a Comparative Analysis of the Distinctive Public Administration Problems of Small States and Territories, primarily as part of its own work programme but also as part of the larger UNITAR study[1] It concentrated its attention on small states which had already achieved independence, and it adopted

B.L. Jacobs is a Fellow of the Institute of Development Studies at the University of Sussex.

a further classification of 'intensive' small states – i.e. those small in area; and 'extensive' small states – i.e. those large in area. It did not quantify large and small areas. Most of the UNPAD report was reproduced in the UNITAR report, the first version of which appeared in 1969, but the UNITAR report refuses to define what it means by a small state, arguing that the use of a single variable is too narrow. However it does identify ninety-six states of 1 million or less compared with the forty-eight *sovereign* states of less than 2½ million identified in the UNPAD report.

What ought to be the aims of the administrations of such states? Their overall goal must be the same as for any state, namely to execute as effectively and efficiently as possible the agreed policies of the leaders holding political power whom they are employed to serve. But the administration, and especially its senior members, not only have an executive role. They also have an important part to play in offering advice to their political masters as part of the process of policy-making. Senior civil servants giving advice in small states will need to bear in mind certain factors which may not be important for their peers operating in larger states. Notably they must recognise the need for policies which leave the maximum amount of room for manoeuvre. They must be aware of the weapons available to small states in order to achieve such leeway. Small ex-colonial states will have inherited values and criteria appropriate to the former metropolitan power. These values and criteria will continue to be brought to bear on them by way of the mass media long after they have achieved independence. They need to be able to consider whether those values and criteria are relevant to the needs of independence. It may be assumed too readily that they are. The need to consider alternative policies is paramount.

Because many political leaders tend to be risk-minimisers and because they may have had little or no experience in the exercise of their powers, they may wish to avoid major changes, or alternatively they may embark on major changes without thinking through the administrative implications. Administrators are subject to similar pressures. They too, at the time of independence, have had no experience of the new situation brought about by independence. They too have to feel their way with political leaders before a satisfactory *modus vivendi* can be established. They have often failed to achieve this years after independence. Thus it is not surprising (although I suggest it is to be deplored) that many former British dependencies have accepted without demur a continuation of the Westminster/Whitehall pattern of government. Even if ministries are not all equal, it will usually be assumed that all Permanent Secretaries are – and paid accordingly. The administrative resources invested in ministries may bear little relation to the relative importance of the ministries to the independent state. Moreover, relative importance changes. For example, the importance of the role of, say, the Permanent Secretary of the Ministry of Local Government will change if central government decides to *recentralise* its administration. This has happened in a number of states. But the relative status and pay of the Permanent Secretary remains unchanged, even when the holder of the post is changed. The allocation of resources may thus reflect the relative importance of the ministries in the colonial situation. It will not be possible to break away from these administrative patterns as long as the Westminster/Whitehall model is retained. Similarly the model will not be adequate if an attempt is to be made to change the political and administrative levels at which functions and decisions are carried out. Thus when politicians have sought to diverge from the Westminster/Whitehall model in matters of appointment and promotion, they have usually and understandably run into strong opposition from entrenched civil servants and Public Service Commissions. Often the fiction of the colonial model is retained and supported by pre-independence legislation, but new practices inconsistent with the legal position are introduced.

II.

The following problems with administrative implications have been identified as of particular significance for small states:

1. A small state has *small manpower resources* from which to draw its administrators. Also, there will be a shortage of skilled manpower — especially of specialists and technicians for many of whom training facilities will not exist locally.

2. Public services tend not to increase in direct proportion to population: there may be *economies of scale in administration.*[2] The size of the public service expressed in terms of percentage of total population tends to be higher for small states.[3] This will be particularly so if the state employs more people than all other employers combined, as will often be the case where natural resources are few (v.7 below).

3. Because total numbers are small, *the civil service clientele will be small.* Administrators will be reluctant to provide certain specialist services for very small numbers of potential clients. Thus, whilst it may be possible to justify a university for an isolated state of under a million inhabitants (there are a number of examples), it becomes more difficult to justify, say, a post-graduate school in such circumstances. The long-term effects can clearly be very serious and extend beyond implications of merely administrative significance.

4. Administrative organisations of new states reflect (indeed are often little different from) the organisation inherited from the colonial power. Colonial powers tended to be inadequately concerned with *the economics of administration* despite the UK principle of colonial finance, whereby budgetary assistance was supposed to be the

exception. Their resources were such that the cost of administering individual small dependencies was of little significance. Funds could always be found for the maintenance of law and order – even if this was at the expense of the local population. Their administration, in terms of size, structure and excessive departmentalisation, often reflected these facts. The cost of administration becomes a much more critical factor once it has to be borne by a small sovereign state. But small independent states may find it difficult to reduce, say, the salaries of the civil service, or even the number of ministries.[4] Expanding budgets have usually been accompanied by expanded Cabinets, often justified on the grounds of the increased services expected of an independent state (v.5 below). Chief executives of new states will not find it easy to reduce the number of appointments which it falls to their discretion to make: rather the pressures will be to widen the 'spoils' element of their administrations.

5. One of the factors conducive to an expanded administration will be *the need to provide services which may not have existed – or scarcely so – in the era of dependence.* A notable example is of the need for some long-range planning facilities. Viable planning machinery hardly existed for many small dependencies. Frequently the planning machinery which existed before independence was part of a larger regional machine which was dismantled at independence or, at any event, was not at the disposal of the newly independent successor. Advice to 'minimise managerial systems and keep units few, small and "lean"'[5], cannot be expected to be well received, especially when it comes from an organisation whose own officials have often been responsible for advice diametrically opposed to the sentiment of smallness and leanness.

6. *The distribution of population* may create special problems in small states. The problems caused by the fact that 50 per cent of agricultural land is on privately-owned estates will be of quite a different order in a small country from that in a large country. It may result, for example, in a far higher proportion of the population having no alternative to living within urban areas (e.g. Mauritius), a factor clearly of administrative significance. Some small states (in the Caribbean, for example) have their population spread out unevenly on a string of islands. To provide basic services on those farthest from the capital at a level comparable with those in the capital can be very expensive.

7. Usually, small states (oil countries are a notable exception) have *small natural resources* (indeed, this is so by definition as far as manpower, one of the main natural resources, is concerned). Moreover, the *range* of these natural resources is limited. This makes them vulnerable to natural disasters and world price variations – a further factor of importance to planners and administrators.

8. In small states there is a greater likelihood than in larger states

that people will know each other or even be related to each other, even if the relationship is of the extended African family type. This poses administrative problems, especially if an attempt is being made to pursue policies of merit-based recruitment and promotion. Nearly all civil servants will know each other, and 'knowing each other' includes a knowledge of political sympathies and political party affiliations.[6]

9. Individuals can affect administrations in a manner impossible in larger states. This may be reflected in the *increased direct accessibility to ministers of the public* (not without its implications for civil servants) or in the ease with which junior civil servants have access or even 'rights' of appeal to politicians over civil service matters, including matters concerned with discipline.

10. Because the society is numerically small, the sub-groups within it will be small. *They may therefore tend to use informal means of communication.* As I have suggested elsewhere,[7] the effect may be a failure to record decisions and the reasoning on which those decisions were based, with resulting discontinuities which are inimical to efficient administration.

11. *The isolation of some small states* constitutes a problem with – *inter alia* – administrative implications. The remark does not apply only to islands (cf. Botswana, Lesotho, and Swaziland). Advice, or even mere information, becomes more difficult to obtain. This factor should not however be exaggerated at a time when international communications are improving, especially when advice or information available near at hand is less acceptable than that available far away. Paradoxically, it can be cheaper for, say, Uganda to send a civil servant for training at Sussex in Britain than to send him to the East African Staff College course in Tanzania.

12. The smaller the administration, the smaller will be the *opportunities for a life-time career* within it because of the reduced number of promotion opportunities towards the top. This situation can be exacerbated by an unnecessary profusion of cadres with rigid rules preventing progress from one cadre to another. These bars to progress will not always be of a hierarchical nature. Thus, one small state maintains two police forces: one large, concerned with the normal duties one associates with the police, and another miniscule and offering no prospects for promotion, concerned with airport security. Elsewhere, the dichotomy between general and railway police might be questioned.

13. *Small administrations tend to have small spare capacity.* This makes for difficulty when trying to free suitable civil servants for further training, and places a disproportionate strain on those who remain. The effect can be observed in a score of small states: either the least suitable people are sent for training, good people are sent on inappropriate training courses, or training does not take place.

14. The assumption is made too often by small states, looking at

the examples in larger states, that their *training needs* can only be met in prestigious training institutions, and until such institutions are available training can only be done overseas. And when technical assistance produces the training institutions, the small state may find itself having little control over what is taught. *International or regional schemes for training* have proved very difficult to arrange successfully, although there have been some notable exceptions in Eastern and Southern Africa.

15. It is in the area of *decentralisation and local government* that the inconsistencies of the colonial inheritance can be most clearly seen. The extent and operation of the inherited system of local government in small states have been questioned less than in large states which have tended to experiment more adventurously, albeit often settling in the event for something approaching a pre-colonial pattern. The fact that small countries have experimented less may be a manifestation of the point made at (4) above. Thus the British Colonial Secretary (Creech Jones) in 1947 encouraged colonial governments to develop democratic local government systems. But the less than discriminating application of this policy in the colonial situation has left anomalies, particularly for small states, which have yet to be reconciled.

The situation which existed in Lesotho (with a total population of less than 1 million) at the time of independence may be cited as an instance. First, the dependence of government on the hereditary chieftainship meant that over 3,600 chiefs were on the Government payroll. Super-imposed on the chieftaincy was a Ministerial system on the British pattern. This included ten Ministries with their own staffs, seven Assistant Ministers and a bicameral legislature of sixty persons in the National Assembly and thirty-three chiefs in the Senate.

Furthermore a colonial-style district administration had been created with nine districts, each with its District Commissioner and supporting staff. This was not all, since in compliance with the Creech Jones despatch, a single-tier system of local government had been developed with nine elected District Councils which it was acknowledged in 1966 had so failed to fulfil their intended duties that they had all been suspended. Nevertheless their executive officers continued to function. This multiplicity of lines of communication between the centre and the periphery was largely uncoordinated.

16. The capacity of small states to obtain appropriate *technical assistance* and use it to the best effect is directly related to size. Small states may have access to technical assistance funds which are relatively high in per capita terms. But in absolute terms the sums involved look less impressive, and even less so in terms of minimum critical size. Problems of processing applications and recruiting counterpart personnel will often be compounded by the absence of a resident regional representative of the fund-giving body. As an example I may illustrate the steps which were taken in Lesotho to

seek remedies for its problems of decentralisation.

The assistance of a number of outside advisers was sought. They included a former Colonial Governor to advise on the structure and administration of Government (provided by the British Government), an Indian civil servant to advise on Local Government (provided by the United Nations), a former Town Clerk of the commercial capital of a British protectorate to advise on the establishment of municipal and other local government authorities (also provided by the British Government), and a former colonial District Commissioner from West Africa appointed to advise on the reorganisation of Local Government (also provided by the British Government). All but one of these advisers spent only a few weeks in the country which none of them had visited before. The inability of the administration to be selective in its choice of visiting advisers and their terms of reference was equalled by its inability to evaluate or even process the often conflicting reports which they left behind them.[8]

17. Independent states frequently assume that they are required to establish *foreign services* with their concomitant overseas missions. Decisions are taken without a study of the likely costs and benefits. The costs and benefits of foreign services are not easy to assess, but a considerable amount of information on the subject is now available and indicates that costs tend to be underestimated and benefits overestimated. Diplomatic accreditation is not the same as resident representation. And the true costs of diplomatic representation cannot be obtained even by the most informed study of published budgets — for example the published foreign service budget will not disclose expenditure on the purchase of information. On the credit side there are problems of quantifying the value of diplomatic mission activities: would that contract to sell an additional 5,000 bales of cotton have been obtained if there had been no mission in the purchasing country? The State which, largely without any surface water supplies, in its first year of independence budgeted to spend as much on the establishment of overseas missions as it planned to spend on the development of underground water supplies, is not atypical. Moreover it is common to find a nation's most favoured sons employed in foreign services on work of low national priority. The establishment of overseas representation may prove to be a highly capital-intensive venture with low returns.

18. Because living in small countries is not easy — especially for people whose horizons are not limited by their national boundaries — *key people may tend to be abroad* more often than their peers in larger states. When, as is common in small less developed countries, one person is holding, for example, two portfolios in Government, which in larger wealthier countries would be held by two ministers, the effect of his absence on the administration can be very serious. The same applies *mutatis mutandis* to civil servants: it is not only Ministers

who cannot be found at home. Indeed there is provision in Civil Service regulations in a number of countries for long recuperative leave overseas — paradoxically still called home leave in some states. Presumably such regulations have not been retained without reason. Some thought has apparently been given to them because the incidence of such leave has been greatly reduced in many countries.[9]

III.

How far do small states themselves wish to encourage the consideration of their position and problems as a special case? Do they feel in danger of exchanging the inferior position of the last of the colonies for an equally inferior position of small independent nation? They have resisted the notion that, in terms of UN General Assembly voting rights, they should be in any way inferior to other larger and more powerful states. Is the concept that small states form a group whose problems can be lumped together repugnant to them? Is it true, as the UN publication suggests, that 'the officials of small states lack the professional interchange and stimulation which is provided in large countries by associations, publications, conventions, etc. . . live in a condition of professional loneliness . . . [and] find great difficulty in meeting colleagues from other countries or learning of administrative development elsewhere'? Certainly, there must be many officials in small states who would question the proposition that their professional activities suffer from the fact that 'appropriate visitors on official business or tourism are few'.

That small states have special administrative problems is scarcely open to doubt: of greater importance is our ability to prescribe solutions. Could not more be done in the interests of administrative efficiency to cut across political boundaries? New states may be largely concerned with nation-building but there are precedents of successful international institutions, cooperation and action.

I think, for example, of the union of civil servants in the Caribbean. There are also organisations of states in Africa, Latin America and the Caribbean. Can such international institutions only be justified when they supplement or reinforce the operations of the national institutions of which they are composed? Would it be feasible as the next step to encourage the demise of national institutions in favour of international ones? Recent history in the Caribbean as well as in the regions does not encourage us to believe so. Federalism may not be the answer. But one hopes more will be done to soften the nationalistic approach. Thus if large states (like the UK and the USA) often fail to be self-sufficient in manpower and are ready to acknowledge the fact, why should small states be expected to be self-sufficient?

For the rest, governments of small states will, despite their vulnerability, have to consider how they can become better informed —

and therefore tougher. In a broader context, they will have to be tougher about their aid policies (what can be done to enable them to understand and identify the various motives of aid donors?) and in resisting pressures from multinational firms. In the more narrowly administrative area they will have to be tougher about their public personnel policies — increasing civil service salaries to bring them into line with private sector salaries related to international salary levels can be counter-productive. They will also have to be tougher over appointment and promotion practices. Established posts should not be filled by the 'best person available' if that person is unsuitable. It may be wiser in such circumstances to make only a temporary appointment so as to avoid being burdened with deadweight later on when better people become available. The brain drain has been one reason for the promotion of inadequate people, but there are dangers in promoting merely because a promotion post becomes available. Governments will have to be tougher too about their training policies — about their attitudes to experts and about policies of decentralisation. But the roots of many administrative problems lie in society at large, and reforms of administrative systems and procedures are not merely a matter for politicians and civil servants.

NOTES

1. Fifteen UN experts who had worked in small states (of whom the author of this paper was one) collaborated with Mr. L.L. Barber, himself a UN expert, in the production of the UNPAD report which was issued in August, 1968.
2. Ved Ghandi has argued, though not entirely convincingly, to the contrary (Nigerian Journal of Economic Studies, July 1970).
3. Reliable comparative statistics have not proved easy to obtain. Notably there are problems which relate to the inclusion or exclusion of unestablished employees, casual labour and those working for parastatal organisations.
4. The real costs of a proliferation of ministries should be brought home. Is it possible to justify Trinidad's 18 ministries compared, say, with the 10 of Lesotho, a country of comparable population? Are the comparable facts even available to governments of small states?
5. *Status and Problems of Very Small States and Territories:* UNITAR Series No. 3, N.Y. 1969, Chapter 3.
6. The following statement was made by a Lesotho Minister after independence, on the first occasion he chaired a meeting of the training committee:
   '. . . the Minister informed the Committee that the Cabinet was very dissatisfied with the Civil Service. Indeed it was beginning to wonder whether it was wise to accelerate Africanisation because of irresponsibility and disloyalty amongst civil servants. If Permanent Secretaries and Heads of Departments were loyal, then their subordinates would follow their example. We know that when we came into power 99 per cent of the service supported the opposition. Even today that figure is 90 per cent. 'We ministers', he said, 'feel that people are appointed by the Public Service Commission because they are

members of an opposition party. We can foresee the time when we shall
have to go overseas for recruitment to the Civil Service.'

7. The role of discussion in the solution of administrative and teaching
problems (International Review of Administrative Sciences Vol. XXXV,
No. 1, 1969).

8. Thus, for example, the UN Local Government report postulated the
creation of 25 elected ward councils as a *sine qua non* of its proposals.
The former Colonial Governor considered that their creation was not
justified.

9. The regulations serve to illustrate what the wife of a prominent citizen
of one of the Caribbean islands had in mind when asked by the author
what she considered to be the main problem of small less developed
states. 'There is only one problem' she said, 'that is the problem of living
in them.'

REFERENCES

Ved P. Ghandi: 'Are There Economies of Size in Government Current
Equality in Developing Countries?' (Nigerian Journal
of Economic and Social Studies, Vol. 12, July 1970).

B.L. Jacobs: 'The Role of Discussion in the Solution of
Administrative and Teaching Problems' (International
Review of Administrative Sciences, Vol. XXXV, No. 1,
1969).

UNITAR: *Status and Problems of Very Small States and
Territories* (UNITAR Series No. 3, New York, 1969).

UNITAR: *Small States and Territories: Status and Problems*
Report by Jacques Rapaport, Ernest Muteba, Joseph J.
Therattil (New York, Arno Press, 1971; particularly
Chapter III).

UN Public *Comparative Analysis of the Distinctive Public*
Administrative Division: *Administration Problems of Small States and
Territories* (August, 1968).

7. THE POTENTIAL FOR AUTONOMOUS MONETARY POLICY IN SMALL DEVELOPING COUNTRIES

Asgar Ally *

Summary

This paper evaluates the potential for autonomous monetary policy in small developing countries (SDCs) in general, and Jamaica in particular. Monetary policies based on the traditions and conditions in the advanced countries have only limited applicability in the SDCs and existing monetary theory is inadequate to cope with their problems. Smallness however has both advantages and disadvantages, and the major limitations to autonomous monetary policy in the SDCs are due not so much to smallness but rather to the structural rigidities which are found in these economies. The potential for autonomous monetary policy resides in skilful manipulation of the 'control' variables and in the process of economic integration. Monetary policy in the SDCs therefore has to operate at two levels — first to service the existing system of production and exchange, and secondly to manage money and credit in such a way as to facilitate the process of structural transformation and economic integration.

1. The concept of autonomous monetary policy

The concept of autonomous monetary policy refers to a situation under which the monetary authority of a country can implement monetary policies to tackle internal economic problems without being hindered by economic and financial relationships with other countries. The concept is therefore closely related to that of 'monetary dependence'.

According to Thomas (1965, p.3), for an economy to be classed as a 'dependent monetary' economy, the following four conditions would have to be evaluated:

   (i) the degree to which the economy is *resilient to changes in the rest of the world*. This would depend *inter alia* on (a) the level and rate at which domestic real per capita incomes are increasing over a relevant period, and (b) the extent of unemployment of existing resources.

   (ii) the degree to which the economy *depends on the rest of the world* to maintain and increase internal levels of employment,

*The author wishes to acknowledge helpful comments on the paper by Mr. C.T. Brown of the Research Department of Bank of Jamaica and participants at the Conference, especially Dudley Seers, Percy Selwyn, and in particular the Governor of the Bank of Jamaica, Mr. G. Arthur Brown, of whom the author is a perpetual student. As is customary the author alone must take responsibility for what is written in the paper.

144

output, demand and prices (generating factors).
- (iii) the degree to which monetary and financial institutions (as well as individuals and government) have *a high propensity to invest in foreign assets.*
- (iv) the degree to which the autonomous elements in the monetary system attach importance to *financing the 'generating' factors* not only by lending to them more of their funds than to other sectors (independent sectors), but also lending to these generating factors at an increasing rate in comparison with other sectors.

In most SDCs an analysis of these conditions will suggest that the economies can be classified as 'dependent monetary economies'. However, some elements of monetary dependence are present even in large countries, especially since modern communications have broken national barriers and have brought nearly all economies into a network of interrelationships.

2. The theory, objectives and scope for monetary policies in SDCs

The scope for monetary policies in the SDCs is related to their basic structural characteristics and major economic problems. The problems of structural transformation in SDCs have been extensively analysed by Demas (1965) from the point of view of economic development in general, and by Thomas (1965, 1972) in the context of 'monetary dependence' and the implications for monetary policy. Both writers agree that structural transformation is synonymous with economic development and that economic policy as a whole must be designed to effect this. Most SDCs are either colonies of a metropolitan power or have been at some stage of their history. Their economies are integrated into those of the metropolitan power in such a way that SDCs, whether politically independent or not, are hardly more than a locus of production made up of a number of fragments tenuously held together largely by government controls — themselves borrowed from the metropolitan powers. Monopolistic conditions of production and exchange prevail in these economies together with a heavy reliance on the export of a few primary products. Manufacturing in most cases is limited by the low level of domestic purchasing power and is confined mainly to import substitution or 'screwdriver' type of operations. High levels of unemployment and underemployment of labour may exist while income distribution is frequently highly skewed. There may be significant economic and social dualism while industrial linkages are normally very marginal. The propensity to import is very high and there is a wide divergence between the structures and pattern of domestic consumption and domestic production.

The economies of the SDCs are highly open both structurally and functionally. Structural openness relates to the fact that foreign trade and payments dominate domestic economic transactions. Exports therefore play a crucial role and contribute more to the determination of income levels and employment than investment changes as in the Keynesian-type models. Functional openness of these economies leads to the integration of domestic money and capital market institutions with other branches of the multinational corporations and with the metropolitan countries. Thus both the real sector and the financial sector are controlled from outside. There is a high degree of capital mobility between the SDCs and the metropolitan countries, and being unable to compete in either 'breadth, depth or resiliency' a substantial portion of domestic savings is channelled overseas and the remainder is utilised mainly to finance imports. Given the high ratio of foreign to domestic investments, long-term capital inflows become crucial to the operation of the economic system: the inflows finance expansion in domestic production and at the same time narrow the deficit in the current account of the balance of payments. In addition the branches of a few multinational corporations dominate domestic production − both in export- and import-substitution industries.

Both Demas (1966) and Lewis (1961) are of the view that the scope of monetary policies is limited by the structural features of the SDC's while Thomas (1972) is of the view that 'the structural relations of these economies (Jamaica, Trinidad and Tobago and Guyana) are sufficiently rigid to make the Central Monetary Authorities nearly impotent'. On the other hand Best (1966, p.31) considers that 'the bulk of the potential for explaining has still to come from a more systematic examination of the instruments of control rather than the "natural" variables themselves'. Consequently such problems as foreign ownership become inevitable in an SDC only when the economy is assumed to be unable to devise techniques of organisation, production and marketing which would free it from reliance on foreign corporations.

On the more narrowly defined monetary issues, many Latin American countries have been unable to cope with the inflation resulting from expansionary monetary policies. This resulted in the debate between the 'monetarists' and the 'structuralists' concerning the usefulness of monetary and fiscal policies. However we agree with Campos (1961) that it is not that monetary policy tools are ineffective but that great care must be taken in the choice of monetary policy instruments and that targets must not be incompatible. We will have to treat the structural symptoms until we are in a position to remove the structural maladies.

It is in this context that the Central Bank is a strategic institution − in terms of both its 'internationality' and its statutory powers of control in such a way that the management of money and credit is closely related to necessary changes in domestic economic structure.

146

In the advanced countries monetary policies are designed mainly to manage money and credit so as to maintain internal and external equilibrium and full employment and to avoid inflation in an already well-developed economic system. In the SDCs monetary policy has to be concerned with the building of an economic system that will reduce economic dependence and render the economy more amenable to control from inside. It is on these criteria that the effectiveness of monetary policy in the SDCs must be judged.

3. The instruments of monetary policy

In this section we will discuss the nature of the instruments of monetary policy and assess their potential effectiveness in the SDCs. Particular attention will be placed on such issues as unemployment, income distribution, the role of the multinational corporation, measures to facilitate economic and financial integration and the overall problem of economic transformation. The main instruments of monetary policy to be discussed will include bank rate, open market operations, reserve ratios, rediscounting, public sector credit, selective credit controls, import deposits, exchange control, exchange rate adjustment and moral suasion. The experiences of the Bank of Jamaica in using these instruments will also be discussed.

(i) Bank rate

The bank rate is the classical monetary policy instrument designed either to expand or to contract domestic credit so as to maintain equilibrium in the economy. In practice, however, unless an economy is virtually closed with regard to both current and capital financial transactions, the chances of pursuing an independent interest-rate policy are small. Most SDCs are necessarily open economies and as such face similar problems to the open developed economy. The effectiveness of changes in the bank rate is further limited by the shortage of loanable funds and the relationship of the multinational corporations — both financial and non-financial — with their head offices in the metropolitan countries.

If domestic interest rates are low in relation to overseas rates there will be a tendency for domestic funds to flow overseas in search of higher earnings. This is facilitated by the integration of domestic and metropolitan money and capital markets. Foreign businesses will tend to borrow locally instead of overseas since it is cheaper to do so. This action will result in a decline in capital inflows and reduce the volume of credit available to local businesses and individuals. On the other hand if domestic interest rates are too high in relation to overseas rates there will be a tendency for 'hot money' to flow into the economy, possibly resulting in an inflationary situation in so far as this causes an increase in the domestic money supply.

In most SDCs, funds available for local long-term investment are scarce, whether for institutional or other reasons, and hence there is a case for Central Bank policy to be directed to keeping interest rates high so as to ensure the efficient use of capital. But such a policy might discourage local development and encourage an inflow of hot money. Equally a policy of low interest rates, while possibly encouraging domestic investment, may make capital artificially cheap and encourage the substitution of capital for labour. However, these arguments may not be of central importance in determining central bank interest policy, since bank rate may have little influence on market rates of interest. In practice, effective or market interest rates are far higher than bank rate, mainly because of demand and supply conditions together with the pattern of mobilisation and use of domestic savings. Bank rate as such is therefore not an effective instrument for dealing with the allocation of credit in the SDCs.

Experience in Jamaica has shown that such factors as the fragmented and underdeveloped nature of domestic capital markets, the integration of the main productive and financial sectors with the economies of the United States and the United Kingdom, and sub-optimal allocation of savings leave the Central Bank with no alternative but to move bank rate in line with the changes of bank rate in the United Kingdom and the United States.

Twenty years ago, when Jamaica was under the Currency Board system, it was pointed out that when the Bank of England raised bank rate, Jamaica was obliged to follow suit although opposite conditions prevailed in the two economies. 'In Jamaica there is great unemployment and underemployment. Investment of new capital, in all fields, is badly needed. Nevertheless what happened was the automatic transfer of the policies adopted in the UK. Interest rates went up, credit was restricted and new investment accordingly made more difficult, thus checking the badly needed expansion of the economy which is required if an inroad is to be made in the heavy body of unemployment and if the standard of living is to be raised' (Analyst 1953, p.54). This is still true of Jamaica in 1972, despite the dismantling of the currency board system and the establishment of a Central Bank over eleven years ago. The underlying structural rigidities in the economic system make any use of bank rate ineffective.

(ii) Rediscounting facilities and loans to commercial banks

As lender of last resort the Central Bank is in a position to influence credit expansion or contraction through its rediscounting and loan facilities to commercial banks. These facilities can also help to make bank rate effective and influence the allocation of credit. But the potential of these facilities for effecting an independent monetary policy is limited by a number of factors. First, in most countries the

Central Bank is a relatively new institution and it takes some time before the commercial banks become adjusted to its presence and the use of its facilities. Secondly, since many of the commercial banks are branches of overseas banks they tend to use their head office facilities when they are short of funds and to reduce their indebtedness when they are in surplus. Thirdly, the commercial banks find it more economical to finance import requirements – an important portfolio in most small countries – through their head offices. Fourthly, some of the commercial banks operating in small countries are branches of large multinational banks with assets many times that of the Central Monetary Authority; the resources of the Central Bank are limited and the amount of funds available for rediscounting facilities and loans to commercial banks may be inadequate to influence domestic monetary conditions. Finally the Central Monetary Authority has to be very cautious in making loans to commercial banks since this could contribute to balance-of-payments problems because of the high propensity to import.

In Jamaica several types of loans and rediscounted facilities are available to the commercial banks.

(a) Direct loans: These are made to assist a commercial bank with a liquidity problem, where for example the bank has incurred a loss in the clearing or has become illiquid because of a loss of a large amount of deposits.

(b) Loans from the Bankers Deposit and Loan Fund: Commercial banks deposit surplus balances in this Fund. Loans are made from the Fund to banks which are short of liquid funds. Banks normally utilise this facility before borrowing under (a) above.

(c) Rediscounting facilities: Banks are allowed to rediscount loans made by them for a variety of purposes including construction projects, export financing, public utilities, tourism, manufacturing, agriculture and other loans for productive purposes. The aim here is twofold: first, to ensure that a temporary illiquid situation does not prevent banks from making loans for productive purposes, and secondly, as a means of diverting credit into the productive sectors as against the non-productive sectors.

(d) Loans tied to long-term deposits with the Bank of Jamaica by the commercial banks: This arrangement was instituted to enable the commercial banks to sell foreign exchange to the Bank of Jamaica in return for Jamaican dollars which in turn would be deposited with the Bank of Jamaica. If the bank making the deposit becomes short of funds it would borrow against the deposit rather than withdrawing it.

The objects of these arrangements are primarily to encourage the commercial banks to make use of the facilities of the Central Bank and, to the extent that they do so, to operate within the framework of domestic policy.

Loans under (a) and (c) above are money-creating. They add to demand and may create price inflation and/or foreign exchange loss. As regards discounting facilities, although they help to divert the flow of loan funds into productive areas of economic activity, the funds released may be used for loans to finance imported consumer goods. Loans under the Bankers Deposit and Loan Fund have a neutral effect: they perform a redistribution function rather than a money-creating function. This has been a convenient device for assisting smaller and younger banks with a relatively small deposit base. It also helps to cushion the effects of a contractionary monetary policy which tends to affect the smaller banks more than the larger and more established banks.

Loans under (d) have a positive money-supply effect and a neutral balance-of-payments effect since they add to money supply but any foreign exchange loss is covered by the original sale of foreign exchange by the banks to the Bank of Jamaica.

The experience in Jamaica has been that as the economy develops and becomes more diversified the influence of the Central Bank over the policies of the commercial banks becomes more significant. Moreover, as the commercial banks become localised their operations become more grounded in the Jamaican economy, and the scope for monetary policy improves.

(iii) Public sector credit

The Central Bank acts as the Government's banker. Government income and expenditure are significant and therefore the operations of Government accounts affect the money supply. Payments by Government serve to increase the stock of money held by the rest of the community, while Government's receipts tend to reduce it. If deficits are financed by borrowing from the Central Bank, the money supply is likely to increase.

Since it is easy for Government to borrow from the Central Bank, there is a tendency in many developing countries for governments to misuse this facility. This leads to balance-of-payments problems and widespread inflation resulting from increases in the money supply without commensurate increases in real product. Consequently, Central Bank loans to government and the amount of government securities that they can hold are usually fixed by law.

In Jamaica, the limit to holdings of Government securities by the Bank of Jamaica is fixed at seven times the Bank's authorised capital. Moreover, the currency issue is required to be backed 50 per cent by foreign assets. In practice the currency issue has been backed by over 80 per cent in foreign assets, mainly sterling. So far there has been little need for Government to borrow from the Central Bank since it has found no problem in obtaining its financing requirements from the domestic private sector and overseas organisations.

(iv) Open market operations

Open market operations involve the Central Bank's intervention into the market on its own initiative to buy or sell Government securities in order to effect changes in the money supply. The efficacy of open market operations therefore presupposes the existence of a broad and active securities market. This exists to only a limited degree in most small countries. Furthermore the existence of a low money multiplier in most small countries necessitates larger open market transactions in order to achieve the same effect on the money supply in the small countries as in developed countries. Consequently successful open market operations would entail wide fluctuations in interest rates. Most governments in the developing world take the view that the price of Government securities must remain within a narrow band of stable and relatively low interest rates. These are usually unrelated to rates outside the supervised markets. It is thought that stable prices and relatively low interest rates are a sign of respectability and engender domestic and international confidence, whereas high rates impede investment. In any event Central Bank activity in most small countries is devoted more to the development of the capital markets than to open market operations. Moreover, financial institutions and individuals in small countries have a high propensity to invest in foreign assets and this is facilitated by the close association of local money and capital markets with overseas financial centres. In addition, the ability of local financial institutions to borrow from their overseas head offices limits the effectiveness of open market operations.

(v) Reserve ratios

Variable reserve ratios of commercial banks have been used effectively as a tool of monetary policy in small countries. Thus, under banking legislation in Sterling Area countries the liquid assets ratios which commercial banks are required to maintain range from a minimum of 15 per cent to a maximum of 30 per cent of total deposits.

Although it may be objected to as interfering with the market mechanism, this system is a direct means of stabilising money and credit conditions and the balance of payments. Whenever there is excessive liquidity in the banking system there is a temptation for banks to expand credit, particularly for consumption purposes. Because of the high import co-efficient, balance-of-payments problems could arise. The Central Bank can prevent this by raising the liquid assets ratio, thereby reducing the banks' ability to expand credit. Funds thus sterilised could then be channelled to productive sectors through rediscounting facilities.

However, a number of problems result from the use of changes in reserve ratios to regulate credit. First, it tends to affect smaller banks more than larger ones. In most small countries the banking system is dominated by a few large banks, and banking practices are very conventional. Efforts are often made to introduce more banks so as to increase competition and force existing banks to adjust their operations to the economic and social environment in which they operate. Thus any measure which inhibits the expansion of the new banks, some of which are indigenous, conflicts with the objectives of reform. The expatriate banks also have access to head office funds, and to the extent that they draw on these resources to lend locally, their action could run contrary to domestic policy.

Because of the undeveloped nature of the money and long-term capital markets in SDC's, and the desire of savers for liquidity, currency in circulation tends to be a substantially higher proportion of the money supply than in other countries, and banks have to remain relatively liquid and have adequate reserves. Thus if currency represents 60 per cent of the money supply and reserves 25 per cent, the money multiplier is only 1.4. In order to obtain a 3 per cent decrease in money supply it would be necessary to raise the reserve ratio by 5 per cent. In the financially mature countries where currency represents about 20 per cent of money supply and bank reserves about 10 per cent, it is necessary to increase the required reserve ratio by only 1 per cent to achieve a 3 per cent decline in money supply.[1]

In Jamaica we have raised the liquidity ratio twice to restrict excessive credit expansion and correct related balance of payments problems. In 1969 the rate was raised by 2½ per cent, from 15 per cent to 17½ per cent, mainly to divert bank credit from consumption to production. In June 1972 the ratio was again increased, this time by 1 per cent to 18½ per cent. In order not to disturb the flow of credit to the productive sectors the Bank has kept open its rediscounting facilities.

(vi) Selective credit controls

Although selective credit controls are a useful policy instrument, their application in small developing countries may be limited by conflicts between various policy goals. Thus in small countries with highly open economies excessive credit creation does not necessarily lead to internally generated inflation, because domestic output is easily supplemented by imports, and hence instead of inflation a balance-of-payments problem arises. On the other hand credit controls must be carefully administered to ensure that domestic production is not affected. But many locally manufactured goods have a relatively high import content: many small countries in a hurry to industrialise have established a large number of 'screwdriver' industries, which require the importation of finished and semi-finished products for their operations. Where the number of workers employed in manufacturing industries is significant, this poses a conflict between employment policy and foreign exchange reserves policy.

Selective credit controls have been used in Jamaica and Trinidad and

Tobago to regulate domestic borrowing by foreign-owned and controlled business enterprises. When liquidity conditions are tight overseas or when domestic interest rates are lower many foreign-owned and foreign-controlled companies tend to increase their local borrowing. By establishing ceilings for these companies the Central Bank can limit the amount of credit that banks may extend to them.

(vii) Import deposits

The use of pre-deposits on imports is becoming popular given high import leakages and the other open characteristics of dependent economies. The purpose of this instrument is to increase the cost of credit and restrict its availability for import expenditure, while at the same time mopping up excessive liquidity. However, structural factors in the dependent economy tend to militate against its effectiveness. First, it is likely that the financial institutions will make credit available to finance the pre-deposit requirement. Such loans are riskless and the deposit in itself guarantees the loans. Also the financing of imports is an important area of the operations of commercial banks, and in order to maintain their level of profits and retain their customers the banks are likely to meet the pre-deposit requirements at the expense of credit to other sectors. Also the local importing houses have long association with overseas exporting houses and these may provide credit.

The effectiveness of import deposits is therefore dependent on the simultaneous imposition of direct controls and adequate arrangements to absorb liquidity at the time when deposits are refunded. The potential of import deposits as a monetary policy instrument would however be significant if used as part of a monetary policy package to restrict imports.

(viii) Exchange controls

In small dependent economies, exchange controls are considered important in preventing the export of domestic savings. They thus encourage the development of the local money and capital markets. Furthermore, since the openness of an economy limits the effectiveness of monetary policy and its potential for independent action, exchange control may be necessary to ensure some degree of independence to monetary authorities in protecting their own economies. The case for exchange control is therefore based on the need to insulate the domestic economy against adverse financial conditions overseas and give the domestic monetary authorities greater power to regulate capital outflows and to some extent capital inflows.

Capital tends to flow from small countries in search of greater security in the metropolitan markets. With exchange control such movements are regulated. This permits greater flexibility in pursuing an independent interest rate policy which reflects the economic conditions of the domestic economy. Exchange controls also make it possible for the monetary authority to pursue a more realistic foreign exchange policy in that the use of foreign exchange reserves becomes more regulated. This facilitates foreign exchange budgeting. The chief arguments against exchange control are largely psychological. As soon as exchange control is imposed some local investors panic because they have been accustomed to invest overseas freely without any consideration for the needs of the domestic economy. It is also claimed that exchange controls deter foreign investors and thus inhibit development. On the other hand the existence of exchange controls prevents nationals from frittering away the foreign exchange reserves and thus ensures that reserves are available to meet the genuine foreign exchange needs of the country, including the returns to foreigners on their investment. Exchange control is therefore welcomed by foreign investors.

(ix) Exchange rate policy

Changes in exchange rates are primarily intended to bring the balance of payments into equilibrium. In the case of small countries however, changes in the exchange rate may be either passive or active. Passive changes reflect a decision to follow the international currency to which the currency of the SDC is linked in instances of devaluation, revaluation or floating. Active changes in exchange rates by the monetary authorities of the SDCs are deliberate policy decisions in the sense that action is taken to change the exchange rate or to establish multiple exchange rates for purely internal economic reasons notwithstanding the position of the reserve currency.

The countries of the Commonwealth Caribbean have been largely passive in exchange rate policy. Some SDCs — especially those in Africa and Central America — have pursued an active exchange rate policy to aid the process of structural change and economic development.

There are two schools of thought on the pursuance of an active exchange rate policy in the Caribbean. First, there are those who regard devaluation as a strategic policy decision to foster economic development; secondly it is argued that given the underlying structural rigidities in the system, devaluation as a policy prescription would be disadvantageous to the domestic economy. Lewis contends that 'nearly all West Indian currencies are heavily over-valued in relation to our foreign trade policies and our current levels of money income and productivity. This is the basic reason for our high and steadily mounting unemployment' (Lewis, 1972, p.4). On the other hand it is argued that for small countries with narrow resource bases and supply inelasticities, devaluation as such does not help the export sector and tends to move the terms of trade against the devaluing country. The welfare or 'cost of living' arguments tend to outweigh the 'production' arguments since there is little likelihood of increasing exports and consequently income and employment. In so far as exports are predetermined, the gains to the small country from a devaluation are likely to be marginal. Even if gains are experienced most of them would accrue to foreign-owned enterprises, which dominate the export sector. In addition the high cost of production in the SDCs could be attributed not so much to high wages — wages account for a relatively low percentage of total costs in such industries as bauxite and petroleum — but rather to inefficient management and high profits as a result of the monopolistic nature of production and exchange.

These arguments assume severe inelasticities of supply. But in circumstances where there is surplus productive capacity, and local producers are uncompetitive both in export and import replacement industries, an adjustment of the exchange rate may well lead to an increase in output and employment. Such a devaluation should however be viewed as part of an entire economic package, designed to ensure that its benefits are not immediately absorbed by rising costs. Moreover, in so far as the benefits of devaluation may accrue to a few foreign firms or there are unfavourable distributional effects, these may be counteracted in other ways, e.g. through taxation.

In any event, to argue that exchange rate policy is ineffective is not to conclude that the rate arrived at by passively following the rate for some international currency is in some sense 'correct'. An active exchange rate policy must feature as an integral part of overall economic policy, whatever the case might be for devaluation in particular circumstances. It is not, however, easy to establish the correct international value of SDC currencies. (Indeed recent events have suggested that it is far from easy to do so for advanced country currencies.) There are no markets for these countries' currencies, and balance-of-payments equilibrium (in so far as it can be arrived at by choice of some hypothetical correct exchange rate) is only one of the policy objectives of such countries. Exchange rate policy must be determined primarily by the needs of the country for development and structural transformation, and it is hardly likely that these needs will be met by an automatic and fixed relation to a metropolitan currency.

(x) Moral suasion

Moral suasion as a tool of monetary policy is used extensively by Central Banks in the more advanced countries, especially where there is close cooperation between the private and public sectors. Commercial bank managers recognising the wide range of powers available to the Central Bank usually respond to moral suasion, making it unnecessary for the authorities to resort to the law.

In small countries the situation is more difficult, especially where the commercial banks are branches of larger banks in the metropolitan countries. Here control is exercised from the head offices in the metropolitan countries; the local bank managers, in as much as they might be inclined to respond to moral suasion, have to abide by the decisions of the head office. In some cases the head office is a substitute for the local Central Bank and this relationship weakens the position of the local Central Bank in dealing with the local branch. Moral suasion was however an invaluable policy tool in the early development for the Bank of Jamaica and is still important. As the economy becomes more sophisticated however, and the Central Bank asserts its role in the economy, moral suasion in some cases is not effective.

Thus, it is those control instruments which interfere with the market mechanism (selective credit controls, import deposits) and those which insulate the domestic economy from the rest of the world, such as exchange controls, that have the greatest potential for both remedial and corrective monetary policy in the SDCs. Experience in Jamaica has shown the importance of both selective controls and exchange controls. Selective credit controls have been used to limit the domestic borrowings of foreign-owned and controlled companies and to divert credit from consumption – mainly of imports – to mainly indigenous productive enterprises, both in the area of import-substituting and of export-oriented activities. The extension of exchange controls to all foreign currencies (including sterling) has enabled the Bank of Jamaica to increase its ability to manage the domestic economy and to regulate the outflows of domestic savings. Thus the Bank of Jamaica is in a better position to manage its external reserves and conserve the use of scarce foreign exchange.

But there are obvious limitations on the effectiveness of such instruments. One of the areas of greatest difficulty is the activities of the multinational corporations. Increasing use is being made of monetary instruments in the advanced industrial countries in order to control the activities of these corporations. 'Multinational corporations, because of their size and international connexions, have a certain flexibility for escaping regulations imposed in one country. The nature and effectiveness of traditional policy instruments – monetary policy, fiscal, anti-trust policy, taxation policy, wage and income policy – change when important segments of the economy are foreign-owned' (Hymer, 1970, p.447). Many of the instruments at the disposal of SDCs in the area of monetary policy may well be feeble in relation to the scale of activity of the multinational corporations.

4. The money supply, balance of payments and inflation

In the process of economic development, the major problems confronting the monetary authorities in the SDCs are the balance of payments, inflation and unemployment. These problems are all related to the level of the money supply, and since the monetary authority regulates the money supply, its role in the process of economic development becomes crucial. In a study on Jamaica, Taylor (1972) has demonstrated that variations in the money supply independent of the autonomous movements in the balance of payments are likely to influence in a very real way the subsequent behaviour of income, imports and the level of reserves.

In Keynesian terms the SDCs can be regarded as economies producing at capacities far below full employment; consequently monetary policy should be geared towards economic expansion. But the monetary authorities are required to walk the tightrope; they have to pursue an expansionary policy in order to increase output and reduce unemployment, but they also have to devise ways and means of containing the consequential balance of payments and inflation problems. Because of the high propensity to import in the SDCs, any increase in the money supply to stimulate employment is reflected in the balance of payments, since a substantial portion of income generated is spent on imports. This interrelationship between the money supply and the balance of payments acts as a powerful constraint on the ability of the monetary authority to expand the money supply. Thus in the final analysis it is the balance of payments which sets a limit to development.

In some Latin American countries where restrictions have been placed on imports excessive increases in the money supply have resulted in chronic inflation and periodic devaluation of the domestic currency. At the same time the stimulus to growth of these policies has been very limited because of rigidities in the domestic productive structure. Thus while monetary policy through selective credit controls, import deposits and exchange rate policies can successfully curtail expenditure on imports of consumer goods, regulate capital outflows and make exports cheaper on foreign markets, there is no guarantee that domestic production will increase and be sufficiently diversified to take up the slack of locally under-utilised resources. Hence the resultant balance of payments and inflationary problems which are basically of a structural nature. In the SDCs this problem is likely to persist since the resource base is very narrow and the size of the internal market does not allow for substantial economies of scale. It may therefore be necessary to live with a moderate degree of inflation since this is a necessary accompaniment to growth and structural change. The crucial choice is between a moderate degree of inflation or a high level of unemployment. However, excessive increases in the money supply without commensurate increases in production could result in both unemployment and inflation of the type which has occurred in some Latin American countries. Here the strain on monetary policies was too great and the targets incompatible.

It is thus necessary to harmonise monetary, fiscal and commercial policies in such a way that they complement each other. It is in this respect that the SDCs, despite their structural problems, are at an advantage because of their small size. The 'importance of being unimportant' in external commercial policies, more unified national markets, and greater potential social cohesion and greater flexibility, all facilitate more effective use of the manipulable variables of control.

How then could monetary policy alleviate unemployment? We have shown that increasing the money supply by financing government expenditures alone will not suffice. However, since the process of economic development requires the more efficient use of idle resources, increases in the money supply at a greater rate than increases in the real product could play a useful role in alleviating unemployment so long as increments in money supply are diverted to idle resources, especially labour. This would entail the institution of a wages, incomes and prices policy to ensure that increments in output and productivity are channelled towards the creation of new jobs rather than an increase in the incomes of those already employed. Increases in the money supply would have to be carefully managed so that the new funds created are channelled to identifiable projects in agriculture, industry, transportation, tourism, etc. This policy would tend to squeeze fixed income earners, but a Central Bank Governor in an SDC has to be more concerned about those who are without employment than those who already have incomes. It is in this context that institutional changes, and in particular wage policies and the establishement of development banks, play a vital complementary role to that of purely monetary policies.

The policy of the Bank of Jamaica over the last ten years has been directed towards the maintenance of internal financial stability and international confidence in the Jamaican economy so as to attract foreign investment. It was only after 1969 that serious consideration was given to changing the structure of the economy by manipulating the control variables. So far increases in the money supply — tightly regulated by statute — have been very conservative and there has been little pressure on the bank to move away from this policy. The economy has relied heavily on foreign investment which provided capital for productive enterprises and helped to bridge the gap on the current account of the balance of payments. The deficit on visible trade rose from J$29.6m. in 1962 to J$175m. in 1971. Imports (largely of consumer goods) grew very rapidly while exports stagnated, especially after 1969 — despite a 'passive' devaluation of 14.7 per cent against the US dollar in 1967. From 1969 to 1971 exports increased by J$40m. — from J$243.7m.— while imports rose by nearly J$100m — from J$363.3m. to J$458.7m. Foreign investment in Jamaica over the period 1962-1971 has been substantial, almost J$1000m.[2] In the meantime the country's external reserves remained in a healthy position and amounted to J$169m. at the end of March 1972. Capital inflows prevented the inherent balance-of-payments problems from coming to the surface and the monetary authority did not find it necessary to take measures to help correct the structural rigidities in the economic system.

Jamaica's current (1972) balance-of-payments problem has brought to the surface the real structural problems of the economy. Capital inflows have tapered off, largely as a result of the completion of projects in the mining sector; exports are relatively stagnant while imports continue to increase. The Bank of Jamaica has tried to divert credit expansion away from imported consumer goods towards the stimulation of domestic production including construction. Complementary commercial policies have also been undertaken, to restrict the importation of luxury goods and to cut off imports of goods which are produced locally. Thus as the process of structural transformation proceeds greater reliance is necessarily being placed on corrective and remedial monetary policies.

5. Monetary policy and economic integration

Economic integration among SDCs is widely accepted as perhaps the only means by which economic viability in the long run can be ensured. Through economic integration the structure of demand as well as the use of resources is integrated and each integrated unit is vested 'with a potential greater than that of its pre-integrated state' (Brewster and Thomas 1967, 1970).

Financial integration is a crucial part of the process of economic integration. As production and trade expand in the integrated unit, the financial sector must be integrated in order to service the system of production and exchange. Monetary policy in the integrated units has to be harmonised to deal with problems which would arise. Harmonisation of interest rates, integration of money and capital markets, the evolution of a common policy towards the multinational corporations and the management of money and credit as it affects economic transformation, have to be tailored to fit the integrated unit as a whole rather than individual components.

The Commonwealth Caribbean has been gradually moving to some form of economic integration especially since the emergence of the Caribbean Free Trade Area[3] in 1967 and the establishment of the Caribbean Development Bank in 1970. As economic links among the territories increase, the monetary authorities have been active in devising ways and means of strengthening them. Regional settlements arrangements were worked out in 1967 while a regional programme of monetary studies was instituted. There are also regular meetings of the heads of monetary authorities to deal with regional problems and to work out a common stand on international monetary matters as far as is practicable.[4]

(a) The regional settlements arrangements

The main objectives of the regional settlement arrangements are:

(i) to eliminate the sterling commission change which was incorporated in the exchange rate applied by the commercial banks in the purchase and sale of regional currencies. and,

(ii) to promote the use of regional currencies for settlement of transactions within CARIFTA and to improve the facilities for the transfer of funds between the respective units.

(b) The regional programme of monetary studies

The general objectives of the programme are:

(i) to facilitate research on matters of common interest to public financial institutions.

(ii) to promote an interchange of ideas on the experience of different countries in the Commonwealth Caribbean in monetary and credit management, on recent progress in central banking and financial legislation and on overseas developments in money and capital markets.

(iii) to provide training of operational value for personnel employed in public financial institutions throughout the region.

As in many other SDCs, and even advanced countries, the Commonwealth Caribbean is discovering that monetary policy is extremely significant in facilitating the process of economic integration. At the same time, the more self-sufficient the integrated unit becomes, the greater is the potential for autonomous monetary policies.

The evolution of a common currency for the CARIFTA countries would mark the culmination of the process of financial integration with a Central Monetary Authority for the entire integrated unit. In the Caribbean there is already administrative machinery for the coordination of exchange rate policies, especially among the Central Bank territories. However, there are many problems which would have to be overcome before a uniform exchange rate policy could be achieved.

First, the Associated States still operate a Currency Board system and their currency is tied to sterling. These territories are free to re-align their currencies with any other currency which they consider to be in their best interest, but it is difficult to achieve consensus to change the existing relationship. It may also be argued that it is in the economic interest of the Associated States to maintain their links with the United Kindgom.

Secondly, some territories may feel that it is in their interest to pursue a positive exchange rate policy while others may not see any advantages in devaluation. For instance, supply elasticities may be greater in Guyana than in Barbados for a product such as sugar. Thirdly, there are divergences in the type of economic system which individual territories consider appropriate for the economic and social advancement of their peoples. Some members may see devaluation as a positive measure to redistribute income and change the terms of trade between the rural and urban areas. In Jamaica for instance a policy of cheap food prices

160

results in welfare benefits to urbanites to the disadvantage of farmers who produce the food. On the other hand, increased prices for imported foodstuffs which would result from devaluation could act as an incentive for farmers to increase production, since imported food would become less competitive with locally produced foods. Thus in territories where a large proportion of the population is urbanised, the government would be hesitant to devalue the currency.

Fourthly, the individual territories of the Caribbean make up twelve units and it is not easy to achieve consensus. Even where consensus is achieved it would have to be ratified by twelve Parliaments. Thus a coordinated exchange rate policy is difficult to achieve since changes in exchange rate have to be carried out at the same time.

Fifthly, there is no uniform value of the various currencies; the international value of individual currencies varies from country to country. For a common currency to evolve it would be necessary for the international values of the individual currencies to be equalised. In order to overcome this problem, it is suggested that the Central Monetary Authority of the Caribbean create a new currency from which the individual currencies would derive their values. All international transactions would be done through the regional currency. This arrangement would exist until economic inequalities were reduced so that the disadvantages of a uniform currency were not too great to the less developed countries. It is interesting to note that the less developed territories of the Caribbean — the Associated States — have a currency with the highest international value in the Caribbean.

Many obstacles will have to be overcome and many compromises made before a common currency evolves in the Caribbean. However, steps are already being taken in this direction. The Central Banks of the region consult with one another before taking action to change the par values of their currencies. Recently Jamaica devalued her currency by 6.5 per cent after consulting with the other Monetary Authorities in CARIFTA.

6. Conclusions

Many of the debates around monetary policy in western countries have little relevance for the small developing countries. Where the money supply and the level of activity, incomes and prices are so powerfully influenced by external factors, and the power of adjustment of the internal economy is limited by structural constraints, no simple prescription, whether of the 'monetarist' or the neo-Keynesian variety, is likely to be adequate. We have argued that the main purposes of monetary policy should be, first, to reduce monetary dependence and increase the power of autonomous decision-making in the monetary area, and secondly, in association with other kinds of policy, to facilitate the process of structural transformation and economic integration. In this policy area these countries may be helped by their very smallness. In matters such as exchange rate adjustment and exchange controls the SDCs are not likely to experience retaliatory measures by other countries because these measures have virtually no effect on trade with the larger countries.

The experience of Jamaica is that in spite of dependence on the larger developed countries the potential for pursuing autonomous monetary policies which are carefully conceived and administered is not insignificant. There is no doubt that the economy has developed to such a stage where skilful management of the money supply in combination with an incomes policy can reduce unemployment without serious balance-of-payments and inflation problems.

However, the SDCs will continue to depend on foreign trade and investment for economic advancement. They thus need to ensure that autonomous monetary policies are not at cross-purposes with commercial, fiscal and development policies. Constant innovations in monetary policy are therefore necessary in order to achieve success.

NOTES

1.   The money multiplier formula is as follows:

$$m = \frac{1}{c + r(1-c)}$$

(a) Thus if currency ratio (c) is 20% or $\frac{1}{5}$ and reserve ratio (r) is 10% or $\frac{1}{10}$

$$m = 3.57$$

(b) when currency ratio (c) = 60% or $\frac{3}{5}$ and reserve ratio (r) = 25% or $\frac{1}{4}$

$$m = 1.42$$

2.   J$1 = £0.5 sterling.
3.   Jamaica, Trinidad and Tobago, Guyana, Barbados, Belize (British Honduras), Grenada, St. Lucia, St. Kitts-Nevis-Anguilla, St. Vincent Dominica and Montserrat. The Bahamas is not a member of CARIFTA but is a member of the Caribbean Development Bank and the Regional Monetary Studies Programme.
4.   For a detailed analysis of the areas of cooperation among monetary authorities of the Commonwealth Caribbean, see G. Arthur Brown, 'Caribbean Central Bank Cooperation' *The Banker*, April 1972, pp.517-21.

REFERENCES

Analyst: 'Currency and Banking in Jamaica' (Social and Economic Studies, Vol. 1, No. 4, August 1953. I.S.E.R., U.W.I., Jamaica).

Lloyd Best: 'Size and Survival' (New World Quarterly, Vol. 2, No. 3. Guyana Independence Issue, 1966).

Lloyd Best: 'A Model of Pure Plantation Economy' (Social and Economic Studies, Vol. 17, No. 3., September 1968).

H. Brewster, and C.Y. Thomas: 'The Dynamics of West Indian Economic Integration' (Studies in Regional Economic Integration, Vol. 1, I.S.E.R., 1967).

H. Brewster, and C.Y. Thomas: 'Aspects of the Theory of Economic Integration' (Journal of Common Market Studies, Vol. 8, No. 2, December 1969).

Roberto de Oliveria Campos: 'Two views of an Inflation in Latin America' (*Latin American Issues*, H.O. Hirschman, New York, Twentieth Century Fund, 1961).

W.G. Demas: 'The Economics of Small Countries' (McGill University Press, 1965).

Stephen H. Hymer: 'The Efficiency (Contradictions) of Multi-National Corporations' (The American Economic Review, Vol. LX, No. 2, May 1970).

H.G. Johnson: 'Monetary Theory and Policy' (in *Surveys of Economic Theory*, Vol. I, London, MacMillan, 1967).

Charles Kennedy: 'Keynesian Theory in an Open Economy' (Social and Economic Studies, Vol. 15, No. I, March 1966).

W.A. Lewis: *President's Statement to the Second Annual Meeting of the Caribbean Development Bank* (St. Lucia, April 1972).

A. McIntyre, and L. Best: 'A First Appraisal of Monetary Management in Jamaica' *(Social and Economic Studies,* Vol. 10, No. 3).

A.N. McLeod: Credit Expansion in an Open Economy *(Economic Journal,* September 1962).

Dudley Seers: 'The Mechanism of an Open Petroleum Economy' *(Social and Economic Studies,* June 1964).

Leroy Taylor: 'Money, the Balance of Payments and Income Determination in Jamaica' (Social and Economic Studies, Vol. 21, No. 2, June 1972).

C.Y. Thomas: 'Monetary and Financial Arrangements in a Dependent Economy (A study of British Guiana – now Guyana – 1945-62, I.S.E.R., U.W.I., 1965).

C.Y. Thomas: 'The Structure, Performance and Prospects of Central Banking in the Caribbean' (I.S.E.R., U.W.I., 1972).

8. DEVELOPMENT AID TO SMALL COUNTRIES

*Barend A. de Vries**

Summary

Small countries receive more development assistance per capita than large countries. This 'small country bias' is documented with data for official assistance in 1967-69. There are various non-economic considerations influencing the allocation of aid, some of which may favour small countries. On the other hand, there are strong economic reasons why small countries require more aid: diseconomies of scale in the administration of development plans, more limited possibilities of domestic diversification such as economic import substitution, exports of manufactures and the mobilisation of financial savings.

The distribution of official development assistance is a result of many interesting forces — political, technical and economic/financial. Whatever the factors determining the flow of public capital, small countries tend to receive more aid than large ones, both per capita and as a percentage of GNP. One may ask whether the more favourable treatment of small countries has been the result of the recognition of their greater needs. This paper explores why the development of small countries may require more substantial contributions of external capital than that of countries with larger and more diversified economies.

This is a rather novel topic. Some studies of trade orientation and development patterns explicitly take the economic size of countries into account (e.g. Chenery, 1966 and 1972, Chapter III). Demas (1965) has drawn attention to the economic forces which make development in small countries more difficult. However, the theory of capital flows to developing countries makes little, if any, reference to country size. In this respect, it is no exception to the more general theories of development which have been based on the experience of larger countries. While this lopsided attention can probably be explained quite simply, it nevertheless has tended to neglect a broad range of development issues which have only recently come to the foreground. The most urgent of these is represented by the plight of the small, resource-poor country.

*The views expressed are those of the author and not necessarily those of the World Bank with which he is associated. The paper has benefited from comments during the Conference and elsewhere, particularly from Arabinda Kundo, Salvatore Schiavo-Campo, Dudley Seers and Ernest Stern. Cynthia Miller assisted in the preparation of this paper.

164

This paper begins with a factual examination of the extent to which small countries receive more aid than large countries. It then briefly reviews the principal considerations in allocating aid among competing claimants (Section II). Next, it explores the impact of country size on the determinants of external financing requirements – the demand for external assistance. Section IV discusses the obstacles which small countries characteristically encounter in export expansion as a means of reducing their dependence on aid. The final section briefly summarises the economic reasons for allocating more aid to small countries.

I. The 'Small Country Bias'

It will be useful first to look at the facts. The Annex Table presents 77 developing countries' average annual receipts of official loans and grants in 1967-69 and the grant equivalent of these receipts (calculated for each transaction at a discount rate of 10 per cent). Countries are arranged in six groups depending on size and income range. 'Small countries' are defined as those with less than five million people. The income ranges are per capita GNP in 1969 of US $0–150, $150–300, and higher than $300.

The criteria for deciding which is a small or a large country must be arbitrary, although the one used here seems satisfactory for the present purpose. The criterion chosen here follows Demas (1965). When classifying countries in an analysis of export performance (de Vries, 1967), it was found that a GDP of $4 billion was a convenient dividing point, as below this size it may be uneconomic and costly for a country to embark on broadly-based industrial development. All the small countries included in the Annex Table have a GNP well below $4 billion (the highest is $1.6 billion). Size criteria may be different depending on the purpose of the classification. Thus, for example, for both aid administration and economic analysis, the 23 countries of Africa with a GDP of less than $1 billion are small. On the other hand, Ghana, with a GDP of about $1.6 billion and official capital receipts of about $60 million a year plus additional amounts from debt refinancing, is small as far as the design of industrial development is concerned but cannot be regarded as a small country in the coordination and administration of external finance.

The following conclusions may be drawn from the summary of the data in Table 1:

(a) In each of the per capita GNP ranges, small countries receive more aid than large countries. This is true for aid (official grants and loans received) and the grant equivalent of aid, both calculated on a per capita basis and as a percentage of GNP. This conclusion is not invalidated by excluding from the category of large and poorest countries the three largest countries (India, Indonesia and Pakistan).

(b) As per capita GNP increases, aid as a percentage of GNP tends to decrease while *aid per capita tends to increase.* This is true for the nominal value of aid as well as its grant equivalent and for both small and large countries. Thus, the *decline* in aid as a percentage of GNP is not rapid enough to avoid an increase in the absolute value of aid receipts with rising GNP (and an increase in aid per capita with rising per capita GNP).

(c) In all three income ranges, the terms of official assistance received by small countries are on the average more favourable than those of large countries. As can be seen from the last column in Table 1, the difference in the grant element of aid to small and large countries becomes larger as the income level rises. One explanation of this phenomenon could be the recognition – when decisions on the terms of assistance are made – that as income rises the development prospects and aid-bearing capacity of small countries do not improve as rapidly as those of large countries.

(d) There is considerable difference in aid receipts per capita between small and large countries. Moreover, this difference does not appear to decrease markedly with per capita income levels in recipient countries. Small countries receive 2.9 times as much aid (grant equivalent) per capita as large countries in the low-income group, 2.4 times as much in the middle income group, and 3.4 times as much in the higher income group. The corresponding ratios for the grant equivalent of aid as a percentage of GNP are 4.0, 2.2, and 3.7.

(e) The decline in aid as a percentage of GNP with rising income levels is less marked than the difference between small and large countries. Small countries in the highest income range receive more aid as a percentage of GNP than large countries in the lowest income range.

In order to check the conclusions stated under (a) and (b), a regression analysis was carried out, using the data in the Annex Table, with aid and grant equivalent of aid per capita and as a percentage of GNP as dependent variables. The equations with statistically significant results are shown in the Annex. With the exception of equations (19) and (20), generally more significant results were found with logged coefficients. The signs of the coefficients of the equations confirm the conclusions under (a) and (b) as follows:

Conclusions (a) and (b) for all countries: equations (9) – (12);

Conclusion (a): for all countries (1) – (4); for low income countries (21) and (22); and for high income countries (23) and (24);

Conclusion (b): for all countries (5) – (8); for small countries (13) – (16); and for large countries (17) – (20) (except for the latter category no significant results were found for the grant equivalent of aid per capita).[1]

166

Table 1: Aid (Official Grants and Loans) and Grant Equivalent per capita, and as a percentage of GNP in 1967-69.

Country Group[1]	Population (millions)	GNP per capita ($)	Aid[2] US $ per capita	G.E.[3] US $ per capita	Aid Percentage of GNP	G.E. Percentage of GNP	Grant Element Aid[3] Percentage
A1	< 5	≤ 150	8.51	6.36	11.3	8.4	74.8
A2	> 5	≤ 150	3.07 (3.37)[4]	2.17 (2.53)	2.9 (3.7)	2.1 (2.8)	70.7
B1	< 5	150—300	16.77	10.87	7.1	4.6	64.8
B2	> 5	150—300	9.65	4.59	4.5	2.1	47.6
C1	< 5	> 300	27.26	13.26	4.6	2.2	48.6
C2	≥ 5	> 300	14.60	3.85	2.5	0.6	26.4

1. Countries in each group as given in Annex Table. Group averages are weighted by population for per capita data, by GNP for data on percentage of GNP, and by gross aid for grant element.
2. Annual average of official loans and grants in 1967-69.
3. Grant equivalent of grants and loans obtained by multiplying their nominal value by the grant element (at 10 per cent discount) shown in last column.
4. Data in brackets exclude India, Indonesia, and Pakistan.

Source: Annex Table.

II. Consideration in allocating aid

The bias in favour of smaller countries observed in the previous section
need not, of course, reflect purely economic factors. The considerations
underlying the global allocation of official development assistance are
complex and not based exclusively on an assessment of needs. They do
not fit into a precise model.

Bilateral relations may exert considerable influence on the level and
character of assistance e.g. former colonial ties (which may extend to
more intensive cultural and educational contacts), present political-
military alliances, and the investment interests of the donor country.
Donor countries may possess deeper and broader knowledge about
certain recipient countries either historically or recently acquired and
may therefore be more interested in extending assistance to them.
Certain donor governments give special attention to newly independent
countries which suffer from weak administrations and face special
difficulties in establishing social and economic unity. These considerations
may weigh heavily in the allocation of aid to the smaller countries. On
the other hand, special aid relationships between former colonies and
metropolitan powers are far from general and may be diminishing.
Their effect on total aid given to any country could be offset by the
distribution of multilateral aid.

Willingness of a recipient country to 'work with' donor agencies may
extend to receptivity to technical assistance, project preparation and
execution, and sector or macro-economic policy. Donor-recipient
cooperation may increase the effectiveness and volume of aid. Again,
it may be that the smaller countries are more interested in building up
more effective donor-recipient relationships.

The use of country programmes as a framework for operations of
donor agencies may also work in favour of small countries. When it is
not practical to cut these programmes below a minimum, the smaller
countries will tend to receive more aid per capita. On the other hand,
the largest of the LDCs tend to receive proportionally less aid because
of the more substantial absolute amounts involved (Demas, 1965).
Thus, while many small and poor African countries receive aid up
to 8–10 per cent of GNP (and some as much as 25 per cent), the three
largest countries in the poorest category in the Annex Table receive aid
equal to only 2.8 per cent GDP. Total aid to these countries (India,
Indonesia and Pakistan) amounted to US $2.3 billion or 23 per cent
of the total annual aid received by all 77 countries. If these three large
countries were to receive the same proportion of GNP as the smallest
countries in this income group (11.3 per cent), the additional amounts
involved (some US $8.5 billion) would exert a strong claim on
available resources and require significant shifts in the overall
allocation of aid and corresponding bilateral relationships.

A further important consideration is the availability of development projects or, more broadly, absorptive capacity. Most aid is provided for a specific purpose – a development project or sector programme. Through technical assistance, donors can influence recipient countries' ability to utilise aid. Thus absorptive capacity, even over five to seven years, can be improved and may not operate independently in the allocation process. It has been argued that project assistance may increase the supply of aid to small countries.

Donors prefer to make project loans in excess of a minimum amount so as to use staff and technical assistance resources more efficiently. Thus, a combination of project loans could easily overshoot a country's overall requirements. It is difficult to prove this from available data, although it should be recognised that project lending may be bunched. The availability of many different types of projects in development programmes and the possibility of changing the percentage of project cost to be externally financed make the link between project finance and total aid somewhat less rigid and permit, in practice, considerable flexibility in the phasing and level of aid.[2]

A comprehensive assessment of a country's development priorities and prospects and its overall financing requirements would seem to be the most fundamental and conceptually satisfying approach to determining the level and distribution of aid. On this basis, aid allocation would allow for all available relevant information including achievable growth rates, natural endowments, plan preparation and project readiness, fiscal performance, likely composition of investment, production incentives, private investment, etc. It can therefore be considered as a starting point for deciding *total* requirements, with the contributions by individual, bilateral and multilateral donors being decided through an iterative process which involves the above-mentioned considerations.

Objective assessment of a country's aid requirements cannot be expected to be more definitive than the knowledge of the development process itself. It involves a projection of the economy for which no generally accepted and fully satisfactory methodology has been worked out. These projections are subject to conceptual and methodological difficulties which have been extensively discussed in the literature. See, for example, Bruton (1969), Chenery and Strout (1966), and Hawkins (1968). The projections are also subject to data problems and a wide range of value judgements. Built into the assessment of a country's development programme and its domestic and external financing requirements, one finds judgements and assumptions about the country's policies and performance. These judgements may be based on what will or what should happen. Clearly, the projections of future policy intentions are highly uncertain. Furthermore, despite several attempts, no-one has come up with a generally accepted definition of performance; there is no general agreement on what constitutes satisfactory performance or what weight should be given to criteria in determining it. Finally, the emphasis on more equal income distribution, employment and other social aspects of development has thrown doubt on elements of development policy which had been regarded as universal marks of good performance, e.g. high returns on capital investment, rapid pay-off projects, and low increase in current public expenditure.

Against the complexities of aid allocation and the conceptual and practical difficulties of determining overall financing requirements of country programmes, the test of how much aid each country receives per capita would appear to be simple and straightforward. This test also has a welfare connotation, assuring that each national gets an appropriate share of global aid regardless of his country's size. Yet its very simplicity hardly justifies its many shortcomings — it does not, for example, allow for self-help, natural or locational endowment, and the stage of development. Furthermore, it does not account for the impact of country size on overall aid requirements discussed in the next section. The welfare element in this test can be refined by *reducing* the per capita aid allocation to countries in the higher income brackets. When applied to aid concessionary terms, a lowering of the per capita allocation as income rises is also justified by creditworthiness. Countries' debt-bearing capacity should improve with per capita income, although in practice a number of other factors (not necessarily correlated with income) are also important. This is discussed in more detail in de Vries (1971).

III. Do small countries require more aid?

The demand for aid might best be determined by estimating the resource gap which would prevail were the country to maintain a reasonable pace of growth compatible with its natural resources and absorptive capacity. The gap is determined by many factors, including resource endowment, policy orientation, stage of development, trade position, location and economic size. Economic size itself may affect the other factors, in particular trade position and policy orientation. For the present purpose, a distinction should be made between the magnitude of the gap at any given moment and a country's ability to reduce the gap. The following considerations suggest that small countries may have a larger gap and may find it more difficult to reduce their dependence on external capital. It would appear that the 'small country bias' in aid allocation observed in Section I is consistent with the larger needs of small countries or their greater difficulties in reducing the external resource gap.[3]

The small size of the domestic market is an obstacle to diversified industrial development in small and poor countries. The few small less-developed countries which have been able to develop export-oriented industries have had the advantage of location and/or resource base, particularly human resources (education and literacy). In general it is difficult and more costly to develop economic import substitutes in small and poor countries. Consequently, the most direct way to reduce the external resource gap is closed off to small countries. This contrasts sharply with the success of some larger countries in constraining their import growth in the development process. Admittedly, import substitution in the larger countries has been associated with many uneconomic practices and has often led to increased, rather than reduced, import pressure. Yet their economic size and diversity enables them to overcome these difficulties. Despite past 'mistakes', they have a rather diversified industrial structure which makes possible growth with reduced dependence on external aid.

Industrial diversification permits large countries to develop exports of manufactured goods. For many countries manufacturing growth may well be the most favourable base for longer-term export growth. This view is supported by the more dynamic growth of world trade in manufactured goods and the sluggish growth of many agricultural staples. As industrial development is less feasible and more costly in small countries, they have poor prospects for exports of manufactured goods. Thus, countries such as Brazil, Korea, and Taiwan, which recently have been able rapidly to increase manufactured exports, have a far better chance to close their gap then smaller countries like Ivory Coast, Jamaica or Senegal, let alone landlocked countries like Chad or Mali, all of which are still far removed from diversified industrial development.

Larger countries may also be in a better position to close their *domestic* resource gap. The income level is the primary determinant of domestic savings. However, it is increasingly recognised that a financial system with suitable institutions and the development of popular attitudes towards the facilities they offer, plays a crucial role in the growth and efficient utilisation of financial assets and savings. It would seem that larger and more diversified countries have more means to build up a financial system and a variety of financial policy instruments which facilitate the mobilisation and efficient allocation of financial savings. Thus, the larger countries, although poor, already have a sizeable urban and industrial sector. This enables them to build up the financial institutions needed in a modern system — domestically-owned commercial banks, savings institutions, and viable specialised credit institutions. Furthermore, with their broader economic and regional diversification, larger countries have greater scope for fiscal measures to increase savings and channel resources to selected activities or regions. For example, the tax and investment incentives for industrial development in the north-east of Brazil presuppose, first, the existence of a substantial industrial-urban sector whose resources can be tapped and, secondly, the possibility of introducing tax incentives in a well-developed fiscal system. Neither of these conditions applies in most small and poor countries.

Finally, the diseconomies of government in the smallest countries also enlarge their needs for external assistance. The task of building up the machinery of public administration would appear more extensive in most smaller countries than in larger countries. This expands both the current and the capital cost of government administration in general and of development in particular.[4] It would also seem that larger countries have more means of overcoming shortages of administrative, managerial, and technical skills. Consequently, the need for technical assistance is larger in smaller countries – increasing both the cost of development and the amount of external assistance required.

IV. Reducing aid requirements through export development

Export growth may be the key to reducing the dependence on aid in small countries, since the possibilities of doing so through import substitution are limited by the small size of the domestic market. However, the contribution of export growth to development will hinge on its impact on the income and employment of broad layers of the population.

Development of natural (particularly mineral) resources has provided considerable export impetus in many small countries. It is widely recognised that the often spectacular resource development in enclaves still leaves countries with a major problem of structural transformation. Enclave development may accentuate and aggravate the dualistic nature of the economy. An adequate contribution by the enclave to fiscal revenues provides countries with the financial resources needed to accelerate their structural transformation. Consequently, the relations between enclave companies and national governments are a critical element in development. This assumes special importance when enclave operations are large in relation to the rest of the economy. It may be noted that in a number of small countries the enclave contribution to fiscal revenue is proportionally below its share of total GDP. Small countries may find it harder to cope with enclave problems than large countries. They are more dependent on enclave earnings because of their lack of diversification. They have less bargaining power with the enclave company because of their small economic power and their limited alternatives.

Countries which have a relatively small share of the market of their primary exports may be in a stronger position to expand their exports than countries which have relatively large market shares (de Vries, 1967). Smaller countries can be expected to have smaller market shares than large countries, although there are significant exceptions (e.g. Mexico with small and Ghana with large market shares). On the other hand, small countries are relatively more dependent on trade than large countries. Export instability may have greater consequences for economies of smaller countries, which then may have greater need for extraordinary assistance to overcome the effects of instability.[5] Furthermore, in the longer run the growth of commodity exports must depend on the relative cost-advantage of the supplying countries and there is no reason why small countries should be in a stronger position.

Ivory Coast is an example of a small country which successfully improved its share in the world markets of its export commodities, coffee and cocoa. It has had a remarkable export growth. Its recent experience shows, however, that rapid export growth leaves many development problems still to be tackled. Despite its diversification efforts, the country is crucially dependent on commodity markets. Its three major export commodities (coffee, cocoa and timber) still account for 80 per cent of export earnings. The decline in cocoa prices during 1969-71 caused a reduction in import capacity equivalent to 3.8 per cent of GDP and 36 per cent of public investment in 1972. Continued diversification efforts are not likely to increase export earnings for some years, even though the level of investment should remain high – thus, the need for external assistance is growing rather than subsiding. At the same time, despite its rapid output growth, the country suffers from increasing problems of unemployment and the presence of many immigrant workers (who account for some 26 per cent of the total labour force).

It has already been noted that diversification of exports (and of production in general) via manufacturing industry is severely limited in small countries. Their small domestic markets do not permit many industries to get an economic start from which to expand into export markets. Very little is known about the possibilities of industrial development in small and poor countries. Most of the studies of import substitution and industry have been based on the experience of countries which, in the present context, must be regarded as large.[6] Small and poor countries must place much greater reliance on small-scale industry and the development of indigenous entrepreneurship. Systematic work on the problems of small-scale indigenous industry is only just beginning (e.g. John de Wilde's study, 1971). From the available evidence it would seem that while small-scale industry is a key element in labour-intensive development, it is not likely to have a strong export-orientation in its early phases.

Conclusion

There are strong economic reasons for allocating more aid to small countries. A number of systematic forces make the relative aid requirements of small countries exceed those of large countries. While the difference in aid requirements has not been quantified, this can be expected to be most marked for small countries with a poor resource base, especially undeveloped administrative and infrastructure facilities and locational disadvantages (e.g. the landlocked countries in Africa). The main considerations why small countries have greater aid requirements may be summarised as follows:

(a) Many developing countries need help in overcoming weakness of government administration, but small countries suffer more from this handicap than large ones. In addition, small countries have a proportionally smaller reservoir of trained talent than larger countries. Thus, small countries tend to have a greater need for technical assistance and as a result the cost of development projects may be larger. The higher cost of government will tend to depress public savings.

(b) Small and resource-poor countries have much greater problems in diversifying their economies than large poor countries. The cost of diversification may be higher, while its absence may prolong the country's dependence on external capital.

(c) The small size of domestic markets limits the potential for industrialisation and, consequently, the possibility of reducing dependence on aid through economic import substitution and development of exports of manufactures.

(d) Lack of domestic diversification – especially the absence of a relatively advanced modern sector – reduces the potential for mobilisation of financial savings through development of a domestic financial system and of application of a variety of fiscal incentives.

(e) Small countries have a disadvantage in dealing with enclave companies which develop their mineral or agricultural resources. They may not, in these circumstances, be able to reap the same benefits from export growth as large countries.

NOTES

1. The regression analysis by Davenport (1970) with 1962-64 data confirmed that as per capita income increases, aid per capita also increases while aid as a proportion of GNP decreases. In a comment on this study, Pyle (1970) pointed out that the increase in aid per capita occurred only up to a per capita income of $184. Although Davenport found the size distribution of aid highly unequal, in his (linear) regression the population variable was not statistically significant. Pyle did find statistically significant results in a non-linear form.

2. Projections by the IBRD/IDA suggest, for a group of eleven West African countries over the next five years, that project loans will average US$4.8 million, well above the minimum regarded as desirable by lending agencies. For the mid-point of the projection period (1975), these countries have the following average profile: population – 3.8 million; GNP – about US$650 million or US$170 per capita; average number of of IBRD/IDA projects – 1.8 per year. In 1967-69, these countries

received official aid equivalent to 7 per cent of GNP. On the basis of cross-section data for countries in this income range, this level of aid would seem in line with overall requirements in the next five years, covering a net resource gap of 4 per cent of GNP, debt service of 2 per cent of GNP (roughly equivalent to 10 per cent of exports) and factor payments (not financed by private capital) of 1 per cent of GNP. Gross aid at 7 per cent of GNP would be US$45 million per country and provide financing for nine projects (at an average US$4.8 million). This aid level would finance projects in all major sections for a diversified development programme.

3. Section I presented data on gross capital inflows while the present section discusses the reasons for inter-country variations in the resource gap. At any given level of the resource gap, and assuming reserves are unchanged, the gross inflow of public capital must increase as the debt service increases and the net contribution of private capital (i.e. net of factor income payments and remittances) decreases. There is no *a priori* reason to assume a systematic influence of country size on the debt service and the *net* contribution of private capital.

4. Cf. Percy Selwyn (1971) in his criticism of Gandhi. Gandhi found that available statistical data did not confirm the *a priori* reasoning that, in general, small countries suffered from diseconomies of public expenditure.

5. Erb and Schiavo-Campo (1969) found that in 1954-66 small countries experienced more export instability than large countries.

6. For example, the analysis in Little, Scitovsky and Scott (1970) is based on studies of seven large countries: Argentina, Brazil, Mexico, India, Pakistan, the Philippines and Taiwan. Balassa (1971) also bases his empirical work on studies of large developing countries: Brazil, Chile, Mexico, Malaysia, Pakistan and the Philippines. However, Balassa also includes Norway as an example of an open economy, small in population but, in the present context, large in terms of GDP.

Average Official Loans and Grants in 1967-69 for 77 Developing Countries

Country	Population[1] (Million)	GNP[2] ($ million)	GNP[2] per capita ($)	Aid[3] ($ million)	Grant[3] Equivalent of Aid ($ million)	Aid ($ per capita)	Grant Equivalent of Aid ($ per capita)	Aid (% of GNP)	Grant Equivalent of Aid (% of GNP)	Grant Element[3] ($)
GROUP A1 (GNP per capita ≤$150) (Population <5 million)										
Botswana	0.6	60.0*	100*	15.7	15.6	26.17	26.00	26.2	26.0	99.3
Lesotho	0.9	72.0*	80*	13.2	12.8	14.67	14.22	18.3	17.8	96.9
Mauritania	1.1	154.0	140	11.9	9.4	10.82	8.55	7.7	6.1	78.9
CAR	1.5	195.0	130	18.2b	16.0b	12.13	10.67	9.3	8.2	87.9
Togo	1.9	190.0	100	14.7b	13.4b	7.74	7.05	7.7	7.1	91.1
Dahomey	2.6	208.0*	80*	15.4b	14.4b	5.92	5.54	7.4	6.9	93.5
Somalia	2.7	162.0*	60*	32.7a	28.4a	12.11	10.52	20.2	17.5	86.8
Burundi	3.5	175.0*	50*	12.8b	12.5b	3.66	3.57	7.3	7.1	97.6
Chad	3.5	210.0*	60*	24.3b	17.7b	6.94	5.06	11.6	8.4	72.8
Rwanda	3.7	259.0*	70*	13.1	12.9	3.54	3.49	5.1	5.0	98.4
Guinea	3.9	269.0	69	70.0c	21.0c	17.95	5.38	26.0	7.8	30.0
Niger	3.9	343.2*	88*	32.3b	25.0b	8.28	6.41	9.4	7.3	77.4
Malawi	4.4	220.0*	50*	38.8	31.4	8.82	7.14	17.6	14.3	80.9
Mali	4.9	441.0*	90*	19.7	18.1	4.02	3.69	4.5	4.1	91.8
Average	2.8	211.3	83.4	23.8	17.8	8.51	6.36	11.3	8.4	74.8

1. 1969.   2. 1969. Data marked * are 1968.
3. Aid is official loans and grants. Grant equivalent is product of nominal value of aid and grant element (at 10 per cent discount) shown in last column. Annual averages for 1967-69 unless stated as follows: a) 1967, 1968 average; b) 1968, 1969 average; c) 1968 only; d) 1969 only.

Sources: *World Bank Atlas*, 1971.   *IBRD/IDA Annual Report*, 1971.

Average Official Loans and Grants in 1967-69 for 77 Developing Countries

Country	Population[1] (Million)	GNP[2] ($ million)	GNP[2] per capita ($)	Aid[3] ($ million)	Grant[3] Equivalent of Aid ($ million)	Aid ($ per capita)	Grant Equivalent of Aid ($ per capita)	Aid (% of GNP)	Grant Equivalent of Aid (% of GNP)	Grant Element[3] (%)
GROUP A2 (GNP per capita ≤$150) (Population >5 million)										
Upper Volta	5.3	265.0	50	18.0b	16.0b	3.40	3.02	6.8	6.0	88.8
Cameroon	5.7	855.0	150	65.9d	43.5d	11.56	7.63	7.7	5.0	66.0
Malagasy Republic	6.7	737.0	110	42.5	34.9	6.34	5.21	5.7	4.7	82.0
Uganda	9.5	1045.0	110	33.4	28.8	3.52	3.03	3.1	2.7	86.2
Kenya	10.9	1417.0	130	71.6	54.9	6.57	5.04	5.0	3.8	76.6
Tanzania	12.6	1008.0*	80*	66.3	46.9	5.26	3.72	6.6	4.7	70.7
Afghanistan	14.0	1120.0*	80*	46.9	39.4	3.35	2.81	4.2	3.5	84.0
Sudan	15.2	1672.0	110	61.2a	26.3a	4.03	1.73	3.6	1.5	42.9
Zaire	17.9	1611.0*	90*	76.2d	69.3d	4.26	3.87	4.7	4.3	90.9
Ethiopia	24.8	1736.0*	70*	66.8	43.9	2.69	1.77	3.9	2.5	65.7
Nigeria	64.6	5426.4	84	81.2a	70.2a	1.26	1.09	1.5	1.3	86.4
Indonesia	116.6	11660.0	100	364.5	243.1	3.13	2.08	3.1	2.0	66.6
Pakistan	126.7	13937.0	110	624.7	370.4	4.93	2.92	4.4	2.6	59.2
India	526.0	57860.0	110	1315.2a	986.4a	2.50	1.88	2.2	1.7	75.0
Average	68.32	7167.8	98.9	209.6	148.1	3.07 (3.37)	2.17 (2.53)	2.9 (3.7)	2.1 (2.8)	70.7

Note: Data in brackets are averages for group excluding India, Pakistan, and Indonesia

Average Official Loans and Grants in 1967-69 for 77 Developing Countries

Country	Population[1] (Million)	GNP[2] ($ million)	GNP[2] per capita ($)	Aid[3] ($ million)	Grant[3] Equivalent of Aid ($ million)	Aid ($ per capita)	Grant Equivalent of Aid ($ per capita)	Aid (% of GNP)	Grant Equivalent of Aid (% of GNP)	Grant Element[3] (%)
GROUP B1 ($150 < GNP per capita ≤ $300) (Population < 5 million)										
Swaziland	0.4	72.0	180	9.7	8.9	24.25	22.25	13.4	12.3	91.7
Mauritius	0.8	184.0	230	8.6	6.3	10.75	7.88	4.6	3.4	73.2
Liberia	1.5	300.0	200	14.9	13.2	9.93	8.80	4.9	4.4	88.5
Jordan	2.2	616.0	280	59.0[a]	52.8[a]	26.82	24.00	9.5	8.5	89.4
Paraguay	2.3	552.0	240	29.2	20.1	12.70	8.74	5.2	3.6	68.8
Honduras	2.5	650.0	260	30.0	19.4	12.00	7.76	4.6	2.9	64.6
Sierra Leone	2.5	425.0	170	10.1	8.6	4.04	3.44	2.3	2.0	85.1
El Salvador	3.4	986.0	290	21.3	13.4	6.26	3.94	2.1	1.3	62.9
Senegal	3.8	760.0	200	45.5	39.1	11.97	10.29	5.9	5.1	85.9
Zambia	4.0	1160.0	290	69.2	38.1	17.30	9.53	5.9	3.2	55.0
Dominican Republic	4.0	1120.0	280	60.8	42.4	15.20	10.60	5.4	3.7	69.7
Bolivia	4.8	768.0	160	58.7	39.7	12.23	8.27	7.6	5.1	67.6
Ivory Coast	4.9	1176.0	240	111.0	51.1	22.65	10.43	9.4	4.3	46.0
Tunisia	4.9	1127.0	230	176.7[a]	103.4[a]	36.06	21.10	15.6	9.1	58.5
Average	3.0	706.9	232.1	50.3	32.6	16.77	10.87	7.1	4.6	64.8

Average Official Loans and Grants in 1967-69 for 77 Developing Countries

Country	Population[1] (Million)	GNP[2] ($ million)	GNP[2] per capita ($)	Aid[3] ($ million)	Grant[3] Equivalent of Aid ($ million)	Aid ($ per capita)	Grant Equivalent of Aid ($ per capita)	Aid (% of GNP)	Grant Equivalent of Aid (% of GNP)	Grant Element[3] (%)
GROUP B2 ($150 < GNP per capita ≤ $300) (Population > 5 million)										
Rhodesia	5.1	1224.0	240	1.0	1.0	0.20	0.20	—	—	100.0
Syria	5.9	1534.0	260	22.7[c]	12.7[c]	3.85	2.15	1.4	0.8	55.9
Ecuador	5.9	1416.0	240	52.3	24.7	8.86	4.19	3.6	1.7	47.2
Ghana	8.3	1577.0	190	75.4[d]	49.8[d]	9.08	6.00	4.7	3.1	66.0
Ceylon	12.2	2318.0	190	98.3	46.2	8.06	3.79	4.2	1.9	47.0
China, Republic of	13.8	4140.0	300	174.5[a]	60.2[a]	12.64	4.36	4.2	1.4	34.5
Morocco	15.1	2869.0	190	146.7	87.0	9.72	5.76	5.1	3.0	59.3
Colombia	20.5	5945.0	290	297.7	137.8	14.52	6.72	5.0	2.3	46.2
Korea	31.1	6531.0	210	688.5[a]	296.1[a]	22.14	9.52	10.5	4.5	43.0
Thailand	35.1	5616.0	160	100.3	69.5	2.86	1.98	1.7	1.2	69.2
Philippines	35.9	7539.0	210	164.8	82.4	4.59	2.30	2.1	1.0	50.0
Average	17.2	3700.8	225.5	165.7	78.9	9.65	4.59	4.5	2.1	47.6

179

Average Official Loans and Grants in 1967-69 for 77 Developing Countries

Country	Population¹ (Million)	GNP² ($ million)	GNP² per capita ($)	Aid³ ($ million)	Grant³ Equivalent of Aid ($ million)	Aid ($ per capita)	Grant Equivalent of Aid ($ per capita)	Aid (% of GNP)	Grant Equivalent of Aid (% of GNP)	Grant Element³ (%)
GROUP C1 (GNP per capita > $300) (Population < 5 million)										
Malta	0.3	213.0	710	18.5ᵃ	14.6ᵃ	61.67	48.67	8.6	6.8	78.9
Gabon	0.5	160.0	320	20.8	14.0	41.60	28.00	13.0	8.7	67.3
Cyprus	0.6	582.0	970	12.2	6.1	20.33	10.17	2.0	1.0	50.0
Guyana	0.7	238.0	340	27.7	17.4	39.57	24.86	11.6	7.3	62.8
Trinidad and Tobago	1.0	890.0	870	21.0	7.4	21.00	7.40	2.3	0.8	35.2
Panama	1.4	924.0	660	40.1	28.5	28.64	20.36	4.3	3.0	71.0
Costa Rica	1.7	867.0	510	44.4	20.6	26.12	12.12	5.1	2.3	46.4
Nicaragua	1.9	722.0	380	55.9	28.0	29.42	14.74	7.7	3.8	50.0
Jamaica	1.9	1045.0	550	24.3	10.8	12.79	5.68	2.3	1.0	44.4
Singapore	2.0	1600.0	800	61.1	27.7	30.55	13.85	3.8	1.7	45.3
Uruguay	2.9	1624.0	560	79.2	21.6	27.31	7.45	4.8	1.3	27.2
Average	1.35	805.9	608.2	36.8	17.9	27.26	13.26	4.6	2.2	48.6

180

Average Official Loans and Grants in 1967-69 for 77 Developing Countries

Country	Population[1] (Million)	GNP[2] ($ million)	GNP[2] per capita ($)	Aid[3] ($ million)	Grant[3] Equivalent of Aid ($ million)	Aid ($ per capita)	Grant Equivalent of Aid ($ per capita)	Aid (% of GNP)	Grant Equivalent of Aid (% of GNP)	Grant Element[3] (%)
GROUP C2 (GNP per capita > $300) (Population ≥ 5 million)										
Guatemala	5.0	1750.0	350	49.3	25.1	9.86	5.02	2.8	1.4	50.9
Greece	8.8	7392.0	840	87.3a	19.6a	9.92	2.23	1.1	0.2	22.4
Iraq	9.4	2914.0	310	18.8a	12.1a	2.00	1.29	0.6	0.4	64.4
Chile	9.6	4896.0	510	511.5a	161.1a	53.28	16.78	10.4	3.2	31.5
Venezuela	10.0	10000.0	1000	116.0	37.5	11.60	3.75	1.1	0.3	32.3
Malaysia	10.6	3604.0	340	113.8	51.6	10.74	4.87	3.1	1.4	45.3
Peru	13.2	4356.0	330	169.0	59.2	12.80	4.48	3.8	1.3	35.0
Yugoslavia	20.4	11832.0	580	199.5	58.5	9.78	2.87	1.6	0.4	29.3
Argentina	24.0	25440.0	1060	531.6	102.6	22.15	4.28	2.0	0.4	19.3
Iran	28.5	9975.0	350	401.3a	94.3a	14.08	3.31	4.0	0.9	23.5
Spain	33.0	27060.0	820	378.4	80.6	11.47	2.44	1.3	0.2	21.3
Turkey	34.5	12075.0	350	310.5	162.4	9.00	4.71	2.5	1.3	52.3
Mexico	49.0	28420.0	580	852.4	121.9	17.40	2.49	2.9	0.4	14.3
Average	19.7	11516.5	570.8	287.6	75.9	14.60	3.85	2.5	0.6	26.4

The following regressions are found for data on all countries or country groups with significance level and R^2 as shown; the t-ratio is indicated in brackets. No multicollinearity was observed between $\frac{Y}{N}$ and N.

K	=	Gross Aid ($ million)
GK	=	Grant of equivalent of K (at 10 per cent discount) ($ million)
Y	=	GNP ($ million)
N	=	Population (million)

For all countries:

			Signif.	R^2
1)	$\log \frac{K}{N}$	$= 2.806 - .309 \log N$ $\quad\quad\quad (-4.60)$	.000	.22
2)	$\log \frac{K}{Y}$	$= 1.873 - .241 \log N$ $\quad\quad\quad (-2.45)$	.017	.07
3)	$\log \frac{GK}{N}$	$= 2.443 - .410 \log N$ $\quad\quad\quad (-7.66)$	.000	.44
4)	$\log \frac{GK}{Y}$	$= 1.506 - .349 \log N$ $\quad\quad\quad (-3.29)$	.002	.13
5)	$\log \frac{K}{N}$	$= -.782 + .570 \log \frac{Y}{N}$ $\quad\quad\quad (5.00)$	.000	.250
6)	$\log \frac{GK}{N}$	$= .612 + .209 \log \frac{Y}{N}$ $\quad\quad\quad (1.720)$	.090	.038
7)	$\log \frac{K}{Y}$	$= 3.875 - .453 \log \frac{Y}{N}$ $\quad\quad\quad (-2.670)$	.009	.087
8)	$\log \frac{GK}{Y}$	$= 5.398 - .843 \log \frac{Y}{N}$ $\quad\quad\quad (-4.925)$	.000	.244
9)	$\log \frac{K}{N}$	$= -.005 + .515 \log \frac{Y}{N} \quad -.274 \log N$ $\quad\quad\quad (5.069) \quad\quad (-4.671)$	.000 .000	.421
10)	$\log \frac{GK}{N}$	$= 1.750 + .127 \log \frac{Y}{N} \quad -.401 \log N$ $\quad\quad\quad (1.370) \quad\quad (-7.495)$	.175 .000	.453
11)	$\log \frac{K}{Y}$	$= 4.670 - .510 \log \frac{Y}{N} \quad -.280 \log N$ $\quad\quad\quad (-3.141) \quad\quad (-2.993)$	.002 .004	.185
12)	$\log \frac{GK}{Y}$	$= 6.567 - .926 \log \frac{Y}{N} \quad -.412 \log N$ $\quad\quad\quad (-6.082) \quad\quad (-4.684)$	.000	.417

For all small countries:
(Groups A_1, B_1 and C_1)

			Signif.	R^2
13)	$\log \frac{K}{N}$	$= -.245 + .547 \log \frac{Y}{N}$ $\quad\quad\quad (5.20)$	.000	.42
14)	$\log \frac{GK}{N}$	$= .550 + .324 \log \frac{Y}{N}$ $\quad\quad\quad (2.89)$	.007	.18
15)	$\log \frac{K}{Y}$	$= 4.376 - .456 \log \frac{Y}{N}$ $\quad\quad\quad (-4.17)$	.000	.32
16)	$\log \frac{GK}{Y}$	$= 5.215 - .690 \log \frac{Y}{N}$ $\quad\quad\quad (-6.08)$	.000	.50

	Signif.	R^2

For all large countries:
(Groups A_2, B_2 and C_2)

17) $\log \dfrac{K}{N} = -1.623 + \underset{(3.78)}{.648} \log \dfrac{Y}{N}$ .001 .28

18) $\log \dfrac{GK}{Y} = 5.325 - \underset{(-3.37)}{.949} \log \dfrac{Y}{N}$ .002 .24

19) $\log \dfrac{K}{Y} = 4.647 - \underset{(-2.11)}{.003} \dfrac{Y}{N}$ .042 .11

20) $\log \dfrac{GK}{Y} = 3.141 - \underset{(-4.37)}{.004} \dfrac{Y}{N}$ .000 .35

For low income countries:[1]
(Groups A_1 and A_2)

21) $\log \dfrac{K}{N} = 2.394 - \underset{(-5.31)}{.314} \log N$ .000 .52

22) $\log \dfrac{GK}{N} = 2.233 - \underset{(-6.95)}{.362} \log N$ .000 .65

For high income countries:[1]
(Groups C_1 and C_2)

23) $\log \dfrac{K}{N} = 3.301 - \underset{(-3.23)}{.275} \log N$ .004 .32

24) $\log \dfrac{GK}{N} = 2.685 - \underset{(-6.32)}{.489} \log N$ .000 .65

---

1. No significant fits were found for middle-income countries (Groups B_1 and B_2)

REFERENCES

Bela Balassa, et al: *The Structure of Protection in Developing Countries,* (Baltimore, John Hopkins Press, 1971).

Henry J. Bruton: 'The Two Gap Approach to Aid and Development' (Comment, *American Economic Review,* Vol. 59, June 1969).

Hollis B. Chenery, and Alan M. Strout: 'Foreign Assistance and Economic Development' (*American Economic Review,* Vol. 56, September, 1966).

Hollis B. Chenery: *The Developing Economy* (New York, John Wiley and Sons, Inc., forthcoming 1972).

Hollis B. Chenery, and Lance Taylor: 'Development Patterns — Among Countries and Over Time' (*The Review of Economics and Statistics,* Vol. 50, November 1968).

Michael Davenport: 'The Allocation of Foreign Aid: A Cross-Section Study, with Special Reference to the Pearson Commission Report' (*Yorkshire Bulletin of Economic and Social Research,* Vol. 22, May 1970).

William G. Demas: *The Economics of Development in Small Countries with Special Reference to the Caribbean* (Montreal, McGill University Press, 1965).

Barend A. DeVries: 'The Debt-Bearing Capacity of Developing Countries: A Comparative Analysis' (*Banca Nazionale del Lavoro Quarterly Review,* No. 96, March 1971a).

Barend A. deVries: *The Export Experience of Development Countries* (World Bank Staff Occasional Paper, Baltimore, John Hopkins Press, 1967b).

John C. DeWilde: *The Development of African Private Enterprise,* (International Bank for Reconstruction and Development, mimeographed, 10 December 1971).

Guy F. Erb, and Salvatore Sciavo-Campo: 'Export Instability and Economic Size of Less Developed Countries' (*Bulletin of Oxford University Institute of Economics and Statistics,* Vol. 31 November 1969).

Ved P. Gandhi: 'Are There Economies of Size in Government Current Expenditure in Developing Countries?' (*Nigerian Journal of Economic and Social Studies,* Vol. 12, July 1970).

E.K. Hawkins: 'Measuring Capital Requirements' (*Finance and Development,* Vol. 5, June 1968).

Ian Little, Tibor Scitovsky, and Maurice Scott: *Industry and Trade in Some Developing Countries: A Comparative Study* (London, Oxford University Press, 1970).

Percy Selwyn: 'Are there Economies of Size in Government Current Expenditure in Developing Countries?' A Comment, (*Nigerian Journal of Economic and Social Studies,* Vol. 13, November 1971).

David Pyle: 'The Allocation of Foreign Aid' (Comment in Michael Davenport, *Yorkshire Bulletin of Economic and Social Research,* Vol. 22, May 1970).

E.A.G. Robinson (ed): 'Economic Consequences of the Size of Nations: Proceedings of a Conference held by the International Economic Association' (London, Macmillan and Company Ltd., 1960).

184

9. SOME CONSIDERATIONS ON DEVELOPMENT AID TO SMALL COUNTRIES*

Salvatore Schiavo-Campo

Summary

Various possible meanings of the concept of country size are discussed. The explanations in DeVries' paper of higher *per capita* levels of aid to small countries are disputed, although there may be good reasons why such countries should receive more aid. Possible relations between country size and institutional efficiency are worth more detailed examination, as are constraints on import-substitution policies in small countries.

This short paper offers some general considerations of relevance to the problems specific to small developing countries and hence to their needs for development aid. It takes the lead from Barend DeVries' study of that subject — also presented at this conference. The principal findings of that interesting work — that small developing countries generally receive proportionately more aid, and on softer terms, than their larger counterparts — is certainly worthy of attention. It is no reflection on the merits of that paper to note certain omissions and ambiguities which it shares with some of the literature on small countries and much of the writing on development aid.

First, an unfortunate frequent tendency is the evasion of even a skeletal discussion of what a 'small country' is. (There is in DeVries' paper a mention of the criterion which he uses to define size, but little explanation of its meaning.) It might be argued, to paraphrase H.W. Singer, that a small country is like a giraffe: difficult to describe, but you know one when you see it. In my opinion, the intellectual surrender implicit in this point of view is unnecessary. The following considerations — though rather obvious — may assist in clarifying the definition of a small country. The concept of the production function gives us the basis for a useful taxonomy.

A country may be classified as small because its availability of a specific input is limited, or because its total production is small. If, to begin with, one is interested in the problems arising from the size of the raw materials base, the country's territory is probably the best single proxy measure. Many of the obvious exceptions — such as territorially small countries with abundance of an important resource (the oil kingdoms come readily to mind) — can be eliminated if territorial size is understood to reflect the variety of the natural resources base as well as its total endowment. If one is instead

*(Dr. Schiavo-Campo's paper was not prepared for the Conference. It was written in response to the foregoing paper by Barend DeVries, ed.)

interested in problems of the availability of human resources, then clearly the criterion of country size ought to be population. As in the case of raw materials, weighting the number of people by some appropriate index of skill distribution would yield an improvement over the simple population criterion. If capital is the main concern, the appropriate measure of country size would be some estimate of the capital stock; neither territory nor population would necessarily be related to capital availability. Recognising the conceptual and practical difficulties of capital stock estimates, especially in developing countries, a proxy measure could be the total supply of savings (public as well as private).

Is the population criterion a better indicator of country size than the territorial or the capital criteria? The question itself is incorrectly posed: each is appropriate, or incorrectly used, depending on the purpose of the definition of size. It is, however, true that these criteria are partial ones: each of them measures country size in terms of only one type of input. One is normally interested in an *aggregate* measure of economic size — and not in a specific set of problems relating to one input. It then seems reasonable to look at national product as a measure of a country's economic size, since total output will in fact reflect the weighted impact of country size with respect to each factor of production, in addition to being the best single measure of the aggregate size of the domestic market. (It does not matter much which technical definition of national product or income is actually used, provided of course that it is used consistently.)

A potentially troublesome issue in the definition of size lies in the arbitrariness (which DeVries recognises) of the boundary set between the 'large' and the 'small' countries. Thus, with respect to territory 'space is virtually and practically a continuum' (as Rutledge Vining puts it): countries vary in territory from a few hundred square miles to several million. Any grouping of 'large' and 'small' is of necessity arbitrary. The same is true of population, capital, national income. The extremes are easy: the country with the smallest number of people is unequivocally small in population, and China is unequivocally large. The country with the smallest national income is clearly small, and the United States large; and so on. But the classification of all other countries is in doubt. As several other papers presented at this conference have made clear, size of country is a relative matter: it is relative to the size of its partners or opponents, to the historical circumstances, to the specific policy issue at stake. Indeed, one of the main contributions of this conference has been to show that a country too small for the exercise of certain conventional attributes of statehood may be a perfectly 'viable' state in other respects. (It is, of course, fundamental to realise that in this context it is the country's own goals and terms of reference that matter and not necessarily the standards of performance prescribed from the outside

186

or derived from the historical past of industrialised nations.)

There is thus an inevitable circularity of any discussion of the effects of economic size: the problems specific to small countries obviously cannot be identified – much less analysed – until we first settle on a criterion of smallness. But the criterion, in order to be meaningful, must depend on prior identification of the particular problem at issue. This difficulty is conceptually very serious. The saving grace, fortunately, is that with notable exceptions the several possible criteria of size yield the same broad groupings of countries (as DeVries also recognises). A territorially small country usually has also a small population, a limited resource base, a small supply of savings and, as a result, a small absolute national income. Therefore, while it is essential to keep in mind the conceptual arbitrariness of any discussion of the effects of country size, it is possible in practice to treat 'small countries' as a group and to try to identify their common characteristics, if any.

One such common characteristic, Barend DeVries argues, is their greater need for aid. His argument, however, shares the Pangloss-like nature of many of the attempts to explain the international allocation of aid funds. The argument often seems to be: small countries receive proportionately more aid; it must be because the have a greater need for it; hence, they should receive more aid. To quote from DeVries' paper:

> 'One explanation of this phenomenon [that the difference in the grant element of aid becomes larger as the income level rises] could be the recognition – when decisions on the terms of assistance are made – that as income rises the development prospects and aid-bearing capacity of small countries do not improve as rapidly as those in large countries'.

It might well be that, as the old Rheingold beer commercial in the United States says: 'We must be doing something right!' But surely the mere existence of a pattern is far from sufficient to prove it to be desirable – or even economically rational. We may well choose to frame the issues of development aid in normative terms (at their root they are inevitably normative anyway) but should be careful not to pass this off as positive description. A clear-cut example of this normative-positive mix in the argument is found in DeVries:

> 'As suggested by the data in Section I, the *total* (and per capita) requirements of aid tend to rise with income levels even though they decline as a percentage of GNP'.

This sounds like a perfectly straightforward factual conclusion. The trouble is that the data referred to are on aid *receipts,* not requirements. To confuse the two entirely begs the main question. Thus, the argument *assumes* that aid needs underlie the allocation of aid funds; the finding that the small countries receive proportionately more aid is then taken as proof that they need more aid.

Having assumed the economic rationality (in terms of the recipients' needs and capabilities) of the international allocation of aid, the paper proceeds to list a number of possible reasons why the smaller countries' needs are in fact greater. Any or all of these reasons, though unsubstantiated and inadequately explained, may be quite valid. I would argue, however, that DeVries' list — as other treatments of the subject — almost entirely disregards the political realities of aid. This may, in DeVries' own case, be due to his particular vantage point as an official of a multilateral institution. I willingly accept the implicit claim that much IBRD aid is in fact allocated on the basis of recipients' needs and absorptive capacity. I utterly reject the possible inference that the allocation (as distinct from the volume) of bilateral aid is made principally on that basis. (This has already been commented upon during the debate at this conference by Dudley Seers: aid is dispensed, among other reasons, in order to obtain strategic and political benefits — e.g. support in UN bodies — and this can be done most efficiently by concentrating aid in small countries. This point is quite telling and surely valid.)

I may advance here two other possible explanations for the DeVries finding — neither of which partakes of the nature of a dispassionate *ex ante* assessment of recipients' needs and economic capabilities. First, there is a minimum size of aid loans and grants owing to the complexities of the administrative paperwork involved; if *any* aid is given to a small developing country in a given fiscal year, the amount of it is likely to be proportionately greater than the aid given to a larger country. Second, it is well known that economically small countries have a greater import/GNP ratio. Consider that during the 1960s (the period to which DeVries' data refer) nearly all bilateral aid was tied to donor country goods or technical services, and conversely, that purchases from a developed nation were likely to be financed on concessionary terms. It should follow that countries for which trade has a relatively greater importance tend to receive a proportionately greater amount of aid which is tied to their imports.

Leaving now aside the question of how international aid is in fact allocated, can one reasonably expect *a priori* that the smaller countries' aid needs are greater? DeVries' positive answer to this question is, I think, correct and his emphasis on the role of limitations of domestic market size — while not new — is at the root of the matter. There are, as I see it, at least two development problems which acquire particular intensity in small developing countries. First, it has been shown that export instability is mainly related to the degree of commodity concentration of exports, and that the smaller developing countries exhibit a considerably higher degree of export fluctuations — with their attendant drawbacks on development planning and prospects. To this extent, it can then be argued that if aid is required for successful export diversification the need for such

188

aid is greater in the smaller developing nations. Second, the issues of taxation and effective control of foreign equity investment probably have a special dimension in small countries. That there is a minimum scale of foreign equity investment in any given activity can hardly be doubted. For the smaller countries this almost certainly means that foreign investment is more concentrated on a few activities. It may also mean that foreign investment in the aggregate has a relatively greater weight in the country's economy. The problem of taxation and control is thus probably of a different nature — and of more difficult solution — in small countries. If the economic weight of foreign equity investment is greater in a relative sense, presumably its potential political influence within the country is also; and the expected discrepancy between the foreign investor's technical and administrative know-how and the host government is greater too. If so, the small country's specific need would be for a proportionately greater amount of technical assistance of a specialised nature (rather than financial aid) to fill the larger gap between the foreign investor's knowledge and information about his own industry's technical and financial characteristics and the host country's knowledge of that industry. (It would be highly unrealistic to expect this kind of technical assistance to come from bilateral sources — since its stated purpose runs directly counter to the interests of foreign investors. It would probably be confined to multilateral institutions, and hence subject to those institutions' resource limitations.)

An important proposition advanced by DeVries (and hinted at in other papers of this Conference) is the direct relationship between country size and the efficiency of government administration and of the financial and credit system of the country. One implication is of course the small country's greater need for technical assistance in these areas. It is unfortunate that this hypothesis is unsupported and inadequately elaborated in DeVries' paper. Still, while as yet substantially unproved and speculative, this possible connexion between country size and institutional efficiency must be considered as potentially one of the most important differences between small and large developing nations. It deserves rigorous analysis and testing. It also deserves disaggregation into its separate components. The hypothesis of economies of scale in public administration is quite different in its practical impact and theoretical underpinning from, say, the proposition of a direct association between national economic size and the efficiency of financial markets or intermediaries.

Finally, DeVries' hint that import-substitution possibilities offer a potentially fruitful focus for distinguishing between large and small developing countries is a useful one. In this respect, a possible systematic difference between 'large' and 'small' arises from the following consideration. We may assume that the acquisition of a comparative advantage at some future time is the only long-run economic justification for import-substitution policies. Given the difficulties of accurately forecasting the sector or sectors which have a potential for developing such comparative advantage, a developing country is led to protect a number of different activities in the hope that at least one will eventually emerge as internationally competitive. A small developing country is likely to have less scope for a variety of import-substituting activities than a larger country. If import-substitution attempts must be confined to a smaller number and *range* of activities, the probability that one of them will acquire international competitiveness is *ipso facto* lower. (This is a mixed disadvantage, however, for the efficiency losses are smaller too.) Thus, judicious selectivity in the use of protection — necessary in any case for all countries — is probably even more essential for the smaller developing nations.

10. ECONOMIC INDEPENDENCE: Conceptual and Policy Issues in the Commonwealth Caribbean[1]

William G. Demas

Summary

The paper discusses some conceptual and policy aspects of economic independence in Third World countries, with special reference to the small Commonwealth Caribbean countries. It distinguishes between economic interdependence and economic dependence. Five aspects of economic dependence are identified – foreign ownership and control of key sectors of the economy; dependence through aid; dependence through trade; dependence through imported consumption and production patterns; and dependence on foreign know-how. The forms of dependence are part of the total structure of underdevelopment in the Commonwealth Caribbean, as in all Third World countries. The reduction of dependence in the Commonwealth Caribbean involves changes in policies and institutions; changes in values and attitudes; a sound incomes policy; a meaningful scheme of regional integration; and, above all, the development of greater technological, managerial and organisational know-how.

I. Introduction – Discussion of Concepts

(a) Definition of economic dependence

Economic independence is a vague and elusive phenomenon. It is perhaps easier to demonstrate what it means by first examining its opposite – namely, economic dependence. Economic dependence refers to a situation in which economic relationships between a country and other countries tend to be unequal and one-sided rather than equal and mutual. It thus has to do with relative power in the field of international economic relations.

Two actors (whether persons, firms or countries) – A and B – may be said to have equal power when A's capacity to make decisions for himself and to influence decisions of B is equal to B's capacity to make decisions for himself and to influence decisions of A. On the other hand, where A's decisions about himself are frustrated by the action of B, and where A cannot influence decisions by B about B, it is clear that B has more power than A.

The fact that economic dependence is essentially a manifestation of unequal power relations between countries is clearly seen when we consider that economic circumstances in another (superordinate) country are the most important factor *conditioning* the economic welfare of the subordinate country. Economically independent countries can prosper on their own momentum; economically dependent countries can do so only if circumstances in the dominant country are favourable. A situation of unequal power clearly exists; and it is the subordinate country's dependence on circumstances in the dominant country for its prosperity that provides us with the crux of dependence.

But it should not be thought that the limits of the relative power of two parties are immutably fixed. A distinction must be made between *latent* and *actual* power. In the longer run the limits of relative power are more elastic and flexible than in the shorter run. Latent power has to be mobilised. This is the problem of moving from a state of dependent underdevelopment to a state of more autonomous development.

(b) Size, dependence and integration

The question of economic dependence is not at all unrelated to that of the size of countries. In its attempt to overcome dependence by increasing and diversifying production and reducing its reliance on foreign suppliers for the bulk of the goods and services which it requires, a small country suffers from the basic constraints of a narrow range of natural resources and inadequate market size, stemming from a small population. Other things being equal, imports and exports will accordingly comprise a larger percentage of total production in a small country than in a large country. Moreover, unless the small country produces a significant proportion of the world's supplies of a strategic raw material (such as petroleum), it will usually lack the bargaining power to take the necessary steps to obtain satisfactory prices and tax receipts for its exports and to promote greater national ownership and control of its economy and hence of vital decisions over its economic life.

As will become clear later in the paper, small size is by no means the only factor making for economic dependence — it is, however, an important one that we must bear in mind.

It is partially in this context that economic integration becomes important. Such integration can go a long way towards overcoming the two constraints of small size mentioned above. It can make for — among other things — a wider range of natural resources and a larger local market. It could also improve the bargaining power of the integrated group of small countries with respect to trade, aid and private foreign investment in their relations with extra-regional entities, including powerful metropolitan trading blocs and powerful metropolitan-based multinational corporations.

(c) Distinction between dependence and interdependence

The goal of economic independence is often criticised by those who say that developing countries should seek to have interdependence with other countries since, it is argued, all countries in the world that have economic relations with each other are interdependent.

This is obviously true: no country can be fully independent. It is a question of degree. But there is also a very important distinction in kind between interdependence and dependence. In interdependent relationships there is an element of mutuality and equal balance. In cases of economic dependence there is a one-sided non-reciprocal relationship — one of super-ordination and subordination.

(d) Distinction between independence and isolation

It is often suggested that Third World countries such as the Caribbean should not even seek to be interdependent with other countries but should turn inwards and sever all economic links with other countries, particularly metropolitan countries. They should rely entirely on their own financial and human resources and close off their economy by shutting off a great part of their imports, thus forcing the people of the country to be completely self-reliant.

This is an extreme position. While it is true that one must make the economy less open in order to promote internally-propelled development, to seal off one's economy completely is to choose economic stagnation and a much lower standard of living. There is an optimum degree of economic contact with the outside world which is required to promote economic independence and internally-propelled development. The real issue is to determine the optimum degree of openness in every particular case. What is required is a controlled and regulated relationship with the metropolitan countries, in order to avoid the danger of economic satellisation or even absorption into the metropolitan economy or economies.

Consider the examples of Cuba and Tanzania. Cuba has substituted very close relations with the USSR for the pre-revolutionary dominance of her economy by the United States. Undoubtedly one can argue that the new relationship is different from the old; but nevertheless, Cuba is in many ways dependent on the USSR, a great power. It is a dependence, however, which is of a very different nature from what existed before the Revolution. The Cuban economy is owned and controlled by Cubans, the phenomenon of direct ownership by large, multinational corporations has been one of the victims of the Revolution. One can argue further that Cuba's new form of dependence is in principle transitional, depending upon how soon she can solve her foreign exchange problem. Foreign direct ownership of all the key sectors of a subordinate economy can in principle easily become a cumulative self-reinforcing process. On the other hand, again in principle, heavy foreign borrowing can induce dependence for only a finite period. Cuba's lingering dependence must be seen then, in terms of her reliance on the USSR for foreign exchange in the form of aid and trade. As regards the former, the Cubans have landed themselves in a heavy foreign debt burden; concerning the latter, the Cubans are clearly dependent on the USSR for highly favourable marketing conditions for sugar, their main export.

Tanzania, contrary to popular belief, has not completely cut itself off economically from the rest of the world, even though it is employing a self-reliant strategy of economic development; what it is seeking to achieve is a controlled and regulated relationship with the rest of the world, particularly the metropolitan countries. It is often forgotten that Tanzania and its other two partners in the East African Community — Kenya and Uganda — have an association relationship with the European Economic Community and that Tanzania still receives a fair amount of aid from both international agencies and national governments (both Socialist and non-Socialist). Even though she has nationalised (with compensation) many basic industries and the banking and financial system, she still continues to receive foreign private capital from European countries in the form of joint ventures.

II. Five Forms of Economic Dependence

There are five ways in which economic dependence is manifested in Third World countries. These are:

(a) dependence through foreign ownership and control of key sectors of the economy.

(b) dependence through foreign aid;

(c) dependence through trade.

(d) dependence through reliance on foreign human resources and foreign know-how.

(e) dependence through imported consumption and production patterns.

(a) Dependence through foreign ownership and control

Foreign ownership and control of the key sectors of the economy is usually regarded as the principal form of economic dependence. The Caribbean countries have for centuries had ownership and control over key economic sectors in foreign hands. Today this control is exercised by the multinational corporations. Heavy foreign investment is not all bad. It can raise per capita national income, create some relatively well-paid jobs and (after the end of tax-holiday periods in manufacturing and from the start in the case of minerals) pay considerable tax revenues to the Governments. On the other hand, a long period of foreign ownership and control of key economic sectors can prevent the creation of a genuine national economy, even though it may produce economic growth in the sense of a rise in total and per capita income. When a country is dominated by foreign private investment over a long period of time, the effect is to distort development; to fail to produce linkages between economic activities and sectors; to cripple

194

and discourage the development of local initiative, local entrepreneurship and local institutions for mobilising savings; and to remove from national control powers of effective decision-making in economic matters.

In the past foreign investment was highly exploitative – paying low wages and the minimum of taxes to government, and draining the country of its surpluses. Today, the modern international corporation is much more sophisticated and pays relatively high wages and salaries, employes more local persons in skilled and middle-management positions and usually tries to be a 'good corporate citizen'. Even so, foreign domination can still distort a country's development. One must see economic development as not merely a process of growth in per capita income but also as a process where nationals of the country are involved in economic decision-making at all levels; where the impetus for development comes from within and not from outside the country; and where there is not too much unemployment. It is doubtful whether heavy reliance on foreign private investment over a long period of time can produce this kind of autonomous development.

Accordingly, countries heavily dependent on foreign private investment have at some stage or other to achieve greater national decision-making through a programme of 'localisation' of the key sectors of the economy under foreign control – whether through nationalisation (with compensation) or through participation of the State or private individuals in existing key foreign controlled enterprises. In addition, national participation in *new* important economic activities must be sought. Such control and participation in both new and existing activities must be done on a careful and selective basis and must focus on the key sectors of the economy.

It is often argued the government or national private acquisition of existing key enterprises is bad economics in that:

(a) scarce foreign exchange is wasted;

(b) national savings are scarce and should be used only for new investment and not to 'buy back' existing activities.

Much depends on whether payment by the country is made in cash or in phased payments over a number of years. But even where the payment is made in cash (assuming that it could be raised), foreign exchange is eventually saved. So long as the acquired asset continues to be well-run and well-managed, it will produce income, and (by definition) future payments of dividends, profits and interests abroad will no longer be necessary.

The second objection – about scarce national savings – also takes too short-term a view. A company usually finances much of its investment out of the internal funds (or savings) generated by its own expansion. Provided that the enterprise acquired continues to be well-managed and to expand, in a dynamic context the flow of company savings accruing to the *national* economy will be increased over time.

This is not to deny the useful role that foreign private investment can play not only in bringing in capital but, much more important, in bringing in know-how, management, technology and, in some cases, access to foreign markets. There is a vast world of difference between foreign domination of an economy and 'normal' flows of private foreign investment within a clear-cut framework of Government policy. Once national control of key sectors and activities is achieved, there should still be much scope for, and less suspicion of, foreign private investment.

To achieve such national control requires an increase in the proportion of national income saved by nationals — including companies, individuals and the public sector. In the Caribbean national savings as a percentage of national income are scandalously low, in spite of fairly high levels of per capita income. This is so partly because, as we have seen, so many of the companies themselves are foreign-controlled and do not issue shares to local investors; partly because of high and growing wage and salary rates, which reduce the surpluses (or savings) of government and public enterprises for further investment; and above all, because of the cultural impact of the North American and West European 'consumer society' on the Caribbean, coming partly through advertising and partly through the images of the affluent society projected on television. This cultural impact has raised aspirations for consumption that the economies of the region could never satisfy in the foreseeable future. It also leads to excessive demands for higher wages and salaries in an attempt to equip oneself with the (often unnecessary) gadgets of modern North American society. In the level of national savings, as in the level of production and attitudes towards work generally, only a change of values can bring about a more autonomous pattern of development in the Caribbean.

(b) Dependence through foreign aid

Most developing countries receive external financial assistance from the Western or the Socialist powers, or both. The need for financial aid depends on the level of the country's per capita income, the ability to mobilise the maximum amount of domestic savings for national productive investment and the ability to avoid the foreign exchange bottleneck in development (see next Section). At higher levels of per capita income, with greater mobilisation of local financial resources and with economic policies which prevent the emergence of a foreign exchange bottleneck to development, a country really does not need foreign aid. (However, a pattern of all-pervading foreign ownership of the economy, combined with a pattern of high personal consumption expenditure on imported goods and services, may reduce 'surpluses' retained for new investment in the local economy and so perpetuate the need for foreign resources in the form of aid, even at fairly high levels of per capita income.)

(c) Dependence through trade

Whether a country is dependent or interdependent through trade
depends on the composition of its exports, the marketing arrangements
for its exports and the character of its imports. At one extreme we
find countries engaging in tropical monoculture, exporting one or
two primary products, the world demand for which is declining and
which may also be very unstable. Often, too, because of high costs of
production, these products may require preferential shelter in
metropolitan markets. This is accompanied by heavy dependence on
imports not only for capital and intermediate goods, but also for the
most elementary and simple consumer goods, including food. This is
clearly an extreme form of trade dependence.

Other countries export minerals which may be in high and great
demand abroad but which are marketed through vertically integrated
multinational corporations. This again is a form of trade-dependence –
although not as extreme as in the former case.

At certain higher levels of economic development where there is
a fair amount of industrialisation by import-substitution for the
national market, promoted by high tariffs and quantitative restrictions,
many countries cannot finance their essential requirements for
capital goods and raw materials for their industries from their foreign
exchange earnings. There is a foreign exchange bottleneck. This is the
position of many of the semi-industrialised Latin American countries
and of India. The problem of foreign exchange arises from the inability
of the country to increase the volume of exports of manufactured goods
to the outside world (or to produce for export or home consumption
agricultural products) to a sufficient extent.

Finally, one finds countries whose exports are highly diversified
(consisting particularly of manufactures) and going to many different
geographical markets, without the need for special preferential
shelter. Further, the proceeds of such exports are sufficient to
finance all the country's import requirements and there are no chronic,
as against periodic, balance-of-payments problems. This is the position
of most of the developed, highly industrialised countries of Western
Europe.

Irrespective of the level of development, the need to rely on foreign
trade depends very much on the size and range of natural resources of
the country. A very large country (such as the USA, the USSR or
India) exports and imports only a very small proportion of its total
production and requirements respectively. For a small underdeveloped
country seeking to develop, foreign trade must always be important.
(Cuba is still as heavily dependent on foreign trade as in pre-
revolutionary days.) What matters is the commodity composition of
trade (the importance of exports of manufactures or processed primary

products as against raw or unprocessed primary products); the geographical diversification of export markets and sources of imports; the ability to compete without preferential shelter in external markets; and the marketing arrangements for its products (whether they are sold in 'administered' markets through vertically-integrated multinational corporations or in competitive markets). On the side of imports, heavy dependence on imports of food and light manufactured consumer goods (as against imports of raw materials, components and capital goods which the country could not under any circumstances produce economically) signifies dependence.

Thus economic dependence as manifested in trade is very much linked with the internal structure of the economy and its stage of development.

(d) Dependence through the need for foreign know-how and foreign human resources

Human resources are perhaps the key element in autonomous development. One can have as much ideology as one wants. One can have the will to develop and the right attitudes among the population. Unless, however, the population develops the know-how and capacity, development will not take place.[2] Know-how and capacity include not only knowledge of technology but also managerial and organisational skills. Know-how and capacity are the scarcest factors of production in all developing countries. One can implement programmes for localisation or nationalisation of the key sectors of the economy, one can encourage greater self-reliance and one can attempt to encourage development from below through small- and medium-sized farms, small industries and cooperatives. But without know-how in technology, management and organisational capacity, these efforts are likely to prove futile. Moreover, in small countries with a limited range of natural resources, the factor of production of trained human resources and technological capacity becomes crucial for economic independence.

It is useful to distinguish here between the need for foreign human resources and the need for foreign technology.

The use of foreign human resources takes two forms: first, technical assistance to governments of Third World countries extended by international and multilateral agencies and bilaterally by governments of developed countries; and second, the use by government or by local private enterprise of foreign technologists and managers. The answer to this is obviously the production of more local cadres of trained personnel. (In many Third World countries, however — and particularly in the Commonwealth Caribbean — the production of more local trained personnel may simply swell the 'brain drain'.) Training by itself is insufficient when it comes to local personnel developing certain essential aspects of organisational and managerial skills: this is an art that is difficult to develop except by learning-by-doing and this is

198

usually not a short-term process.

The other aspect of dependence on foreign know-how and human resources relates to technology in its material aspect. Many Third World countries have come near to being self-sufficient in technologists and managers but still import nearly all their requirements of material technological processes.

In fact, all Third World countries are technologically dependent on metropolitan countries — whether or not they have 'neo-colonialist' or independent economies. This is because most of the Research and Development expenditure on technological innovation takes place in the advanced countries, particularly the United States. What Third World countries need is a vast increase in expenditure on Research and Development which would enable them to utilise their own domestic raw materials and ultimately to produce and export products based on their own resources or on their own designs and styles. Even more important, technological innovation in Third World countries is required to develop efficient labour-intensive techniques of production. The problem that modern technology poses for Third World countries suffering from heavy unemployment is that Western technologies are highly capital-intensive and are becoming increasingly so, as continuing efforts are made in the advanced countries to economise on labour. Capital-intensive modern technology is imported into all Third World countries and is one of the main causes of unemployment. Any effort to make a breakthrough in technology requires Third World countries to come together to establish facilities for such research on a regional or even a continental basis. This means that reducing technological dependence is a matter for the long run. In the short and medium run, however, Third World countries can do much to adapt imported technologies to local situations and to employ 'intermediate' technologies.

Finally, it should be observed that technological innovation is required in Third World countries not only to develop efficient labour-intensive technologies but also to put to economic use local raw materials and other natural resources so that local patterns of consumption and production can take the place of imported patterns of consumption and production (see following paragraphs).

(e) Dependence through imported consumption and production patterns

Another manifestation of dependent underdevelopment (closely related to both trade and technological dependence) which is particularly glaring in the Commonwealth Caribbean countries is the importation of the consumption patterns of the affluent societies of North America and Europe. This phenomenon has multiple causes: these include the easy availability of credit to finance imported consumer goods; the influence of advertising and the mass media, particularly commercial television; the proximity to and relatively inexpensive means of travel to North America (particularly through 'fly now, pay later' credit plans); the frequent return home for short visits of West Indian emigrants to North America; and, in many of the countries, the presence of large numbers of North American tourists, whose presumed tastes in food, drink, entertainment and low or zero-duty luxury goods are catered for.

Historical factors also operate, such as the centuries-old concentration in the West Indies on export of agricultural staples and the importation of practically everything else, including food. Moreover, tehncological dependence itself leads to a failure to develop production of indigenous resources, including processing and preservation of local food, vegetables and fruit and the development of indigenous materials, designs and styles.

The effects of such imported consumption patterns are fairly obvious. They put pressure on the balance of payments; reduce local savings; cause domestic natural resources (including agricultural resources) to be under-utilised; and lead to more local unemployment than would otherwise exist.

Finally, imported consumption patterns themselves lead to excessive demands for higher wages and salaries, which, as we shall see, in turn create more local unemployment. And, of course, as prices of imported goods go up because of inflation in the metropolitan countries, the more eagerly are large increases in wages sought to enable wage and salary earners in the dependent countries to purchase the much desired goods.

It should also be noted that high tariffs are not really effective in reducing the volume of imports or in changing consumption patterns, especially when the effects of hire purchase (consumer credit) are taken into account. People either save less or get into debt to acquire the foreign goods.[3] The only real answer seems to be the use of quantitative restrictions or prohibitions.

Dependence on imported *consumption* patterns is closely connected with dependence on imported *production* patterns. This is most clearly seen in the distinction between two types of import-substitution: 'import replacement' and 'import displacement'.[4]

In the former case, a taste among the local population is created for, say, imported Scotch whisky or imported General Motors automobiles. A local plant may then be set up to replace imports of Scotch whisky or General Motors automobiles, in both cases with production relying heavily on imported inputs. In many cases such local plants are set up by branches or subsidiaries of multinational corporations. The phenomenon described by J.K. Galbraith of wants being deliberately created by large innovating companies for their new products applies with equal force to dependent underdeveloped countries as to the affluent North American society about which Galbraith was writing in

The New Industrial State. This phenomenon is, of course, highly dysfunctional in Third World countries, since such imported production patterns often make use of inappropriate capital-intensive technology, fail to use local inputs and resources, and inhibit local creativity and innovation.

In the other case of 'import-displacement', we have products based on local inputs 'displacing' imports – examples being mangoes or oranges being consumed instead of apples or pears, or mango-juice being drunk instead of apple-juice. It will be seen that 'import-displacement' is much easier to achieve in the case of agricultural products or agriculture-based industries than in the case of the usual run of manufactured items.

III. The tasks of promoting economic independence in the Commonwealth Caribbean

Economic independence is of course the situation that one progressively approximates as one brings about the progressive breakdown of the kinds of relations of dependence that we have been discussing. In other words, the less dependent we become in terms of foreign ownership and control, aid, trade and human resources and technology, the more independent we become.

Thus economic dependence through foreign ownership can be overcome through programmes for achieving national ownership and control over key sectors of the economy. Dependence through foreign aid and foreign technical assistance can be overcome through the generation of more national savings and through more development of local human resources. Dependence through trade can be overcome by internal development which changes the structure of the economy by increasing the supply of locally grown foodstuffs; by import substitution in manufactures; by changing imported consumption patterns; by increasing the share of manufactures in total exports; by increasing the degree of local processing of products hitherto exported in raw or semi-processed condition; and by reducing the costs of production of those exports which cannot compete in competitive markets abroad but require preferential shelter. Dependence on foreign know-how can be reduced partly by the people of the country 'learning-by-doing'; partly by a massive programme of scientific and technical (including vocational and agricultural) training for young people; and partly by integrating the world of school and the world of work.

These are the tasks to be accomplished to reduce economic dependence or dependent underdevelopment. This is familiar to everyone. The real question is, *how* can these tasks be accomplished? Fundamentally, four kinds of changes are required in the Commonwealth Caribbean countries (as in all developing countries) if these tasks are to be accomplished.

IV. Means of promoting economic independence in the Commonwealth Caribbean

(a) Changes in policies and institutions

First, there must be a re-orientation of economic policies and institutions deriving from colonial days. Thus imports that can be locally produced or that are 'inessential' must be reduced — both by reducing consumer credit for such purchases and, where necessary, by severe quantitative restrictions or prohibitions. Agriculture producing food and livestock products for the home market must be vigorously promoted. Greater use of local raw materials by manufacturing industries and greater use of local inputs (including local food) by the tourist industry must be encouraged. There must be an adoption of all the well-known methods of increasing exports of manufactures. New financial institutions must be created and old ones restructured in order to mobilise more local savings for local productive investment. Steps must be taken to achieve more effective national control over key sectors of the economy. Local managerial and technical cadres (including young people trained in modern scientific agriculture) must be developed. The educational system must be made more relevant and must serve the purpose of building a national identity and integrating the world of school with the world of work.

(b) Changes in values and attitudes

Second, and this is the key to promoting autonomous development in the Caribbean, the values and attitudes of the people (especially the young) must be re-oriented and the necessary motivation of the people to perform all the tasks involved must be created by the political leaders. These changes in values, attitudes, and motivations — towards hard work, towards agriculture, towards vocational training, towards production as against consumption, and towards tastes for local as against foreign goods and services — can only be achieved through the development (and practice) of an authentic, indigenous West Indian ideology of development and social change — one in keeping with the historical experience of the West Indian people. Moreover, as part of this programme of changing values, attitudes and motivations, the educational system and the mass communications system need to be sharply re-orientated.

(c) The wage and salary problem, unemployment and agricultural stagnation

Many of the broad lines of approach suggested above should help indirectly to overcome the unemployment problem. But one fundamental aspect of the problem should be discussed. It is also connected with agricultural stagnation and low national savings in the public sector. This is a significant and growing gap between earnings in agriculture and in other low-productivity sectors on the one hand and in modern manufacturing, mining, modern tourism and the public sector on the other hand. The higher wages and salaries in the latter sectors are the result of several factors – the higher productivity of these sectors; trade union action; the fact that many of the modern sectors are controlled by branches and subsidiaries of international corporations, which usually pay relatively good wages and salaries; and the attempt of governments to stem the brain drain by raising salaries (and consequently, through trade union action, wages).

This state of affairs causes people to leave the land, thus reducing agricultural output. Such people migrate to the towns where jobs are difficult to find and many remain unemployed. Public sector savings are reduced. Under these circumstances, in the Caribbean as in all Third World countries, an incomes policy is needed to restrain the widening gap in earnings within the countries, to restrain (as far as is economically feasible) rises in prices, and to ensure that the richer people and local and foreign companies pay a fair share in taxes. Only in this way will it be possible to develop agriculture and to reduce unemployment among young people. Tanzania, for example, has a definite incomes policy: wages and salaries in the public sector have been cut and no person can get an increase in wages and salaries amounting to more than 5 per cent per annum.

(d) Acquisition of know-how and technological skills

Earlier we discussed the question of technology and organisational and managerial skills and mentioned the need for technological innovation and for more know-how in Third World countries, including the Caribbean. This cannot be overemphasised. What we are talking about is, however, more than just a question of capital- versus labour-intensive technology. It is also more than just a question of machine technology. It is a recognition of the need for underdeveloped countries to overcome their technological dependence in its broadest sense, because such dependence comprises the very definition of dependence. For anyone who has thought seriously about the development of the Third World, it is difficult to find fault with Streeten's perceptive observation:

'Dependence derives from the lack of an indigenous range of technological and organisational inputs; from not having the know-how, the organisation and the management, the social institutions (land tenure), to respond to investment and trade opportunities. It is something like this that lies behind the important idea of *technological dependence*. It is in the complex links between technology, marketing, private investment, bargaining, trade and aid policies that some of the remedies to poverty and underdevelopment have to be sought'.[5]

Overcoming technological dependence and shortages of managerial and organisational skills presents the Commonwealth Caribbean with one of its greatest challenges to moving away from dependent underdevelopment. With respect to the limited aspect of developing managerial and organisational skills, there are grounds for optimism: there is now a clear recognition of the need to provide higher standards of managerial and organisational attainment through a combination of formal and on-the-job training and through 'learning-by-doing'. But the broader aspect of technological innovation will certainly pose a much more severe challenge to the creativity of the people of the region. Councils and Institutes for Scientific and Technological Research are being established; but only time will tell how much fruit they will bear.

(e) Caribbean integration

The possibility of achieving economic autonomy in Caribbean countries also requires meaningful regional economic integration. This is so for three reasons.

First, it is necessary to widen the small national market in each country and to create a larger regional market, effectively protected by a Common External Tariff and a Common Protective Policy, thereby facilitating the continuing development of both agricultural and manufacturing production.

Second, when we 'combine' all the natural resources of the Caribbean, we have a useful basis for self-sustained growth for the countries in the Region. We in the Carribbean must pool and combine our natural resources to create linkages between the economies of the Region and to develop local industries drawing their inputs from different parts of the Region. In this way we can reduce the need for certain types of imports from the metropolitan countries, create more value added regionally and so strengthen our economies. This of course requires regional programming in the agricultural, manufacturing and mineral sectors.

Third, in this age of powerful metropolitan governments, powerful metropolitan trading blocs and powerful international corporations, the countries of the Caribbean must to some extent pool their sovereignty through joint actions and common policies in order to increase their collective power and hence their bargaining strength in dealing with these powerful external entities.

These then are the three essential reasons for Caribbean economic integration: the need to widen markets; the need to pool and combine natural resources and to programme regional economic activities; and the need to strengthen our collective bargaining power vis-a-vis powerful external entities and forces. Continuing special measures will also have to be implemented to enable the less developed countries of the Region to benefit from economic integration as much as the more developed countries. A greater degree of economic independence for each country can, paradoxically, be achieved only through meaningful economic integration in the Region. This is the 'paradox of sovereignty'. A greater degree of *effective* sovereignty is attainable by each Caribbean country only through some surrender to the regional collectivity of some of its *formal* sovereignty.

Caribbean economic integration must be ultimately extended to the non-English-speaking countries of the Region, after the present CARIFTA arrangements are consolidated and 'deepened' among the existing members into the Caribbean Community (including the Caribbean Common Market). Simultaneously, the Caribbean countries need to develop economic collaboration with other Third World countries in Latin America, Asia and Africa. There are already indications of this through the active participation of Guyana, Jamaica and Trinidad and Tobago in the Economic Action Programme of the Non-Aligned Countries, which aims both at developing greater economic cooperation among the developing countries and at supplementing this 'horizontal' thrust by the developing countries bringing greater collective bargaining-power to bear upon their 'vertical' relations with the developed metropolitan countries.

There is also a strong case for political unity in the Caribbean Region, beginning with the English-speaking countries in the Eastern Caribbean. Such political union would automatically provide even closer and more meaningful economic integration among the countries involved than is envisaged in the Caribbean Community and Common Market to be established in August 1973, and would, quite apart from economic considerations, provide the West Indian peoples with a much needed sense of identity.

V. Concluding observations

The foregoing analysis suggests that overcoming economic dependence amounts to the same thing as overcoming underdevelopment. In fact, 'dependent underdevelopment' is the state of affairs that characterises most Third World countries. The overcoming of economic dependence must be part and parcel of an overall strategy of development and employment creation. Much of what has been said above about ways and means of overcoming dependent underdevelopment is, indeed, being increasingly recognised and acted upon by Caribbean Governments. For example, in all West Indian countries, governments are beginning to give greater priority to agriculture; to the creation of linkages between the manufacturing, tourist and mineral sectors and the other economic sectors; to promoting exports of manufactures; to localising the economy in various forms (Guyana's nationalisation of bauxite being only the most dramatic example); to trying to change imported patterns of consumption and production by banning goods capable of local production and 'inessential' imports; to re-orienting the educational system and providing more vocational and agricultural training; to developing programmes for training persons in the private, public and cooperative sectors in business management; to setting up Institutes and Councils for Applied Scientific and Technological Research; and to creating new indigenous financial institutions. The Caribbean Free Trade Association (CARIFTA), established in May 1968, is to be converted into a Caribbean Community and Common Market in August 1973.

However, a very big gap still exists in the area of incomes policies. Governments all over the world find it very difficult to harmonise trade union activities with national development and employment objectives.[6] But unless this problem is solved, many of the features of dependent underdevelopment will persist in Third World countries, including the Commonwealth Caribbean.

NOTES

1. This paper originated in a simple talk given to a Caribbean Youth Conference in mid-1972. I am grateful to Mr. Swinburne Lestrade of the Secretariat for much constructive comment and some assistance in redrafting the original text of the talk. Mr. Edwin Carrington and Mr. Byron Blake, both of the Secretariat, also made helpful comments on a section of the paper.
2. Compare this, however, with the Mao Tse-Tung's conception of the development of technical know-how through 'right thinking'.
3. Not only is the demand for such 'prestige' products price-inelastic but the demand curve itself is constantly shifting over time to the right (as a result of the growing orientation of tastes towards such goods). The result is that the upward shift to the left of the supply curve (resulting from higher import duties) does not restrain the volume purchased, as the following diagram illustrates:

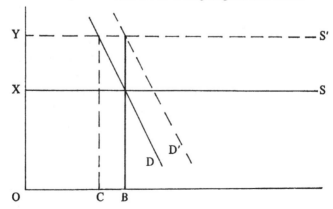

Import Duty raises price from OX to OY but OB (i.e. Quantity) remains unchanged.
If Demand Curve had not shifted, price would still rise from OX to OY, but Quantity would have fallen from OB to OC.

4.	This distinction is due to Lloyd Best of the University of the West Indies.
5.	Paul Streeten, 'The Trade Game', in *World Development*, Vol. 1, Nos. 1 &2, Feb. 1973.
6.	It should be noted that in Socialist countries with centrally planned economies trade unions do not really exercise in any meaningful fashion their 'traditional and Western' role of free collective bargaining. A very elementary fact which West Indian so-called radicals are inclined to ignore is that a Socialist transformation of an underdeveloped country always involves a shift of real income not only from capitalists, managers and bureaucrats but also from better-off unionised workers towards the unemployed, underemployed and workers and peasants in the agricultural sector.

LIST OF PARTICIPANTS

Mr. George C. Abbott:	Department of International Economic Studies, University of Glasgow.
Mrs. Joy Allsopp:	Centre for Multi-Racial Studies, University of the West Indies, Barbados.
Mr. Asgar Ally:	Bank of Jamaica.
Prof. Fuat Andic:	Chairman, Department of Economics, and Senior Researcher, Institute of Caribbean Studies, University of Puerto Rico.
Mr. Eric Armstrong:	Barbados Development Bank.
Dr. Lloyd Best:	University of the West Indies, St. Augustine, Trinidad.
Dr. Courtney N. Blackman:	Governor, Central Bank of Barbados.
Mr. A. Braithwaite:	Ministry of Education, Government of Barbados.
Prof. Harold Brookfield:	Department of Geography, McGill University.
Mr. Arthur Brown:	Governor, Bank of Jamaica.
Mr. N. Duncan:	Department of Politics, University of the West Indies, Barbados.
Mr. S.E. Emtage:	Director, Economic Planning Unit, Government of Barbados.
Mr. J.S. Holder:	Ministry of External Affairs, Government of Barbados.
Mr. B.L. Jacobs:	Institute of Development Studies, University of Sussex.
Mr. Graham Kelly:	United Kingdom High Commission, Barbados.
Dr. Kari Levitt:	Institute of Social and Economic Research, University of the West Indies, St. Augustine, Trinidad.
Dr. Vaughan Lewis:	Deputy Director, Institute of Social and Economic Research, University of the West Indies.
Dr. George Reid:	Economic Planning Unit, Government of Barbados.
Dr. Bernard Schaffer:	Institute of Development Studies, University of Sussex.
Dr. S. Schiavo-Campo:	Visiting Professor, University of Puerto Rico, Associate Professor, University of Massachusetts at Boston.
Mr. Dudley Seers:	Institute of Development Studies, University of Sussex.
Mr. Percy Selwyn:	Institute of Development Studies, University of Sussex.
Mr. Charles Skeete:	Permanent Secretary, Ministry of Trade and Tourism, Government of Barbados.
Dr. Barend A. deVries:	Chief Economist, Western Africa Department, International Bank for Reconstruction and Development.
Mr. Michael Ward:	Department of Applied Economies, Cambridge.

For Product Safety Concerns and Information please contact our EU
representative GPSR@taylorandfrancis.com Taylor & Francis Verlag GmbH,
Kaufingerstraße 24, 80331 München, Germany

Printed and bound by CPI Group (UK) Ltd, Croydon, CR0 4YY
01/05/2025
01858329-0001